# *Start Your Own*

# Additional titles in *Entrepreneur's* **Startup Series**

## *Start Your Own*

Bar and Tavern

Bed & Breakfast

Business on eBay

Business Support Service

Car Wash

Child Care Service

Cleaning Service

Clothing Store

Coin-Operated Laundry

Consulting

Crafts Business

e-Learning Business

Event Planning Business

Executive Recruiting Service

Freight Brokerage Business

Gift Basket Service

Growing and Selling Herbs and Herbal
   Products

Home Inspection Service

Import/Export Business

Information Consultant Business

Lawn Care Business

Mail Order Business

Medical Claims Billing Service

Personal Concierge Service

Personal Training Business

Pet-Sitting Business

Restaurant and Five Other Food Businesses

Self-Publishing Business

Seminar Production Business

Specialty Travel & Tour Business

Staffing Service

Successful Retail Business

Vending Business

Wedding Consultant Business

Wholesale Distribution Business

Entrepreneur® MAGAZINE'S

*startup*

*Start Your Own*

# e-BUSINESS

*Your Step-by-Step Guide to Success*

*Entrepreneur Press, Robert McGarvey, and Melissa Campanelli*

**EP**
Entrepreneur®
Press

Editorial Director: Jere L. Calmes
Managing Editor: Marla Markman
Cover Design: Beth Hansen-Winter
Production: Eliot House Productions
Composition: Ed Stevens

**Library of Congress Cataloging-in-Publication Data is available**

ISBN 1-932156-74-7

Printed in Canada

11 10 09 08 07 06                    10 9 8 7 6 5

# Contents

▲

# Preface

In 1994, during an interview, Stewart Alsop (then an influential tech editor, now a venture capitalist) told me, "Get on the web—that's where the excitement is."

Huh? I'd been using e-mail since 1988, when I signed up with General Electric's GEnie online service. I primarily used GEnie for checking out prices for airplane tickets (via the incredibly cumbersome Sabre system) or sometimes stock market movements. It was a toy, and not a very interesting one.

A few years later, I migrated to CompuServ (now owned by Time Warner Inc.)—same toy, but with somewhat better e-mail capabilities and message boards—then to AOL. Sometime in '94, Time Warner Inc. "discovered" the internet and began promoting various net tools to members: FTP (file transfer protocol) and Archie (a file search tool). Boy, was this internet stuff boring and truly useless! Sure, I could use Archie to find the faculty roster at some irrelevant Virginia college, but so what?

Then Alsop explained what the buzz was about—the web, a graphical internet that was invented, sort of, by Tim Berners-Lee in 1991 when he posted a little program on the internet that allowed the creation of hyperlinks. The web languished, though, until 1993, when a group of students working in a University of Illinois computer lab cobbled together Mosaic, the first browser that allowed a truly graphical look at the web.

Whoosh! The race was on. The internet, founded in 1969 with a Defense Department-sponsored linking of four university computers but until '93 merely a plaything for supernerds, was ready to go prime time.

So I did as the man suggested, got a version of Mosaic, and I was hooked. I immediately knew this was going to be big, really big. I had no idea an Amazon loomed before us, but I did know that suddenly we had in our hands a communications tool like no other. "The web lets everybody be a publisher," Steve Wolff, an internet pioneer who now works at Cisco Systems, told me. The web lets us communicate in ways previously unimagined. Not only can everybody be a publisher, but an international audience is within easy reach. Suddenly, the web emerged as a platform that would forever change how business would be done.

Not that anybody anticipated what was in store when Mosaic hit the streets: "When the net was invented, nobody envisioned a Yahoo! or an eBay, but that's the way technology is," says Barry Leiner, director of the Research Institute for Advanced Computer Science (www.riacs.edu), a NASA-funded laboratory for tinkering with the outer limits of computer science. "Nobody saw that the automobile would spawn shopping malls and suburban sprawl, and with the internet, nobody saw what would happen as information became more accessible."

It has been an incredible few years. Who would have thought that Yahoo!, begun as a project by some Stanford graduate school geeks, would eventually have a stock market capitalization of more than $17 billion. And not too long ago, a guy was jawboning with his girlfriend about her mania for collecting Pez dispensers, when—poof—eBay arrived on the scene, reaching a market cap north of $31 billion.

Or consider Pete Ellis, a down-and-out car dealer who'd watched his Orange County, California, dealerships go bankrupt. Ellis was in his condo and—with little else to do—was playing with his wife's computer. He signed onto Prodigy, and a lightbulb went on. Everybody hates buying cars, thought Ellis, and as a onetime dealer, he also knew many dealers despise the slime that shapes so many of the industry's traditional selling techniques. What if, somehow, buyers could buy new wheels on the net? What if? Shazam—Autobytel was born. Although Ellis is no longer involved with the company, it is still going strong. Autobytel now owns and operates the automotive web sites Autobytel.com, AutoWeb.com, and CarSmart.com, as well as the popular automotive research center, AutoSite.com, and its market cap is currently more than $172 million. It also recently reported its first-ever profitable quarter.

As Miranda gushes near the close of Shakespeare's *The Tempest*, "How beauteous mankind is! O brave new world, that has such people in't!"

Where is your place in this "brave new world?" Nowadays, the answer is yours to write because in the internet economy, everything is different. Really. And forever.

# Introduction
## Riding the Web to Riches

Despite the crash of the dotcom economy after its skyrocketing ascent, the internet continues to offer a virtual universe of opportunity. While it may be more difficult to find the cheap funding that fueled the explosion of dotcom startups, driven entrepreneurs with good ideas are still devising ways to build solid businesses that harness the power of the internet to reach millions of people worldwide.

For every dotcom business that flourishes, hundreds—maybe thousands—go bust. What does it take to build a dotcom that will succeed? Read this book and you'll know, because in these pages you'll find recipes for success, road maps that pinpoint the hazards, and dozens of interviews with dotcom builders who have cashed in.

What separates the winners from the losers? Poor ideas, poor execution, poor marketing, and poor funding.

Worse, the competitive field has become crowded with companies that were online innovators and with traditional companies that reconfigured their operations to include an internet component. In some cases, launching a national, full-scale consumer-oriented site today may require more than $100 million to cover marketing, hardware, software and staffing costs. Gulp! That's a big leap from the graduate school project days that gave rise to Yahoo!.

Low-budget web sites are still launching—and making it to the big time—but now more than ever, they require a unique combination of customer insight, business understanding, technical know-how, financial resources, and entrepreneurial drive. The possibilities of success remain enticing, even when wallets are thin—if your ideas are smart and your execution persistent. The one inescapable fact is this: It's war on the monitors, and more web sites will die than will survive. What will yours do?

The goal of this book is to give you the tools and knowledge you'll need to emerge among the victors. In these pages, you'll find the soup to nuts, the A to Z, of taking your idea through funding, building partnerships, launching, getting more funding, winning eyeballs, and laughing all the way to the bank. This is not a technical book. It's a book about business, consumer psychology, and even sex (because it's sex sites that first proved people would use credit cards online).

While the internet's roots are in technology, that technology has become much more accessible to a wider group of entrepreneurs through the efforts and investment of many companies and people. Not only are there better software tools that make it easier for nontechnical people to manage web sites, but there are also many more people with web expertise who have added internet usage into their daily work or personal routines.

We'll tell you what you need and where to get it, and for hard-core do-it-yourselfers, there's even a chapter on building your own web site. Either way, there's no longer a reason to say "I don't get this internet stuff." You've got to get it, or get out of business.

Some words about how this book is organized: Interspersed among the chapters are "Cheap Tricks," mini-interviews with low-budget web site builders. Since some time will have passed between when these portraits were assembled and when you have this book in your hand, there will doubtless have been casualties among the low-budget sites; nevertheless, you can learn from how these thinly funded site-builders put their online businesses together. The book also features interviews, called "e-Chats," with CEOs of big-budget name-brand sites—among them drugstore.com, Netflix.com, OneTravel.com, Autobytel.com, eBags.com, and WorldRes.com.

You'll also find different kinds of tip boxes designed to hammer home key points.

- *Smart Tip:* bright ideas you want to remember
- *Beware!:* pitfalls and potholes you want to avoid
- *Budget Watcher:* money-saving ideas and practices

Here's the promise of this book: If you need to know it to do business online, you'll find it between these covers. Read on to find out how to make your internet dreams a reality.

# 1

# The Internet
# Gold Rush

This is it—your chance to strike it very rich because, suddenly, the internet has changed all the rules. For a half-century, the big players in business, from IBM to Exxon, have dominated the game, leaving little room for newcomers to move to the top of the heap. Then in 1994, a little start-up named Netscape introduced a web browser—and the race for cash was on. Amazon.com, eBay.com, Yahoo!, 1-800-Flowers.com, drugstore.com, Priceline.com, WebMD.com are today million-, and in some cases billion-dollar businesses, but where were they ten years ago? Out of nowhere these companies, and hundreds more, have emerged to challenge the gods of commerce. They are succeeding because the new rules favor small companies that are flexible, smart, tough, and ultra-quick to react to changing market conditions.

Chew on these numbers: e-business research firm IDC expects the total worldwide value of goods and services purchased by businesses through e-commerce solutions will increase to $4.3 trillion by 2005, from $282 billion in 2000.

By 2007, total online retail spending will reach $105.2 billion, up from the $51.7 billion consumers were expected to spend by the end of 2003. And, in the 2002 Christmas shopping season, consumers spent $7.92 billion online, a 23 percent increase over the 2001 holiday season, according to e-commerce research firm BizRate.com.

The internet is for real, and in the 21st century, if you're not on it, you're not in business. That is today's reality byte.

## A New Set of Rules

On the web, the advantage is yours—it belongs to the entrepreneur. Why? Consider Compaq. It makes fine computers—maybe no better than its competitors, but certainly no worse. So why has it been stumbling while a comparative upstart like Dell has soared into market leadership? Dell long ago made the leap into full-steam web retailing. It yanked its merchandise out of retail stores and threw the dice, betting the company's future on direct selling to corporations and individuals via catalogs and the web. Compaq, meanwhile, has faltered at every step because it doesn't want to alienate its established retail channels, convinced they would be irked if suddenly the same computers were available for less on the internet. So Compaq dithers, and that indecisiveness makes it lose momentum and leadership while upstarts grab market share.

The web is both a new distribution channel and a new way of doing business. Don't miss either part of that statement. Think of the web only as a new channel—a different way of putting products and services in front of customers—and you miss the threat and the promise of the internet, which is that it will utterly change how you do business.

For one thing, the web is ruthless in the squeeze it puts on pricing. Fat and waste have to go, and good riddance because many large companies (and too many small companies) have grown comfortably wealthy by exacting indefensible margins out of the retail process. No more. Because the web stomps margins flat to make profits, companies have to rethink where their dollars will be earned. Most big companies have responded to these new rules by shutting their eyes and praying the moment will pass. (Think of the big banks that treat customers terribly, pay laughable interest rates, and are forever hiking fees. Most are doomed to be dinosaurs.) All this is good news for you because it means you have a wide-open playing field before you.

Better still, the opportunities are unlimited. Would it be wise to go head-to-head against Yahoo! or Amazon? Not directly, because these companies are among the few internet businesses that can legitimately claim to have established major consumer brands. But the web is so young, and possibilities are everywhere. Want proof? Read on for a few amazing stories of internet success popping up where most people would least expect it.

**Smart Tip**

Just because your idea might seem a little out of the ordinary, don't quit if you're a believer. Charles Brofman didn't quit, and his Cybersettle is clearly a big winner in reinventing the way insurance claims are settled.

Tip...

Charles Brofman is an internet entrepreneur who has found success pairing fast-paced internet technology with the slow-paced process of settling insurance claims.

Brofman started Cybersettle Inc. (www.cybersettle.com) in 1996. Cybersettle is a White Plains, New York-based online dispute resolution company. Its web-based system facilitates high-speed, confidential claim settlements by matching offers and demands. Parties can settle disputes instantly, 24 hours a day, seven days a week via the internet, or by calling its customer service center during normal business hours.

Why did he start the company? "The courts today literally cannot handle the onslaught of litigation they face," says Brofman, a seasoned trial attorney. "As a result, people who are entitled to get compensated for their injures have to wait long periods of time, and insurance companies that have an obligation to pay—and want to pay—have to wait a long period of time. Cybersettle really just came out of our frustration with this process, where everybody wants to settle, and we just can't get there because of the way the system has been set up."

Here's how Cybersettle works: An insurance company receives a statement of claim from a plaintiff's lawyer. When the insurance adjuster reviews the case and is ready to settle, he then enters three offers into the computer. The plaintiff's lawyer is e-mailed, faxed, called, and sent a hard copy letter that the insurer has made an offer. The lawyer then enters three demands. The Cybersettle main server compares the lawyer's first offer with the insurer's, and when the demand falls below the offer, the software splits the difference and settles the claim.

Brofman says the system mirrors the way our industry does business. "There's this bidding war that goes on" says Brofman. "It's a numbers game. We just expanded the day—it now can go on 24 hours a day instead of 8 hours a day."

Insurance companies like the service, which can be used in all 50 states and in Canada, because it helps them cut down on the $34 billion worth of claims administration they cope with every year. Claimants like it because they get paid far faster than they would if they wound their way through the legal system. And lawyers like it because they still get paid by their clients.

To date, Cybersettle has handled more than 70,000 transactions and has facilitated over $450 million in settlements, including bodily injury and other types of insurance claims.

In addition, Cybersettle was awarded a U.S. patent for its Computerized Dispute Resolution System and Method. Cybersettle also has similar patent coverage in 14 other countries, and currently there are 28 additional countries where Cybersettle patents are pending approval.

Brofman says there are several reasons why his internet venture is successful. One, his company has a "fabulous" investor, a strategic partner who understands his business. Another is that his business does what the internet was designed to do, and that is to conduct transactions, 24 hours per day, seven days per week. "If you are going to do something on the net," says Brofman, "you have to do something that the net was designed to do."

## Reaching Their Peak

Now, remember just a few lines ago I advised against challenging Yahoo!? That only applies to Yahoo!'s own turf. If you're willing to expand your horizons a little, as two entrepreneurs discovered, the sky's the limit. Consider Jim Holland and John Bresee, who in 1996 founded BackcountryStore.com (www.backcountrystore.com), a Herber City, Utah-based online retailer of outdoor gear for skiing, kayaking, camping, and backpacking.

Holland, a two-time Olympic ski jumper and six-time national champion Nordic ski jumper, and Bresee, a former editor of *Powder* magazine, founded the company with the purpose of providing outdoor adventure gear to the hard-core recreational athlete. Holland and Bresee's online store has had 20 consecutive profitable quarters with exceptional year-over-year growth. Pretty amazing, considering the fact that they began the company without any outside investment.

"We developed the site ourselves and banked about $10,000 of our own money to get started, which we used for inventory," says Bresee. "We took a risk but knew there was an interest out there for what we were doing."

What's the company's secret to success? There's not one answer to that question, but a key reason is that the company decided to focus on a narrow niche—selling gear to hard-core sports enthusiasts—instead of competing with mass-market retailers like REI that might sell the same items, but without the same knowledge and expertise.

BackcountryStore.com, for example, populates its call center staff with hard-core skiers and trekkers who are out there using the equipment the site sells. Therefore, when a customer calls with a question, the staff member can answer it using his or her own unique personal experience.

Excellent customer service, in fact, is the company's mantra. "We do things like put our phone number on every page of our site because we want to make it as easy as possible for people to reach the company, as well as give people the opportunity to buy products from us if they feel uncomfortable about entering their credit card number into the site," says Bresee.

Other reasons for its continued growth? Cost-effective online and word-of-mouth advertising that increases customer confidence in the site.

They seem to be doing the right thing: In its year-end results for 2002, the company reported revenues that rose 132 percent over 2001.

## Fighting Irish

Now, what about treading on Amazon territory, a biggie in books, video, and now practically every aspect of the internet pie? Hop back in time to the Belfast, Northern Ireland, of a few years ago: a war-torn, drab, aging industrial town with no future and a past only worth forgetting (its major claim to fame is that the HMS Titanic was built in its shipyards). It's 1998, and three guys, all under the age of 30, are talking about two things they love—movies and the net. They wonder "Why couldn't there be an online store that sold videos?"

You need to keep in mind one technical curiosity: While U.S. VCRs are made to run videotapes in the NTSC format, in the United Kingdom and most of Europe, the prevailing standard is PAL. That's been a nuisance for world travelers (buy a special video in London, and it won't run back home in New Jersey), but for these Belfast boys, it was the key that unlocked a treasure. The big, U.S.-based online video retailers largely ignored PAL tapes, so this was virgin turf.

Still, the lads had virtually no cash and no connections, so what was to be done? They decided to pool a few thousand dollars and build a demo site, just a test to prove what they could do if they had the money. As they cobbled it together, they found themselves liking it more and more. One day they said, "Why not?" They plugged it in, and BlackStar (www.blackstar.co.uk) was live, open for business. Then what happened? As customers stumbled in, they loved BlackStar. Word spread. Investment money came in, and, within a year, BlackStar could claim to be the UK's biggest video store. It had beaten Amazon, Virgin, and bunches of others. Although the original owners are no longer there, the company did manage to get

### Smart Tip

*Tip...*

Always look for a niche the big corporations have neglected—then exploit this opportunity swiftly, before the mega-companies come to their senses. And guess what: There always are such opportunities. Find yours and move fast.

## The e-Commerce Quiz

Think you're ready to become a "netpreneur"? Prove it. Before moving on to the next chapter, take this quiz. Answers are true or false.

1. I'm comfortable in a game in which tomorrow's rules are invented the day after tomorrow.
2. I see inefficiencies—waste and delay—in many current business practices.
3. I'm willing to delay this year's profits to potentially make more money next year.
4. I know how to size up customers I've never seen or talked with.
5. The Net excites me—I honestly like surfing around and seeing what's new.
6. I can live with thin margins.
7. Customer satisfaction is the most important thing a business can deliver.
8. I'm not afraid of battling Titans.
9. I see opportunity where others see risks.
10. I am willing to work harder and smarter than I ever could have imagined possible.

*Scoring:* Guess what—"true" is always the right answer for any netpreneur. But you knew that already because you're ready to compete on this merciless playing field.

second-round funding, which enabled it to continue to build its business. In addition, in the past year, the company was taken over by a privately owned company that had an interest in the VHS and DVD wholesale market—enabling both companies to gain advantages in the market. Incredible stories? You bet, but the internet is filled with them because—I'll say it again—all the rules are new in the internet economy. Even the biggest players can be successfully challenged by the upstart who sees an opportunity, and then seizes it.

Better yet, the odds are stacked in your favor because you are little. How? When a big company such as Toys "R" Us fumbles its e-commerce debut—which it did by disappointing many 1999 holiday season shoppers—it makes headline news. That company has a well-established brand; consumers who shop there, offline or on, come with expectations. When it made hash of its web storefront, it hurt.

What if you do likewise—drop a few balls at start-up? Customers don't know you, don't have expectations, and odds are you'll be forgiven. A few years ago, business guru Tom Peters' mantra was that the moment had come for business to practice "Ready, Fire, Aim" because no longer was there latitude to spend months scoping the target. On the web, too, action counts. Take it—as BlackStar did—and you just may come out way ahead.

# Sweet Dreams

Sometimes even when your dreams aren't so lofty, the internet can still save the day, as Barbara McCann found out. She and her husband, Jim, own The Chocolate Vault, a hometown store in Tecumseh, a village about 60 miles west of Detroit. They'd watched traffic—and customers—veer away from little towns, and they'd watched their cash flow dry to a trickle. "We were on the verge of closing our shop," says McCann. Then she decided to give the internet a whirl.

On a skimpy budget—a few thousand dollars—she personally built her web site, www.chocolatevault.com, and then she watched an amazing thing happen. "People from all over the country found us, and they started buying our chocolates!" she says.

McCann doesn't have the money to buy major advertising space and instead puts all her energies into offering exceptional customer service.

"We are trying to give our customers the kind of personal service online that they would receive if they walked into our store," she says.

McCann also says that most of her customers are return customers who keep coming back because the site is easy to maneuver and understandable.

Will The Chocolate Vault rise to the top and challenge the biggies in that space, such as Godiva and others? "Never," says McCann, who knows her budget and her ambition. But the big miracle is that "the internet has been a lifesaver for us," she says. "We would've closed our shop without it."

Set the scale of your internet ambtions—dream large in the way of Charles Brofman, or dream on a more diminutive scale like the McCanns—because there is no "right" approach to the internet. Good, steady money can be earned by strictly local players who open on the net and find a stream of global business pouring in. Or big bucks may be yours if you invent a new eBay or Monster.com.

## Budget Watcher

Think small, and a net business's operating costs are nigh unto nil—meaning fast profits can come your way if you've watched your costs going in.

# Ten Reasons
# You Should Be
# Online

**N**eed convincing that the web is the place for your business to be? It would be no sweat to list 25 reasons—even 50 to 100—but to get you started, here are 10 reasons why you have to be online.

1. *It's cheap.* There is no more inexpensive way to open a business than to launch a web site. While you could spend many millions of dollars getting started, low-budget web sites (started with as little as $100) remain viable businesses.

2. *You cut your order fulfillment costs.* Handling orders by phone is expensive. Ditto for mail orders. There's no more efficient—cheap, fast, accurate—way to process orders than via a web site.

3. *Your catalog is always current.* A print catalog can cost big bucks, and nobody wants to order a reprint just to change one price or to correct a few typos. A web site can be updated in minutes.

> **⚠ Beware!**
> Not only can online catalogs be updated in seconds, they must be! A sure way to frustrate electronic shoppers is to take them through the buying process only to annoy them at the last moment with a "Sorry, out of stock" message. Never do that. If merchandise is out of stock, clearly note that early in the buying process. Customers can accept inventory problems, but they'll never accept you wasting their time.

4. *High printing and mailing costs are history.* Your customers can download any information you want them to have from your web site. Sure, you'll still want to print some materials, but lots can be distributed via the web.

5. *You cut staffing costs.* A web site can be a low-manpower operation.

6. *You can stay open 24 hours a day.* And you'll still get your sleep because your site will be open even when your eyes are closed.

7. *You're in front of a global audience.* Ever think what you sell might be a big hit in Scotland or China but feel clueless about how to penetrate foreign markets? The web is your answer because it's truly a borderless marketplace. Watch your site log, and you'll see visitors streaming in from Australia, New Zealand, Japan, Malaysia—wherever there are computers and phone lines.

8. *There are no city permits and minimal hassles.* This could change, but in most of the country, small web businesses can be run without permits and with little government involvement. As you expand and add employees, you'll start to bump into laws and regulations, but it certainly is nice to be able to kick off a business without first filling out reams of city and state forms.

> **Budget Watcher**
> On a really tight budget? Hire local college students or interns and have them work part time. Many young people are willing to work for low or no pay in exchange for getting in on the ground floor of an e-business start-up.

9. *There are no angry customers in your face.* You can't ignore unhappy customers in any business; in fact, how well you deliver customer service will go far toward determining how successful you are. But at least with a web business, you'll never have to stand eyeball-to-eyeball with a screamer.

10. *It's easy to get your message out.* Between your web site and your smart use of e-mail, you'll have complete control over when and how your message goes out. You can't beat a web site for its immediacy, and when a site is done well, it's hard to top its ability to grab and hold the attention of potential customers.

You have other reasons for wanting a web business? Fair enough. The key is knowing your reasons, knowing the benefits of doing business online, and being persistent through the launch. This isn't always an easy road to take, but it's definitely a road that has transported many to riches, with much less upfront cash, hassle, and time required than for similar, offline businesses. And that's a tough value proposition to top.

# Dotcom
# Dreams

Remember the waves of glum news of internet hopes gone awry that washed over us a few years ago? You'd be forgiven for thinking dotcom dreams are just another route to bankruptcy. Probably the scariest finding came from Webmergers.com, which tracks the merger and acquisition activity of technology companies. In a recent report,

▲

Webmergers found that since January 2000, some 962 internet companies have shut down or declared bankruptcy. Yikes! That's rotten news to read over your morning coffee. But is it news that should get you thinking about another business direction? Should you tear up your dotcom business plan?

Probably not. Webmergers' findings may be hard to swallow, but many of those 962 companies were heavily funded blockbuster dotcoms that entered the scene spending wildly (buying everything from Super Bowl advertising minutes to multipage spreads in *People* magazine, and multiyear exposure deals on AOL) in a madcap race for "mind share," or customer awareness. The big trouble: Many of these dotcoms had little (often no) cash flow and only investment money to spend. As those dollars began to run out, wise heads started looking at the outflow and the income of these dotcom enterprises—and very quickly realized the businesses as initially conceived could never prosper. There is no way around the fact that when you consistently spend much more than you bring in, sooner or later you will find yourself with angry creditors beating down your door.

Case in point: DrKoop.com's auditor issued a statement wherein it questioned how DrKoop could remain "a going concern," which is polite accountant speak for "the money is going to run out." The company later filed for bankruptcy, and in 2002 its assets—including its brand name, trademarks, domain names, web site, and e-mail addresses of its registered users—were acquired by Vitacost.com for $186,000. Vita cost.com is a privately held online source of consumer health information, health products and nutritional supplements. All this surely is grim, but it doesn't have to be the end of your dreams. For starters, in another study, Webmergers.com found that 29 internet companies shut down in the third quarter of 2002, which is 76 fewer than the 119 that folded in the third quarter of 2001. Webmergers.com also says it believes internet housecleaning is nearing completion, clearing the way for the gradual rebuilding of the sector along a more traditional growth trajectory.

Another area of impact: Venture capitalists (VC) and angels have gotten skittish—and far more selective about where they will put their money.

You likely are not a richly funded dotcom and need not sit around worrying about the day the VCs show up at the door demanding some kind of return. So breathe normally—but do not make the mistakes the dotcoms that crashed and burned made. Like what?

- *Bad balance-sheet math.* At no point did these companies generate financial statements that indicated any reasonable relationship between income and expenses. And yet they spent wildly, renting expensive offices in Silicon Valley and New York's Silicon Alley, hiring deep staffs (and often paying salaries upwards of six figures for minor positions), and buying fantastic exposure in ads of every medium. No genuinely small start-up could long afford these lush business habits. Sure, every start-up has a day or a week or a few months when income lags way behind outgo, but at least the math makes some kind of sense, and in the lean period, spending is lean, too. You do not need the ritzy office, the high-powered law firm, or the Stanford MBA employees, so you should be able to keep your expenses in some kind of rational alignment with income.

- *No revenue model.* The core question that is supposed to be asked of dotcom start-ups is "What is your revenue model?" This is shorthand for "How do you envision bringing in income? What will be your revenue streams?" Potential investors will ask this, as will would-be employees, partners, and anybody considering a financial future with your dotcom. Strangely, however, when the question has been asked, the questioners have typically accepted formulaic answers. In the past, dotcoms have vaguely explained that their revenue model involved a mix of ad

## Budget Watcher

When you start with little funding, do as small businesses have always done—operate on a shoestring. Dell Computers, for instance, got its start in a dorm room. Apple started in a garage. Your quarters needn't be that humble, but never, ever spend money you don't have to for the sake of "making an impression." If anything, it's the wrong impression you'll make because funders aren't looking to put money in the hands of CEOs who spend like drunken sailors. A little cheapness is always a good thing for a start-up.

dollars and e-commerce, and in most cases, the answer was accepted. It was a mistake because, as the failed dotcoms proved, nobody had ever really put flesh on the revenue models.

Never open a business without understanding your revenue source. This seems so elemental, but in the heady days when vaporous businesses such as Yahoo! and eBay quickly snagged multibillion-dollar market caps, so many people abandoned this axiom.

Will your predictions be on target? Probably not. They may even be wildly wrong, but that doesn't mean they didn't serve a good purpose. Simply articulating realistic, workable revenue models is good discipline. In practice, businesses usually evolve in ways the founders did not anticipate—a fact that is all the more true in the wild and woolly net—so early drafts of revenue models likely will be discarded quickly. But always know where, approximately, money will originate.

Incidentally, the unspoken revenue model of many dotcoms apparently had been additional rounds of funding—either from VCs or public markets—but, at the end of the day, those spigots will be turned off. Why? Read on.

- *No clearly defined exit strategy.* Every well-conceived start-up comes equipped with an exit strategy for investors. This means how investors will get their money out of the business and when. Founders with hands-on roles in the business probably

▲

don't need to know their exit strategy, but angels, VCs and such want to know how and when they will get their money back. What are possible exit strategies?

1. *Going public:* a prime choice for many dotcoms
2. *Getting bought by a bigger fish:* not as popular as going public, but attractive when public markets turn turbulent
3. *Bringing in new investors to buy out others:* another option but rarely used in the years of net mania, probably because later-round investors have been unwilling to pay the inflated prices sought by early investors

There is no saying which exit strategy is best, but what can be said is that no CEO needs anxious investors calling every few minutes to ask when they might cash out. And that happens all too often when there's been a lack of clarity—even realism—about the investment. This means that, in early talks with investors (even if it's your folks who put up the money), you need to be honest about how you see them getting their money out and when. Be as pessimistic as possible. Sure, you might spook investors, but better to do it now than have them hassling you as you're trying to build the business.

- *Building market share to the detriment of the business.* Market share is not God, although CEOs of the many failed dotcoms who pursued a strategy of building market share at any cost wanted you to believe otherwise. Look through the financial filings of many of the best-known dotcoms, and what's stunning is that a common practice is selling merchandise for less than they paid for it. Pay $300 to a wholesaler for handheld computers, and no matter how many you sell for $250, you won't do anything but go broke.

Yet a wacky mantra-infected Silicon Valley held that somehow, market share was the end-all. Sure, you will get market share when you sell items below cost because nobody can compete. But when pressures build and you have to tweak prices up to survive, how much of that precious market share will you lose? Lots, you can bet, which is why the only way to long-term survival is to price rationally to begin with. It makes sense to use loss-leader pricing on an item or two if that strategy generates orders that in a short-term horizon will produce profits. But it makes no sense whatsoever to consistently sell goods at below-cost prices. How can anybody wonder why so many dotcoms have nearly slid into extinction with such practices?

> **Tip...**
>
> ## Smart Tip
> You don't need a fancy business plan—it's probably a waste of time and money—but you do need to write down the basics of your business. As the business evolves, and as the fundamental assumptions change, take out the business plan and update it. Are you still on track to hit your targets?

- *Ignoring stakeholders.* Investors, your community, your employees, management, your vendors and customers all have a stake in your business. Long debates can explode around attempts to prioritize these stakeholders—whose stake is meatiest or weakest?—but probably the best strategy for most dotcoms is to assume that all stakeholders carry about equal weight (except for your community, which, in the case of an internet start-up, likely carries no weight at all).

  To succeed, businesses want to satisfy all stakeholders. That doesn't mean all will get what they want (stakeholders quite commonly are in conflict with each other, and a management task is seeing that everybody gets enough to feel happy), but it does mean you need to stay aware of your stakeholders, their wants, and what you're delivering. You will not last long if investors, employees, management, vendors, or customers get and stay cranky. Failed dotcoms often had little or no awareness that any stakeholders existed (at least any that were not on Wall Street), but stakeholders always exist and will always get their due.

- *Forgetting what industry you're in.* Guess what? Your online store is still a store, meaning you're competing in a retail universe. Yet CEOs of stumbling dotcoms talk as though they're in any industry but retail, throwing around terms like "new media," "content" and "consulting." Never fool yourself about your industry.

- *Having more ego than profits.* Not only did many CEOs of defunct dotcoms forget what industry they were in; some actually seemed to forget that they were in business at all; and that the essence of a business is to make money from revenue—not from bedazzled stock market speculators and frenzied angel investors pouring cash into the till. The sad fact about many failed dotcoms is that they could have been successful—maybe not on the lavish scale hoped for by the founders, but profitable nonetheless. And they blew it by forgetting that in the end, business is business. While it might be fun to make it on the cover of a magazine, it's ultimately more fun to be on top of a steady stream of black ink instead of managing a business that's dripping red ink.

- *The message for you.* Don't be discouraged by the stumblings of the name-brand dotcoms. They had it coming. That sounds cruel, but really, they did. You can avoid their mistakes and thereby create a very different outcome for your business.

> **Beware!**
>
> Of course you'll start off in the red—that's the norm. But when can you honestly project seeing black ink? You need to know that answer and work hard to make it a realistic forecast. So many dotcoms have been shut down because they never had honest forecasts of when investors could expect to see black ink. Don't let it happen to you.

# 4

# Should You Shutter Your Brick-and-Mortar Store?

Should you shut down your store to focus exclusively on online retailing? That's a question many small-business owners are chewing on. On the one hand, all the buzz is about the web and its many opportunities. On the other hand, the question that has to be asked is "Can the web and offline, traditional retailing coexist?"

E-tailer Sherry Rand has a definite opinion on the subject. "The smartest thing I've done in business is shutting down my store and going exclusively as an online retailer," she says. "Now I have a really neat business. I love it." Rand, 58, has an online store that sells one thing, and one thing only—gear for cheerleaders. You want pompoms in various styles and colors? You want megaphones for leading cheers? Then you should know about Pom Express (www.pomex press.com), where Rand has conducted e-business for two years since she shut the doors of her brick-and-mortar store.

"Online, I don't have to carry the great overhead required of a store, and from a quaint town in North Hampton, New Hampshire, I'm selling globally," says Rand. "We get lots of orders from Europe, where cheerleading is really picking up." Rand, herself a cheerleader from fourth grade until she graduated from college, sold cheerleading supplies as a manufacturer's representative until she opened her own store. Now that she's operating solely on the web, she says, "This is a great niche. And on the internet, I can conduct business wherever I want to be."

# Moving Out

Sounds good—but good enough to persuade you to dotcom? The temptations are potent. Close a brick-and-mortar operation, go strictly cyber, and whoosh—you've distanced yourself from monthly rent payments and dealing face-to-face with grumpy customers, not to mention that you've positioned your business to sell globally. At least that's what it seems like in theory. But can you count on it happening for you?

Probably not, says Jackie Goforth, an e-commerce specialist with consulting firm PricewaterhouseCoopers. While she says a great example of an industry that has shifted to online is antique and collectible retailing, "I would say for the average retailer, this is not the time to shut down your shop. I think we will find that retailers will use their online presence as a great complement to their stores. It may actually drive in traffic by allowing the customer to do some online browsing."

In addition, she says the appeal of being able to return merchandise purchased online at the local brick-and-mortar store gives shoppers confidence in their online purchases. "There still appears to be some fear that online purchases are difficult to return," she says. "The retailer who carries unique and exclusive merchandise could potentially tap into a much larger market by utilizing the web to reach a broad customer group."

## Smart Tip

*Tip...*

What about returns? They are proving to be a real hassle in online retailing—both to e-tailers and to consumers—and that's where e-tailers with brick-and-mortar storefronts have a big advantage because consumers who want to return products can simply take them to the storefront. Smart e-tailers stress this perk, so if it's true for you, flaunt it!

You have to keep in mind, though, that for every dotcom that thrives, there are more that flop, says Mark Layton, author of *.coms or .bombs* (Profits in e-Business), an analysis of the difficulties in mounting an effective e-commerce site. "Many dotcoms will become dot bombs—they'll fail," says Layton. "Online or offline, you need a sustainable business model. If you don't have that, you don't have a business."

## Having It Both Ways

Experiencing second thoughts about burning the lease on your storefront and going strictly virtual? Consider Vino! (www.vino2u.com), the online complement to a Winter Park, Florida, wine store, both owned by 28-year-old Adam Chilvers. Built around the tasty proposition that all the wines it sells are rated 85 or higher by a prestigious publication (such as *Wine Spectator*), both the storefront (opened in November 1998) and the online store (launched a month later) are profitable, according to Chilvers. "Doing business on the web is a dream," he says. "The costs are very low."

But he has no intention of shutting down his brick-and-mortar store, for a flock of reasons. For starters, an online operation still needs some real-world warehousing for merchandise such as his, and the brick-and-mortar store provides that. But it's the second reason that is the clincher: "On the site we sell to many customers outside our area, but we also get many locals coming into our store with shopping lists they've printed out on the web," says Chilvers. For those customers, the combination of the web site and the store offers a great convenience—they hunt for wines they want online, at midnight or 6 A.M., and then they can get in and out of the brick-and-mortar store in a matter of minutes. "I'm happy with how the store and the web site are working together to build this business," says Chilvers. "It's a good combination for me."

> **Tip...**
>
> **Smart Tip**
>
> A big consumer worry about e-tailers is that these cyberstorefronts are fly-by-night scams. When you have a brick-and-mortar storefront, you also have solidity in the minds of consumers. Don't hide it. Put up a photo of it on your web site. And definitely show the street address. Bingo—you are an established retailer. Consumer worries will vanish.

## Double Vision

Still, isn't this dual-channel strategy an unnecessary complication that forces an entrepreneur to focus on two distinctly different venues? The experts don't think so, and in fact, many point to it as the way to go forward into the next century. "There are tremendous advantages to be had by leveraging net sales with a brick-and-mortar store," says Bart Weitz, marketing professor at the University of Florida, Gainesville. Case in point: "You can use the store to promote the web site, for instance," and that means printing the URL on bags, sales slips and advertising fliers. That can be a big step in overcoming the obstacle facing every dotcom today. "It's gotten very expensive to attract people to a site," says Weitz. "Stand-alone sites incur very high marketing expenses because they have to spend the money to get eyeballs."

"A [brick-and-mortar store] can be a billboard for your web site," says Bentley College e-commerce professor Bruce Weinberg, who points to clothier Gap as a for-instance. It already has massive brand awareness, and whenever a customer walks in or walks by a storefront, there's a reinforcement of the URL, www.gap.com. Your business might not be a Gap, but even so, says Weinberg, the fact that you are in a physical location with signage and various advertising campaigns to promote the store will mean that you are also building awareness for a web site.

Another argument in favor of a dual-channel strategy: "Different consumers want different things," says Bill Gartner, business professor at the University of Southern California in Los Angeles. "Some customers want the kind of personal interaction that can only happen in a traditional retail setting. For others, it's simpler to log on to the net. The smart, consumer-oriented business makes it easy to buy, no matter the customer's preferences."

---

# Fortunetelling

**W**ant an easy rule of thumb for assessing how your business might fare online? University of Maryland business professor Jonathan Palmer shares the three factors that green lights such a decision:

1. You sell a product line that can be delivered economically and conveniently.
2. You have a desire to market a product with broad appeal to customers outside your own geographical location.
3. There are significant economic advantages involved in going online.

Chew especially hard on points one and two because if they are on your side, the profits implied in the third point likely will follow.

A fourth decision factor just might be "Can you economically draw customers to your site?" Chasing a mass market—and going belly-to-belly against Amazon, drugstore.com, Priceline, and the like—means you had better bring a seven- or eight-figure advertising/marketing budget to the table to keep up with your competitors. But the good news is that there is still plenty of room for thinly funded players with solid business plans who have targeted shrewd niches. The experts agree: Those are tomorrow's dotcom success stories.

# Who's Minding the Store?

But the big, worrisome question is "Isn't all retailing heading to the web anyway?" Just last year, that was the buzz, but nowadays—with more dotcoms struggling and few breaking through to profitability—a kind of caution has taken hold. Explains PricewaterhouseCooper's Goforth, "There are certain merchandise categories that'll be slow to succeed online—but I would anticipate it will follow the trends seen with the catalog industry. Unique product that is hard to find in stores and expensive for the brick-and-mortar retailer to stock will be the logical players online."

Other types of businesses are going to have a tough time prospering if they're not online as well. Cases in point: bookstores, consumer electronics sellers, and travel agencies, to name a few. Margins are getting squeezed ever lower as hard-charging dotcoms fight for market share by offering ever-lower pricing, and that means it will only get tougher to succeed in a brick-and-mortar context. But other types of businesses—from furniture sellers to clothiers—just may find the going stays smooth in brick-and-mortar stores. "Some products are ideal for online; others just work better in a brick-and-mortar store," says Jonathan Palmer, business professor at the University of Maryland in College Park.

Worried about being a merchandiser in an endangered category? Don't panic, says Goforth. "We heard that catalogs would put traditional retailers out of business, and it didn't happen. In fact, some catalog retailers eventually backed into opening brick-and-mortar stores. Now we hear that the web will put brick-and mortars out of business, and that certainly has not happened. We may see e-tailers going for brick-and-mortar stores."

# Web Site
# Building 101

**W**hat's stopping you from putting up a web site for your business? A big and persistent hurdle is the belief that setting up a web site is hard, technically demanding work. While that might have been true a couple of years ago when the World Wide Web first took flight, web page authoring is no longer solely the province of propeller heads. Plenty of easy-to-use software is on the market, and a web newcomer can usually get an initial page up within a few hours. Better still, all this can be accomplished at a very low cost. "Even the smallest businesses can afford to be on the web," says Mary Cronin, a business professor at Boston College and editor of *The Internet Strategy Handbook* (Harvard Business School Press).

Believe it or not, this is probably the least important chapter in this book. Why? Because putting up a web page has become so simple, it's scarcely worth mentioning. And if you don't have time to spare, a small outlay of cash will buy you the services of a local college student fluent in hypertext markup language (HTML). Web page authoring may be fun for purists, but it is no litmus test of your "right" to be on the web. You have that right just by claiming it, whether you know about HTML authoring or not.

But for those of you who want to do it yourself, this chapter provides step-by-step tips for producing your web site—from picking the right tools and putting them into use to testing your creation. Set aside just a few hours, follow the steps, and you, too, will be in business on the web.

# Know Your Purpose

The starting point for putting up a web site is to determine what you want it to do—and know what it likely won't do. The bad news is that you won't get rich quick with a web site. Very few start-ups have achieved overnight success on the web—the most notable success being Amazon. The web just isn't the fast track to Easy Street that too many commentators have depicted it to be.

Then why do it? Of course, persistence and ingenuity may eventually be rewarded with profits. But there are other sound reasons for putting up a web site. Even if your home page is little more than an electronic billboard for your company, it's still a powerful tool for building a business. On the web, for instance, "distance means nothing," says Jerry White, director of the Caruth Institute of Owner-Managed Business at Southern Methodist University in Dallas. A small business in the United States can use the web as a low-cost tool for reaching customers in other states, even other countries.

The clock, too, no longer matters. "On the web your business can be open 24 hours a day, seven days a week," says Gail Houck, a consultant and web strategist. Another reason for building a web presence: The web lets you serve customers in ways that would

**Budget Watcher**

Try WebExpress for free by downloading the software from www.mvd.com/webexpress/down load.htm. This is full-featured trial-ware, about 4.5MB. And even if you decide not to buy, any pages you have created are yours to use on the web.

be unimaginable in a traditional retail environment. On the web, it's easy to offer far deeper product selection, for instance, and—with clear thinking on your side—prices, too, typically can be driven down.

All good reasons? You bet, and you may have many more. Whatever your motivations, the single most important step you can take is this one: Define your goals and expectations. Do that, and the rest—including the mechanics of site design—will fall into place.

Where so many small businesses (and a few very large ones, too) go wrong is that they haven't taken this clarifying step. The resulting sites are fundamentally confusing because nobody ever took the time to specify their purpose. It's perfectly fine to erect a site that amounts to a company information brochure, but that site cannot be expected to function as a retail platform.

# Getting Started

In the not-too-distant past, building a web site meant hours of laborious HTML writing, but today's leading web-authoring tools are solidly WYSIWYG, which is computerspeak for "what you see is what you get." Building a page now involves little more than clicking a mouse.

Which tool to use? The top choice—both for usability and affordability—is Microsoft's FrontPage (www.microsoft.com/frontpage), which costs about $199. It's a program that's powerful enough to concoct ambitious sites, but user-friendly enough that beginners will find the going easy. Another option is WebExpress from MicroVision Development (about $70), available for download and purchase at www.mvd.com/webexpress. It, too, is powerful but simple to use. Either program will get you live and on the web in a matter of minutes.

A big plus for both programs: They come bundled with an assortment of templates, or forms, that need only a bit of tweaking and customizing to create your own home page. Stick with the templates, and a web page within 30 minutes is a realistic goal. For instance, templates in FrontPage such as "Normal Page," "Feedback Form," and "Guest Book" are reached through the task pane, which automatically pops up when you select "New" from the "File" menu. In WebExpress, click "New Web Site," then click "Create Using Web Site Themes," and you're offered a couple of fleshed-out business-oriented templates, plus lots of templates created for other uses, (which with a little ingenuity can be adapted to serve a business).

## On a Shoestring

Do you need new software to create a web site? Not necessarily. Many programs designed for other purposes include basic web-authoring tools. Full-featured word

27

> ## Tip...
>
> ## Smart Tip
>
> Where the built-in Microsoft Word HTML editor really shines is in converting existing Word documents into web-ready pages. Click on "File" and then "Save As." Under "Save As Type," scroll until you find "HTML." Set that option, press "Save," and, just that fast, the brochure you created in Word is a web page. You'll probably want to edit it before putting it online—spacing and such is often weird after the translation—but for sheer speed and convenience, you can't beat this built-in tool.

processors, for instance, can write web pages. Case in point: Microsoft's Word 2003, which is part of the Office XP suite, includes handsome templates for erecting business home pages. Click on "New/Web Pages" and a wizard pops up along with a home page template.

But if you're serious about getting down to business on the web, you should spend the money to buy FrontPage or WebExpress. Hobbyists and tinkerers can try to coax web pages out of programs intended for other users—and they may well succeed—but you are too busy for that, and you need more polished tools. If you're still looking for a bargain and want an alternative to diddling with the bare-bones HTML editors stuffed into word processors, check out the web page creation tools at CNET's Download.com (http://download.com/3120-20-0. html?qt=web+page+creation). Here, you'll be able to download full copies or trial versions of popular, higher-end web page creation tools such as Dreamweaver MX and NetObjects Fusion MX.

# Puttin' on the Glitz

The web is a graphical medium—words matter, but images are just as important in attracting and holding viewers. That's why both FrontPage and WebExpress come bundled with collections of free art—textured page backgrounds, buttons, arrows and other visual elements for helping readers navigate a site.

Want to go a visual step beyond? There are plenty of software tools for creating customized graphics, but you may want to stick with FrontPage 2003, which features Integrated Microsoft PowerPoint-like graphics editing tools, including AutoShapes, a collection of shapes and drawings, such as banners, arrows and callouts that can be inserted into documents and customized. It also features another PowerPoint-like tool called Shadow Style that lets you add shadows. You can crop images, make them transparent or black and white, create image maps, add text, and more. FrontPage 2003 also includes the Photo Gallery component, which allows you to quickly and easily create an album to display personal or business photos or images. You can add images to the Photo Gallery and select from several different customizable layouts, add captions and descriptions to images, reorder images, change image sizes, and switch layouts. You can buy more powerful image tools, but frankly, the learning curve usually is too steep.

- *Another artistic option.* Forget trying to make your own images and just roam the web in a hunt for free art that has been uploaded by graphic artists who are happy just to get their work in the public view and gladly let others download their images. Start enhancing a web page's graphics with a visit to Webpromotion (www.webpromotion.com), which features several dozen superb animated images. Use of Webpromotion's original animated graphics files is free when Webpromotion's home page is linked from pages that display its animation. When animation is used without a link to Webpromotion, a small fee is charged for royalty-free use.

# Image Boosters

When you play with images, you need specialty software that will let you change the image's size, resolution, and more. Good image-editing software will even let you edit photographs. There's a stain on your white shirt in that photo? Whoosh! An image editor will wipe away all such problems.

Such software used to be tricky to use, expensive, and was mainly aimed at professionals working in graphics and photography. Nowadays, there's a boatload of good, cheap, easy-to-use programs. A top choice is Adobe Photoshop Elements, which costs $99.

More good choices come from Ulead (www.ulead.com), a Taiwan-based software developer that excels at creating wonderful and very cheap graphics-editing tools. For instance, SmartSaver Pro ($59.95) allows nearly instant changes in an image's format and size. Why is that important? On a Web page, you generally want small images that display fast, and with SmartSaver Pro, it's simple to save many versions until you get the right balance of size and graphical quality.

Another must-have Ulead program is PhotoImpact ($79.95). The poor man's Photoshop, PhotoImpact is the solution when you cannot lay hands on Photoshop Elements. It's easy to use, versatile, and powerful, and it will allow for creative reshaping of images to suit your Web site.

You can't create quality Web pages without owning image-editing software— but you don't need to spend big bucks or enroll in college courses to master sophisticated software. For most of us, less than $200 will buy all we need. A big plus with Ulead is that most of its programs are available for free trial downloads. Next time you wish you could tweak an image, visit Ulead, download the tool you need—and just do it!

- *How about this great source?* TuDogs (www.tudogs.com) is a gateway to dozens of graphics houses. TuDogs is free; however, access is restricted to TuDogs' newsletter subscribers.

  Many days can be spent downloading images—the web is swamped with terrific free art. But the chief beef of surfers is long waits for pages to load, invariably caused by creating a page with too many graphics. So use images sparingly. A few brighten a page; too many drown it.

- *Another caveat.* Before uploading any images to your web site, carefully read the fine print on the artist's page. Some prohibit use on commercial sites. If in doubt, ask for permission. That is a sure cure against future complications.

- *Something to keep in mind.* Simple is best with a web page. Better an unglamorous page that loads rapidly than a state-of-the-art page that causes the browsers of your visitors to crash. When a mania seizes you and you want to design pages with fancy looks and the newest bells and whistles, put that stuff on a personal page, not your business site. All those toys are fun to play with—but web visitors hate them.

- *A reliable rule of thumb.* The more times you say "wow" as you design your web page, the worse it is. You want to create a page where the wow factor is minimal in terms of design but high in terms of functionality.

# Testing, Testing

Gremlins often play tricks with web pages, and that's why no professional Webmaster announces a new page to the public before testing it. Surf the web enough, and sooner or later you'll stumble into a test site mounted by a brand-name business that has put it online so that insiders can find the bugs before the public does. Do the same thorough testing before publicizing your page.

A crucial test: Make sure pages work equally well in Microsoft Internet Explorer and Netscape Communicator. Ignore this advice at your own peril. Recently a business acquaintance implored me to look at his site, for which he had paid designers upwards of $10,000. I logged in—and found only blank pages. Incredibly, the site had not been tested on Internet Explorer. When I checked the site with Netscape, it was indeed a spiffy piece of work,

## Smart Tip

*Tip...*

Don't go crazy with colors—this is one of the biggest goofs of new web page designers. Stick with maybe two colors for fonts (words) and use a simple, basic color for the page background (white, off-white, and pale yellow are good choices). Always test your page on a laptop with a very cheap screen—don't assume surfers will have $1,000, 25-inch monitors. If it doesn't look good on a small, cheap screen, it's bad page design.

but not checking Explorer, the leading web browser, was simply nuts. If, in testing your own site, you find bugs, don't fret. Few pages get put up without at least some kinks, and a good place to start is to pinpoint things that show up on your screen offline but don't work online. The standard problem is that an image (or two, or three) isn't displaying, caused by a botched hyperlink. Strip down any web page to its essentials, and you'll find a little text interspersed with many hyperlinks, which are web directions to images and other files stored elsewhere. Put in the wrong hyperlink—and sometimes even web-authoring programs do it—and the online page will show up as a jumble.

This is when it's time to do a spot of dirty work with HTML code. Click "View/HTML," and a screen filled with gibberish opens. Hunt for the code pointing to the image or text that is not displaying. A good bet is that the link reads <img src="C:\Windows\temp\bluediamond.gif"> or something like that. No link that includes directions to local drives will work online. The cure? Erase everything that comes before the image's name, the result will read <img src="bluediamond.gif">, and it will work exactly right online.

Follow the same drill with anything that's not displaying properly. HTML is intimidating at first glance—and at second glance, too. But tinker with it, and soon enough, all images and links will display the way you intended.

A sure way to go wrong with a web site is to put it up and just leave it there. To keep viewers coming back, a page needs regular updating. "If your page is aging, static, it says, 'I don't get it,'" says Boston College's Cronin.

How often does a site need updating? Probably once a month at a minimum because although updating takes time, the investment is warranted, says White. "The internet is a new frontier with limitless possibilities," he says. "Now is the time to experiment . . . before lack of competency puts you out of business."

# Online Storefront Solutions

*Pssst.* Want to know a shortcut that eliminates much of your need to know how to build a web site and still puts you in an e-commerce business? Then you want to know about Yahoo!'s online storefront service that allows you to easily create an online store (http://store.yahoo.com). Granted, this option usually is more expensive

Tip...

## Smart Tip

Never underestimate the instant credibility an e-tailer gains from an alliance with a powerhouse like Yahoo!—even when it consists of nothing more than putting up a storefront on Yahoo! real estate. This name recognition is a real boost.

at the beginning, but spending the extra cash will give you faster ramp-up time. As quickly as you type in your credit card information, you will be in business with a Yahoo! store.

Here's the promise of the service: You do not need to know a speck of HTML code, but within an hour or less, you will have an online store that looks good—and all you have to do is follow a form-driven set of instructions. Think of it as akin to cooking with a recipe. If you follow the instructions at Yahoo! Store, the result will be a credible, attractive site. A plus is that Yahoo! Store offers easy tie-ins with credit card providers so you will be truly e-commerce-enabled in the bargain.

Basically, when you rent Yahoo! Merchant Solutions you get web hosting, software to build a catalog, and management and marketing tools. Another important plus—you get access to Yahoo! Shopping, a fantastic source of traffic. Yahoo! Shopping, for example, is one of the largest shopping destinations on the web today. Am I recommending Yahoo! Merchant Solutions over stand-alone, do-it-yourself storefronts? It depends on what you want and how much time you are willing to invest. As any surfer knows, the web is cluttered with millions of poorly constructed, nonfunctional storefronts that get little or no traffic. It is easy to construct a viable store with, say, FrontPage—but "easy" does not mean effortless. Many, many hours go into the job, and your time investment can be slashed dramatically by turning to the templates offered by Yahoo! Merchant Solutions. It's also nearly impossible to create a truly bad Yahoo! store. Unfortunately, many aspiring e-tailers manage to do that when they go the do-it-yourself route. So think hard about the Yahoo! store option. This could be the solution you need.

How much does it cost to have a Yahoo! store? You pay $49.95 per month for hosting, 10 cents per item per month, and a 5 percent transaction fee on all transactions. You will also be charged a 3.5 percent revenue share on all transactions that originate from anywhere on the Yahoo! Network, such as the Yahoo! Directory. If you decide to participate in Yahoo! Shopping, this revenue share will also be applied to all transactions that originate from Yahoo! Shopping. There is no startup fee, and you can cancel whenever you want.

When setting up a Yahoo! store, there is no software to install—all you need is your web browser. It takes less than a minute to add each new item, and you can upload an item image with a single click.

You can use a customized Yahoo! Store web address like store.yahoo.com/mystore for free, but for $35 per year, you can get a personalized web address such as www.my-web-store.com. For more information, go to http://store.yahoo.com and click on "How To Get Started."

Some e-tailers are turning to eBay (www.ebay.com) for their online storefront services—especially those e-tailers who are already experimenting with eBay. EBay Stores allow you to sell your fixed-price and auction items from a unique destination on eBay. You can build your own eBay Store through an easy series of steps: Create customized categories, include your own logo, or choose one of eBay's online images, and list item descriptions and policies.

Your eBay Store is promoted to eBay's 42 million users in several ways: All your listings will contain an eBay Store icon and link inviting buyers to visit your eBay Store; the

**Budget Watcher**

A Yahoo location in particular may be real gold because of how it promotes its stores. Search for "Turkish coffee" on Yahoo!, for instance, and it's a fast hop into a couple of small e-tailers selling that brew as well as pots, cups and so forth. Just as a brick-and-mortar mall brings its merchants traffic, Yahoo! attracts shoppers to its stores.

eBay Store icon is also attached to your user ID for extra visibility; buyers will be driven to your store through the eBay Store Directory, which is designed to promote all stores; and you will receive your own personalized eBay Store web site address to distribute and publicize.

The price is right, too. EBay offers three subscription fees: $9.95 per month for a basic store, $49.95 per month for a featured store, and $499 per month for an anchor store. Store owners must also pay insertion fees for fixed-price listings that are 5 cents per listing for up to 30 days (and increase after that based on the duration of your listing), and final-value fees based on the final sale price of your item. You'll also need to be registered as an eBay seller by putting your credit card on file, and have a minimum feedback rating of 20 or pay $5 to become ID-verified. For more information on eBay Stores, visit http://pages.ebay.com/storefronts/seller-landing.html.

One of the best things about eBay Stores is that they are very easy for visitors to find. For example, eBay lets you add a "Visit my store" link to your auction listing pages. Also, all stores are listed in the eBay Store Directory, which can be reached from eBay's navigation bar, located at the top of all eBay pages. There are other options: Small merchants can use online storefront solutions from Microsoft's bCentral (www.bcentral.com), and hosting companies such as Interland (www.interland.com), NTT/Verio (www.verio.com), XO Communications (www.xo.com), and Affinity Internet (www.affinity.com).

# Advanced Tools and Tricks

Now that your site is up, how do you make it special and filled with content that attracts visitors and keeps them coming back? That mission consumes site-builders, both full-time professionals and part-timers, but if there is one fact we now know to be absolutely true, it is this: Simplicity is best.

Case in point: The web site for a luxury hotel chain based in India features a huge soundtrack of classical music, which is just annoying. Maybe some sitar tracks—authentic Indian music—might make sense, but classical? It's bandwidth-hogging craziness. Resist the temptation to put something on your site just because you can. Never put up content that slows access to a page but doesn't demonstrably heighten user value.

What works is content that gives users reasons to linger, to absorb more of what you're offering. You'll find there are many, many ways to introduce this content, and

## Budget Watcher

Want to dabble at e-tailing without a major money commitment? Take a look at Amazon's zShops (www.amazon.com). Think of zShops as auctions without bidding. A merchant lists an item for sale at a fixed price— and pays a listing fee of one dime. That's right: 10 cents. When an item sells, the merchant pays a "completion fee" ($1.25 plus 2.5 percent of any amount over $25). Check it out.

you are going to have to exercise real discretion here. Pick a few tools, try them out, monitor user responses, and then delete the ones that aren't proving valuable. Be ruthless here, and never forget that simple is better.

That understood, here are many tasty tools for you to consider using to beef up your site. Just remember, this may be an all-you-can-eat buffet, but the more you put on your plate, the more discomfort your web site viewers will feel.

- *Banners.* A standard of web design, the banner proclaims, in effect, a site's name. Whether it sits at the top of the page or sometimes at the bottom, a banner is a necessity. You could make your own from scratch—tools are included with Microsoft's FrontPage, for instance. But my advice is to first try out the free, easy-to-use banner makers on the web. Usually within five minutes these automated banner makers will produce a spiffy design that you could not easily match on your own. A good place to try your hand at this is MediaBuilder's 3D Textmaker (www.3dtext maker.com). Give it a whirl and, almost certainly, the result will be so eye-catching you will want to immediately splash it on your site. MediaBuilder also gives easy-to-follow directions for doing just that.

- *E-mail lists.* You want to experiment with a tool that lets customers talk among themselves about your products and services? An e-mail list gives you that capability. The smartest, simplest way to create a list is at Yahoo! Groups (http://groups.yahoo.com). Yahoo! Groups offers many options. Lists can be private, open only to members you approve, or public—open to all who knock on the door. My advice: Experiment with several types of lists, perhaps a private one for existing customers and a public one for all comers.

Either way, carefully monitor traffic. To be useful, a list needs a steady flow of traffic and at least a few messages daily. Initially, you might encourage friends and colleagues to post just to get the list going, but eventually you'll need a site that generates sufficient traffic, or your lists will collapse from lack of use. When they work (and

## Smart Tip

Tip...

Keep a banner message very short. Aim to limit yourself to three to five words, plus a small image. You want something that grabs attention fast and instantly says what it's all about.

# On File

**Y**ou've created umpteen wonderful web pages, so now how do you get them onto your web site? You need another piece of software, a program that handles file transfer protocol (FTP). An FTP program lets you shift files from your computer to another via an Internet connection, and that makes it an essential piece of any net toolkit.

FTP is built into Microsoft FrontPage and many other web page editors, but personally, I have long found it faster and easier to use a specialty FTP program. For years I've relied on WS_FTP ($39.95 from Ipswitch Inc., www.ipswitch.com). A free trial version is available for download.

An alternative is Cute FTP ($39.95), available from GlobalSCAPE at www.cuteftp.com. Hunt for still others at CNET's downloads site—http://download.com. Type in FTP, and you'll be presented with dozens of apps that do this work.

Check out several apps and pick the one that works best for you—and know that, even if you've never FTP'd, once you get into web site construction and maintenance, your FTP application will become one that's put to daily use.

A word of caution: FTP software generally seems tricky to use. That's because you need to exactly specify your user name, password, etc., and you must also correctly type everything in the right case (upper or lower). It can be a bit maddening to get an FTP program working right, but once you do, settings will be saved and future transfers will be no harder than making a few mouse clicks. For more tips, head to "Beginner's Guide to Using FTP" at http://en.tldp.org/HOWTO/mini/FTP 3.html, a helpful, free guide that should get you uploading in a matter of minutes.

Also, a vocabulary point: When you transfer a file to your web site, that's uploading. When you transfer a file from a web site to your computer, that's downloading. Keep those words straight, and all you read about FTP will suddenly make sharper sense.

they often do), lists are a fast way to spice up a site with the kind of interactivity that keeps surfers coming back.

- *Polls.* Polls, where surfers register their opinion on an issue, are at the heart of the net because this is interactivity in its most basic form. Ask any question— "Should pornography be banned from the web?" "What's your favorite cocktail?" "Who's your favorite Beatle?" It doesn't matter: Surfers will want to register their point of view and see how others voted. AOL has long used polls as a staple on its pages. Learn from the masters and do likewise.

  Writing a poll from scratch is a tricky bit of coding, but free poll templates are readily available for insertion into your site. All you have to do is fill in the blanks in a template and copy and paste a bit of code into your site, and you're in business. Sources of such templates are plentiful, but a good one is from freetools.com (www.freetools.com or www.freepolls.com).

- *Common Gateway Interface (CGI) scripts.* These are easy-to-use scripts (prewritten code) that you simply pop into your page to create a guest book or the ability to track visitors. CGI is a programming tool that lets many small applications run within a web environment and is one of the web's oldest resources. Newer, slicker ways to do much of what can be accomplished via CGI are plentiful, and a real plus is their price tag: Scripts put together by enthusiasts are free and available for anyone to use. Always test any CGI script thoroughly before going public with a page, however. In several cases, I simply haven't been able to get some CGI scripts to work properly.

  Thousands of these free CGI scripts exist, and one of the best resources for finding the scripts you need is The CGI Resource Index (www.cgi-resources.com). If you can't find the script you want here, it probably doesn't exist.

- *Chat rooms.* Wouldn't it be cool if your site had its own private, real-time chat room? It's both easy to put up and free from Dialogoo.com (www.dialogoo.com). The chat room is easy to set up. All you need to do is add a few lines of HTML code to your web page, and in a matter of minutes you'll be able to get folks chatting.

  Before you do, however, mull on this: Empty chat rooms look very, very dumb. Will you have enough traffic to put people into a chat room on a regular basis? Do you want to monitor it? How frequently? Know that you won't be on call 24 hours a day, seven days a week—but the chat room will, theoretically, be available that often. My advice: For most small sites, this is a tool to avoid.

**Smart Tip**

Use web tools sparingly. Best advice: Introduce one, and only one. If it proves popular, leave it up and add a second. If users ignore it, put up another but take down the unloved tool. Always keep it simple, and you'll invariably do better.

Better by far is to set yourself up with an AOL Instant Messenger account (it's free, from www.aol.com) where visitors can fire off questions to you if you are online. This gives surfers an alternative to e-mail for finding information but doesn't expose you to the ridicule that comes with offering an unpopulated chat room. Do this in combination with providing a message board and surfer needs ought to be very adequately handled.

- *Counters.* Resources for counters are plentiful and, with one in place, it's easy to monitor visitor counts. Pick one up at GoStats.com (http://gostats.com/free). But before installing it, know this: Some counters are visible counters, which are usually signs of amateur page creation, and, worse, if your hit counts are low (as they will be at the beginning), it actually deters viewers from hanging around. It's discouraging to stumble into a page and see that you are Visitor No. 112. Any page that's been around any length of time ought to have had thousands of viewers. Another minus to counters: Often they substantially slow down page loading speed. Typically you will get good counts from your web host anyway, so leave the counters behind.

- *Guest books.* Sure, you could create a guest book using a CGI script, but probably the easier way is to insert some HTML code into your page—you can find it at Bravenet.com. Why would you want a guest book? It's a convenient way to collect more information about your visitors. And incidentally, surfers often like to look through guest books.

## Beware!

It is worth repeating: Don't clutter your site with too many tools, don't use tools that slow server response times, and never use tools that distract surfers from the primary purposes of your site. Sure, it's wonderful if you're getting heavy traffic, but if they're all coming to post messages about gangsta rap and your business has nothing to do with music, that's a waste. Keep your site focused, and never stray too far from that focus.

## Smart Tip

*Tip...*

When putting up a guest book, create the first six to 10 entries yourself or ask friends and relatives to sign in. This gives the guest book and your site a trafficked appearance. Nobody wants to be the first to sign in.

# The Ten Most Deadly Mistakes in Site Design

This chapter could probably be called the 100 most deadly mistakes in site design—there are so many goofs site builders make—but let's narrow the focus down to the most disastrous ten. Avoid these gaffes, and your site will be far better than much of the competition.

1. *Disabling the "back" button.* Evil site authors long ago figured out how to break a browser's back button so that when a user pushes it, one of several undesired things happen: There's an immediate redirect to an unwanted location, the browser stays put because the "back" button has been deactivated, or a new window pops up and overtakes the screen. Porno site authors are masters of this—their code is often so malicious that frequently the only way to break the cycle is to restart the computer. This trick has gained currency with other kinds of site builders. My advice: Never do it. All that's accomplished is that viewers get annoyed.

**Smart Tip**

OK, there are exceptions to the "no orphans" rule. If you want a special page set aside only for invited viewers, send out the URL, but offer no links to the page from any of your other pages. When might you use it? For instance, if you're offering big discounts to a special group of customers, that price list might be put on an orphan page.

2. *Opening new windows.* Once upon a time, using multiple new frames to display content as a user clicked through a site was cool—a new thing in web design. Now it only annoys viewers because it ties up system resources, slows computer response, and generally complicates a surfer's experience. Sure, it's easy to use this tool. But don't.

3. *Failing to put a phone number and address in a plainly seen location.* If you're selling, you need to offer viewers multiple ways to contact you. The smartest route is to put up a "Contact Us" button that leads to complete info—mailing address, phone and fax numbers. Even if nobody ever calls, the very presence of this information comforts some viewers.

4. *Broken links.* Bad links—hyperlinks that do nothing when clicked—are the bane of any surfer. Test your site—and do it weekly—to ensure that all links work as promised.

5. *Slow server times.* Slow times are inexcusable with professional sites. It's an invitation to the visitor to click away. What's slow? There is no easy rule, but I'd say that any click should lead to something immediately happening. Maybe a new page or image will take a few seconds to come into view, but the process should at least start immediately.

6. *Outdated information.* Again, there's no excuse, but it's stunning how many site builders lazily leave up pages that long ago ceased to be accurate. When information changes, update the appropriate pages immediately—and this means every bit of information, every fact, even tiny ones. As a small business, you cannot afford the loss of credibility that can come from having even a single factual goof.

7. *Scrolling text and marquees.* It's an odd fact: Netscape and Microsoft Internet Explorer do not display pages identically, which is one way these site-design tools get easily screwed up by browsers. They can also be maddening to the viewer who wants to know, now, what you're offering, but the information keeps scrolling off the page. Use these tools in personal pages—they are fun and add liveliness to otherwise static pages—but put these tricks aside when building business pages.

**Budget Watcher**

Check your site for broken links, automatically and free, with a stop at Keynote NetMe-chanic (www.net mechanic. com). Type in your URL, and—whoosh!—you will get a report on broken links and page load time, and even a freebie spell check. It can also give a free report on browser compatibil-ity on the spot.

8. *Too many font styles and colors.* Pages ought to present a unified, consistent look, but novice site builders—entranced by having hundreds of fonts at their fingertips plus dozens of colors—frequently turn their pages into a garish mishmash. Use two or three fonts and colors per page, maximum. The idea is to reassure view-ers of your solidity and stability, not to convince them you are wildly artistic.

9. *Orphan pages.* Memorize this: Every page in your site needs a readily seen link back to the home page. Why? Sometimes users will forward a URL to friends, who may visit and may want more information. But if the page they get is a dead end, forget it. Always put a link to "Home" on every page, and that will quickly solve this problem.

10. *Using leading-edge technology.* Isn't that what the web is all about? Nope, not when you're guaranteed to lose most of your viewers whenever your site requires a download of new software to be properly viewed. Three-D VRML pages are way cool—no question about it—but if nobody actually looks at them, they're a waste. Never use bells and whistles that force viewers to go to a third-party site to download a viewing program. Your pages need to be readable with a standard, plain-Jane browser, preferably last year's or earlier. State-of-the-art is cool for techno wizards but death for entrepreneurs.

# e-Chat with
# OneTravel.com's Michael Thomas

## OneTravel.com

**Michael Thomas, CEO and founder**
**Location: East Greenville, Pennsylvania**
**Year Started: 1995**

Time out. So far, you've absorbed the theory of building a web site, but to really understand what is going on, you need to hear from the experts—the entrepreneurs who are really doing it.

Throughout this book, you will find two types of interviews—some with top executives at the internet's most distinguished sites and others with folks at wanna-be sites that show promise but still have a long road in front of them. Why both types? The top execs tell how to get there, but it's the wanna-be top execs who give us insight into the nitty-gritty of the process. Mix them together, and what you have is the reality of success.

You want to stick with learning how to build a site into a monster business success? Skip over the next two chapters and carry on. But I strongly recommend you read the words from the real builders because they truly know where you are and how you can get to the next level. Even if you jump over this material now, come back to it later because what you learn will pay big dividends.

Meet Michael Thomas, founder and CEO of OneTravel.com. Usually ranked among the internet's best travel sites, OneTravel is at the forefront of the race to dominate what is one of the web's richest sectors. The Travel Industry Association reports that 64 million people made their travel plans online in 2002. About 15 percent of travel is now booked online, says Jupiter Research, an online research firm that also says growth will continue, with $37.3 billion booked online in 2003, growing to $64.2 billion in 2007. Plenty of money is at stake here, and Thomas intends to get a thick slice. He explains how.

**Robert McGarvey:** *How much money did you start OneTravel.com with back in 1995?*

**Michael Thomas:** Unlike many dotcom business strategies, which center on securing OPM—other people's money—as fast as possible, I decided to build the business out of cash flow. I know that it is a little old-fashioned in this day and age, but I just felt more comfortable that way. My outlay was about $150,000. In 1995 I had purchased five strategic keywords from Yahoo!!, and these initially represented my largest monthly outlay.

**McGarvey:** *You started OneTravel.com on a sheep farm in Zionsville, Pennsylvania— miles from anywhere. Was this location a disadvantage?*

**Thomas:** We had a lot of fun on the farm. In the spring it was hard to get the employees focused on work, as they all wanted to go out and play with the foals, lambs, and kids.

Our office was located in the loft of a wagon shed on a sheep farm. We did a good job using this as a differentiator in the marketplace and secured significant media and PR as a result. Our loft was only one and a half hours from New York and one hour from Philadelphia, so we could reach civilization easily but did not have the daily hassles and expenses associated with major urban areas. The biggest difficulty was finding employees who were comfortable using an outhouse. We finally outgrew our space and moved to a much larger facility with real plumbing in February 1999.

**McGarvey:** *What's been the biggest challenge you've had in building OneTravel.com?*

**Thomas:** I knew that it was not going to be easy. Nothing worthwhile ever is. When we were smaller, unproven, and on the sheep farm, the biggest challenge was to get suppliers to believe and understand that we were a credible entity and an organization that could fulfill their product distribution. Now that we have demonstrated ourselves as a valuable partner, the biggest challenge for us, given that we are still a small company, is to get our arms around all the technology we need. We provide air, car, hotel, vacations, and cruises, and every one of these business verticals has different technology requirements. So, with a reasonably small technical team, we've had to develop a lot of technology to drive each one of these businesses. We've spent years working on developing all these tools, and we are now really beginning to bear the fruit of all the labor and the investment that we have made.

**McGarvey:** *How do you broaden your product mix outside airline tickets?*

**Thomas:** We have probably the largest database of vacations and cruises of any company out there. In addition, since we have built OneTravel.com out of cash flow, we pride ourselves on having a lean operation. We never had the luxury of fattening up on OPM. We have been smart to ensure that our labor-intensive operations are in low-cost locations. Our ticket fulfillment is being done out of Odessa, Texas, which provides us with a great labor market. Having said that, we are and have been very proactive in diversifying our revenue streams with the addition of other product lines. Our next-generation hotel product, for example, Net Rate Hotels, which allows hotels to manage their own inventory and pricing on our platform, has significantly enhanced our revenue stream. In addition, we are starting to make money with our new auction platform. Our business is firing on all cylinders.

# Fighting the Good Fight

Who are the big players in the travel market? Expedia, which was spun off from Microsoft and is now owned by USA Interactive Inc., a New York-based media and electronic retailing company; Travelocity, which was spun off from Sabre, which, in turn, is largely owned by American Airlines; and Orbitz, which was started by five airlines—American, Continental, Delta, Northwest, and United, all very big, very smart companies with lots of money. But as Michael Thomas proves, an entrepreneur with guts and determination can find a place to thrive, even on fields that have been well staked out by 900-pound gorillas.

Don't ever assume that because some giant is in the way, your idea will never prosper. What if Jeff Bezos had felt that way about Barnes & Noble's dominance of national bookselling? There'd be no Amazon. Instead, Bezos is well on his way to beating Barnes & Noble. If your idea is good, fight it out—and let the marketplace pick the winners.

**McGarvey:** *The big guys in your space are getting bigger. How will you find your niche against Travelocity and Expedia?*

**Thomas:** We've done a number of different things. One is that OneTravel.com has really positioned itself as the leading turnkey travel enabler, where we provide companies that want to be in the business of selling travel with all the tools they need without having to make a significant infrastructure investment. Through the OneTravel.com Partner Program, online businesses gain access to travel inventory, including as many as 500 airlines, 54,000 hotels, 48 car rental companies, and more than 2 million vacation packages and cruises. Our booking engines can be placed anywhere on any web site, enabling the site's customers to book travel directly through their site. With this partner program, we believe we are really serving a need in the marketplace with something that nobody else offers. Our Partner Program partners span the spectrum as well. We just signed a deal with Discovery's Travel Channel and have developed turnkey solutions for Sam's Club, Uniglobe.com, Lowestfare.com, and AMC TV.

The other part of our strategy is to focus on niche opportunities. We have started 11thHourVacations.com, which is a web site for last-minute travelers looking for a great deal. Almost every airline has empty seats at takeoff, and most hotels and cruises have room vacancies. By taking advantage of this leftover inventory, customers enjoy unparalleled savings and value. Travel companies worldwide supply 11thHourVacations.com with a revolving inventory of more than two million vacation and cruise deals, so customers need to act fast and check back often.

Another site we have is CheapSeats.com, a web site that offers the lowest international airfare, anywhere. CheapSeats.com offers a minimum of 200 flight options in a single search—offering the most available international flights of all travel sites. In addition to international airfare, CheapSeats. com delivers results from more than 500 domestic and international airlines, 54,000 hotels, 48 car rental companies, and more than 2 million vacation packages and cruises. There isn't another site out there that focuses purely on international airfare.

We have also sought out niche opportunities within the primary travel markets. In the air market with our "White Label," we have conceptualized a brand-new type of fare, which we have integrated into our existing continuum of negotiated, consolidated, sale, and regular tariff fares. White Label fares are offered to the public without identifying the airline and some details of the route.

We think that our approach to the marketplace and implementation is unique.

**McGarvey:** *Why haven't you gone public?*

**Thomas:** It was not that long ago that we were still in the barn with an outhouse. When all the underwriters started to call regarding an IPO, we were simply not ready. We also believed that running a public company was extremely time-consuming and required a lot of effort in terms of maintaining shareholder relations. Realizing that we needed partners, I went out and found some investment banking partners that made sense, and they helped us build our company and invest in technology. It's been a very successful partnership.

**McGarvey:** *How do you up the look-to-book ratio?*

**Thomas**: We are working on a number of initiatives on this front. The math is simple: 2 to 3 percent of the people who look, buy. Of the other 97 to 98 percent, 70 percent will eventually buy, and the rest are just lookers. The game is about increasing conversion on those 70 percent. Without divulging secrets, we are implementing techniques that are used to generate sales and create urgency to encourage the buying decision in the offline world. Let's face it—the art of selling product is the same as it has been for thousands of years. The only difference is the medium and interface.

**McGarvey:** *How do you market the site? What works; what hasn't?*

**Thomas:** We have used guerrilla marketing techniques and public relations extensively. Those tactics work because of cost efficiency and relationship-building. Guerrilla marketing allows for a hands-on, grass-roots approach with audiences, while public relations helps to establish long-term relationships with constituents. Another tactic that works is newsletters—building databases and establishing consistent marketing help maintain an ongoing dialogue with customers. Newsletters are a cost-efficient way to increase sales.

Untargeted advertising does not work. To be successful, our advertising campaigns must be travel-targeted. A medium that does not work is solo e-mails. Unless a user specifically opts in to receive your company's newsletter, many users consider everything else to be spam. If they're not accustomed to seeing your e-mail ad in their inbox, then most likely, the ad will be deleted and ignored.

# Cheap Tricks with BlueSuitMom.com's Maria Bailey

## BlueSuitMom.com

**Maria Bailey, president and founder
Location: Pompano Beach, Florida
Year Started: 2000**

It is amazing, the opportunities that still exist on the web. Ask Maria Bailey. A onetime marketing executive with AutoNation, she launched BlueSuitMom.com on Mother's Day 2000 with the aim of meeting the needs of executive working moms. Her take on the net was that there were sites geared for working moms in general—but none aimed specifically at executives who also happen to be moms.

So she decided to build one, BlueSuitMom.com, which offers opportunities for networking, news geared for executive moms, and tips (how to manage time, for instance). In addition, what started as a single web site and a big dream has now grown into BSM Media, a full-service marketing firm specializing in marketing to moms. The team behind BlueSuitMom.com now produces Mom Talk Radio, which can be heard on WFTL 1400 AM in South Florida, and BSM Media is currently working on nationally syndicating it. The team also wrote *Marketing to Moms: Getting Your Share of the Trillion-Dollar Market* (Prima Lifestyle). Brilliant as the idea for BlueSuitMom may well prove to be, the ramp-up of Bailey's site wasn't smooth. Read on for her candid—and helpful—comments on building a site.

**Robert McGarvey:** *How much funding did you start with? Where was it raised?*

**Maria Bailey:** We started with a commitment for $1 million from a former boss—but, unfortunately, the money did not become a reality. So we truly began with $100,000 raised from personal savings and a few friends.

**McGarvey:** *What were the first big obstacles you encountered in building a web business?*

**Bailey:** Our biggest obstacle has been getting interested investors to actually write the check. That stems from a historical obstacle: Career women have done such a good job at proving to the wealthy/powerful men they work with that they have achieved a balance between work and family that it is difficult to help my potential investors understand the needs of our market. And on top of it, these men are most likely not married to a woman who is a vice president or CEO. So you say "mother," and they envision their spouse, who is [usually] a stay-at-home mom.

There has been a bit of challenge in learning to manage the young technology pros you need to grow your site. There is little loyalty, and they convey an attitude that they have you by a leash, and without them you wouldn't be able to execute your business plan. They realize that their talents are in demand and are used to changing jobs often. Also, their confidence in technology has led many of them to believe that they also know how to run a business based on that technology. There is a short learning curve to adapt your management style to the new breed of employee you find in the web world.

**McGarvey:** *How do you promote the business?*

**Bailey:** We promote our business mainly by creating very strategic partnerships. For instance, we have a partnership with Stork Avenue, the largest retailer of birth announcements. They were willing to put our logo on 5 million catalogs in exchange for driving traffic to their site. We are relying too on the strong word-of-mouth network moms and businesswomen create and in turn networking within women's professional organizations, HR departments, and parenting organizations. We have also been featured in the media, including *The Wall Street Journal* and *USA Today*. Also, we are sponsoring events such as parenting conferences and distributing our content to other web sites to build brand recognition, and we have been very lucky in creating great press.

**McGarvey:** *What's the business's goal? What's the end game?*

**Bailey:** Our exit strategy is not to go public. Our goal is to create a prequalified niche market that may be attractive to content aggregators, such as iVillage and Women.com, or a search engine. Because there is no one out there exclusively targeting our market, we feel we have a good shot at it. We monitor the women's market regularly and watch the internet strategies of others so that we can identify possible acquirers.

> ## Smart Tip — Tip...
> Building a web business is a road filled with ups and downs for any entrepreneur, but a wonderful thing about it is that it provides genuine equal opportunity. Color, race, gender, creed—none of it matters because all cybercitizens are created equal. Better still, whatever you are, if there are others like you, that's the basis for creating an Internet community that just may become a profitable business.

**McGarvey:** *What unique advantages do you have vis-à-vis other web sites?*

**Bailey:** We felt the best advantage we could have was to be the first to market—and we were. Because we are the first site aimed at executive working mothers, it has allowed us to create all the great press we've received. The other advantage we have is that anytime we are working with a woman to make deals or create partnerships, we almost always get what we need because the woman on the other side of the phone relates immediately to the elements of our site.

**McGarvey:** *What's been your biggest surprise and your biggest disappointment in building this business?*

**Bailey:** The biggest surprise has been how quickly the site and idea have grown. The response we have gotten from other Internet companies and offline retailers, marketers and associations has been overwhelming. We can't keep up with the people who want to do business with us. Also, the international response we have received has been incredible. We receive e-mails from women all over thanking us for our vision to create something that is valuable to them.

The biggest challenge is managing our growth. We have so much growth opportunity now. One of the biggest challenges is not going after every single opportunity, but selecting the smart opportunities.

# 9

# **Nuts and Bolts**
## of Web Hosts
## and Domains

With your web site designed, you need a place to stow it so that visitors can access it—and you have hundreds of choices. Many hosts are free, and few cost more than $20 per month. Truth is, setting up your own host—a dedicated computer that's permanently wired into the net—wastes time and money and, for most small businesses, is a bad idea. Better to outsource hosting to folks who specialize in it.

You could use the free space that comes with your ISP account—most providers, from AOL to EarthLink, offer users at least some space as part of the basic service package. Frankly, though, this space is rarely suited to running a business. Servers are often slow during peak traffic hours, and domain names can be cumbersome (http://members.aol.com/rjmcgarvey, for example). This space may be great for putting up test pages and fiddling with a site before you're ready to go live, but when you want to get down to business, you'll need a dedicated host.

Where to find one? A quirk of the business is that while big-name national online services have emerged to dominate much of the internet (AOL, for instance), hosting remains the province of thousands of usually tiny, home-brewed mom-and-pop shops. Paradoxically, however, there's little advantage to using a host that's based in your neighborhood. I honestly don't know where my host (ProHosting.com) is located and cannot imagine stopping in for a visit.

> ## Smart Tip
>
> Want a fast take on comparative features of web hosts? Log onto Compare Web Hosts (www.comparewebhosts.com), where a few mouse clicks let you specify what's important to you and check out which hosts likely will serve your needs best. For a second opinion, head to TopHosts (www.tophosts.com), a site with a bit less functionality but more layers of detail—meaning it's not the easiest resource to use, but it has lots of information.

The only potential benefit of using a nearby company is that many hosts do not offer toll-free customer service. You'll pay your long-distance provider whenever you run into a snag and need to call the company. Hitches will probably be few, though. In the past year, I believe I've called my host one time, incurring maybe $1 in phone charges. Might you have more phone contact? Not likely: Low-budget hosts are just not geared to provide the in-depth handholding that would involve many phone calls. So, in most instances, you can put host location out of your mind.

When picking a host, you first and foremost want to know if a host can handle e-commerce activities. Some of the most barebones companies simply are not equipped. Other criteria that are important to most users: setup and monthly fees (a typical range for basic web hosting is $9.95 to $49.95 monthly, but the price usually goes up when adding e-commerce functionality, with a setup fee equal to one month's fee); amount of available storage space (you want at least 10 to 25MB to start, as well as the option to add more space as your needs expand); and connection speed (some very low-budget hosts rely on slow 56K modems, while most business-level hosts have high-speed T1 or T3 connections).

Comparing hosts is difficult, so a good policy is to quietly set up an account and test the host—kick the tires, so to speak—for several weeks before announcing your presence to the world. Isn't that expensive? You bet, when setup fees are factored in. But more expensive—and embarrassing—is to make a big push for traffic, only to have your host drop the ball and leave you with cranky visitors who cannot quite make it in. Better to know your host is operating smoothly before inviting guests to the party.

# Master of Your Domain

Before setting up your site, you also need to stake out your domain name, which is the word in between "www," "com," or "net" in web addresses. So what name suits you? Come up with some possibilities, then surf to Network Solutions (www.network solutions.com). Other businesses now offer domain registration, but this place was the first, and it has the technology down pat.

The drill is simple: You type in a name, and Network Solutions tells you if it's available. When you strike out—that is, the names you want are taken—Network Solutions then offers possibilities that are available for registration. Network Solutions traffics in the main U.S. top-level domains— "com," "net," and "org"—as well as the new er domains, such as info, biz, us, cc, bz, and tv. Find a name that suits you, and the charge is $25 for three years. After that, you own the rights to the name.

Don't believe doomsayers who talk of a shortage of good names. Yes, most easily remembered "com" names have been snagged, but entrepreneurial genius spawns new possibilities faster than old ones are foreclosed—and that catchy name may be within your reach after all. How? Every country gets its own country code, and that's created the possibility of registering a name abroad that may already be spoken for at home. A Tonga name, for example, would use the domain "to"; Niue would be "nu"; or "st" for São Tomé. You don't have to be in those places to register a domain there—you don't even have to know where they are. All that's required is authorizing a credit card charge— $189.95, in the case of Tonga, for a one-year registration of a web site with a Tonga address.

Here's where matters get strange or funny, depending upon your perspective. Your site may be registered in Tonga, but your web host needn't be there (and you would probably have a tough time finding one there that met your needs anyway). All you need is a host that handles uncommon locations (which you can find out by asking).

Not every country is quite so cavalier in its sales of domains. Greece ("gr"), for instance,

## Smart Tip

*Tip...*

What is a good domain name worth? Stories abound of names selling for seven figures or more, but proof of such transactions is hard to find. Nonetheless, if you think you have a zingy, saleable name that you want to market, try Yahoo Auctions (http://search. auctions.shopping.yahoo.com/ search/auc?alocale=ous&p= Domain+names&auccat=). If you're curious about the market, GreatDomains.com sometimes has as many as one million domains up for sale.

requires a physical presence in the nation (with the only satisfactory proof being a certificate from a government agency). Hong Kong ("hk"), too, requires a physical presence. In fact, most bustling nations want to hand out domains only to their own businesses.

Where to find out about registering your name in a foreign country? Head to Alldomains.com (www.alldomains.com), a company that sells non-U.S. domains, such as Tonga's "to." Prices usually will be higher than a standard U.S. registration, but for a zingy name, what's a few extra bucks?

# What's In a Name?

There's wide agreement that nothing matters as much as a good name. Yet who would have thought Amazon was one? What most matters in a name is that it's easy to spell and easy to remember. For my money, that's an argument against using a catchy name with an unorthodox country code suffix. Most U.S.-based computer users just automatically type "com," "net," "edu," or "gov." Throw a weird ending at them, and you may lose them. So I would recommend a clunky name with a "com" or "net" ending over a catchy name with an unorthodox ending.

Another argument against really offbeat endings: How stable are some of these countries? In revolutions, it's common to nationalize—that is, grab—holdings of foreign companies. What's to stop a new government from nationalizing its web and taking back all the names sold by a prior government? Here we're venturing into speculation. It has not happened, but it could. Don't forget that when picking your domain, you want something that will last and that's worth investing time and money into as traffic increases. And "com" and "net" names just may be the best bang for those dollars.

## Beware!

Can you "park" a domain name for free? When you park a domain, you reserve it but haven't yet mounted a site. Many outfits tout that they offer free parking, but that's not exactly true: You still have to pay the $70 registration fee. Free parking only means they'll put up an "under construction" sign that anyone who hunts for your domain will find. Big deal, you say? Yeah, that's how I see it, too. You could put up the same sign in 30 seconds on free space you already have access to (at an ISP, for instance).

# The Scoop on
## Business-to-Business
## e-Commerce

**U**sed to be, the dream was starting the next McDonald's, or maybe inventing a new widget that everybody would need, putting you on the fast track to wealth so immense it could scarcely be counted. Today, of course, the dream is to come up with the new Amazon or Yahoo!—but that might be the wrong dream.

Isn't this book all about launching the Next Big Thing? Nope. It's about building businesses on the internet. Nowadays, a very good argument can be made that there's a smarter way to go than scouting around for the idea that will spawn a new Amazon.

# Taking Care of Business

Consider Walt Geer. It was in late '98 that Geer, a partner in an Atlanta promotional products company, faced up to reality. His little business—which sold logo merchandise such as pens and coffee mugs to companies to distribute to employees and customers—was chugging along OK, but it was just one of 19,000 promotional products companies in the country. Plainly put, Geer's company was lost in the mob. So he decided to take the plunge. He cut the cord on his traditional company, dumping his existing customers and putting his business online as eCompanyStore (www.ecompanystore.com).

How is he doing now? Well, there were a couple of months of hard swallowing: "We had no revenue coming in," recalls Geer, "but we had to focus our energy on the internet. We didn't have the resources to do it and run our traditional business." But, he says, "in just a few months, the internet let us move from being a small company to a national player. Before, we serviced lots of little accounts. Now we have Microsoft, for example. The internet lets us go after big accounts."

Geer's eCompanyStore is just one of hundreds of a new breed of business-to-business (B2B) enterprises, where companies sell not to consumers but to other businesses.

---

## In the Know

**W**hat industry do you know, and know well? Substantial expertise is needed to create a viable B2B. What industries have you worked in? Which ones interest you enough that you'll enjoy the long hours of research you'll need to put in?

Ironically, you could probably pick any industry and do well—if it truly interests you and your ideas are good. That's because just about every industry will go through massive structural changes in the next decade as the underlying business processes are impacted by the Internet. Savvy entrepreneurs need to be watching for the turf where their ideas can make a difference.

Marketing glitz doesn't go as far in a B2B context as getting down to the nuts and bolts of what you have to offer businesses that will positively affect their bottom line. Business executives tend to be more cold-blooded about these things, so show them where they will save time and money, and they will follow you.

---

These internet companies may not be winning wide press attention, but they are creating a real buzz in big-money circles. Listen up, because in 2001 Forrester Research—a technology research and consulting firm—predicted that the B2B sector would go vertical, with North American B2B online sales reaching $7.2 trillion in 2006. In the meantime, Forrester predicted online retail—that's the business-to-consumer (B2C) market—would also grow, but the numbers were piddling in comparison. In 2006, Forrester says, B2C e-commerce will reach $219.8 billion. Do the math: B2B will generate 33 times the cash—and that's a multiple that demands attention.

What's more, according to a quarterly review from the Institute for Supply Management and Forrester Research, 84 percent of large companies now use the web to purchase indirect materials. In addition, the overall percentage of purchasing conducted online increased steadily during 2002, the review noted. Why the rush by businesses to purchase on the internet? Simply put, they are realizing that using the internet allows them to drive down costs. How much? "Shift purchasing to the web, and a business can eliminate about 90 percent of the cost of a transaction," says Rob Rosenthal, a senior research analyst at technology research firm IDC. "It can be pretty dramatic."

But more than just cost savings are propelling this mushrooming of business trade on the net, says eCompanyStore's Geer. "The real drivers are speed and efficiency," he says. "And besides, our web store is always open. These advantages are as attractive to our customers as the savings. The internet is a better and faster way for businesses to shop."

# The Many Faces of B2B

Just who is making it in B2B e-commerce? Sure winners have yet to emerge, but lately the web is filled with enticing players that illustrate the breadth of this marketplace. That's because B2B e-commerce offers diverse opportunities, with some players seeking to establish themselves as marketplaces where buyers and sellers meet to do deals, while others are positioning themselves to provide services and products to business customers in a wholly new, web-based way. The bottom line: B2B e-commerce entrepreneurs are limited only by their own imaginations. There are plenty of possibilities in this exploding space.

Want concrete examples of how businesses on the web are serving other businesses? Read on for a sampling of the strategies B2B web sites are pursuing.

## Liquidation.com

A bad economy means good things for Liquidity Services, a Washington, DC-based operator of two online liquidation sites, Liquidation.com and Government Liquidation

LLC (govliquidation.com). Why? Because the company helps other companies shed unwanted inventory and other products via online auctions.

"We convert surplus [inventory] to cash using online auctions," says Bill Angrick, CEO of Liquidity Services. "We have a very simple and transparent business model. People know what we do."

Here's how Liquidation.com and Gov liquidation.com (for government agencies such as the Defense Department) work: Sellers register on the sites for free and start

**Budget Watcher**

Do you buy anything for your business that could be more efficiently purchased on the internet? That thought alone can be the trigger to launch a B2B web site. Get thinking about what you buy and where—and whether the net would make the process cheaper and faster.

selling surplus merchandise in categories such as consumer merchandise, transportation, electronics and audio/video equipment, computers, industrial equipment, construction materials, office supplies, medical equipment, and aircraft parts. The company currently has 2,000 registered sellers.

Then, wholesale buyers register for free and bid to buy the goods and services. Every auction on the sites has an average of nine individual bidders and one winner. The auctions last two to five business days, and it takes another 10 to 15 days for the buyer and seller to complete the payment and shipping process. Liquidation.com and Govliquidation.com manage shipping using their shipping partners, and buyers are responsible for paying shipping costs. Once a buyer's payment has been collected, Liquidation.com/Govliquidation.com books the shipment of the merchandise and notifies the seller when to prepare the goods for pickup.

"This is lightning fast when you look at the alternative method that our clients use to conduct this sort of transaction," says Angrick. "For sellers, it can take months."

Currently, the company markets to 60,000 buyers, and 15,000 buyers have purchased products in the past 12 months on the sites, according to Angrick.

Liquidity Services is paid a success fee by the seller on completion of the transaction that is 15 to 30 percent of the sale. In some auctions, buyers also have to pay a buyer's premium. Liquidation.com and Govliquidation.com complete more than 12,000 bulk sales transactions monthly.

According to Angrick, sellers can obtain 30 to 50 percent higher recovery rates using the web sites, as well as save a significant amount of time, while buyers receive exceptional bargains on bulk surplus in many product categories, and receive the surplus very easily and in a trusted manner.

A bad economy might be good for a company like Liquidity Services, as there is always a need for this type of business. Angrick says that the company's sellers—which are basically Fortune 1000 or middle-market companies in the process of manufacturing, distributing, or retailing consumer goods, retail merchandise, or technology assets—are always trying to get rid of excess inventory. "Roughly 6 percent of revenues a year are returned goods, end-of-season product or excess inventory," says Angrick. "Every month, our sellers are turning out their surplus product. And there is $100 billion of addressable excess inventory each year. It's a huge opportunity."

The company is doing well. Angrick says that by the end of 2003, the company will have $55 million in revenue—a 25 percent increase over 2002 year-end revenues. "In the last four years, a lot of ideas for internet business have come and gone," says Angrick. "But this is a rapidly growing business."

> ## Smart Tip
>
> **Tip...**
>
> In early 2000, the major automobile manufacturers rocked their multibillion-dollar world by announcing a plan to shift, as soon as possible, much of their buying to the web. Why? To save money and gain time and flexibility. The point here is this: When tradition-bound behemoths like the automakers say B2B e-commerce is the way to go, there can no longer be any doubt that it's so.

# Elance.com

Another company with a successful online marketplace model is Sunnyvale, California-based Elance Inc. (www.elance.com). Its Elance Online Services Marketplace allows small businesses to post descriptions of their projects free of charge in categories such as web design, software development, administrative support, business strategy, graphic design, and writing and receive proposals from a global pool of service providers. Once a buyer posts a project, qualified service providers in relevant categories bid on the services. The buyer then determines which is the best service provider by reviewing feedback from previous buyers who have used that service provider, bid amounts, service provider portfolios, and service provider experience. Buyers can create a shortlist of vendors and narrow their choices to, for example, two or three, begin a dialogue with the service providers, and then select the best service provider for their project.

Once a project is accepted, the buyer and service provider can use an online work space and message boards to help manage the project. The system lets buyers pay the service providers online. To gain access to the provider network, providers pay a subscription fee to Elance, which varies depending on the type of service category they are participating in. Additionally, Elance collects a small fee once the service provider is paid. Most service providers build this fee into their price. Buyers can also browse service provider descriptions and, if they find a service provider they want to work with, simply invite the service provider to bid on their particular project.

By the time this book is published, however, Elance will launch an extension of its technology that will allow customers to create a company account (i.e., a master account that supports multiple individual logins for buyers); it may begin charging a fee for this.

Currently, the marketplace is doing well. Elance's online business unit grew by more than 60 percent during 2002, and the number of projects outsourced through Elance Online grew by more than 55 percent during 2002, when more than 30,000 businesses used the service.

"The recent revenue growth has made Elance Online a profitable part of our business," says president and CEO of Elance Fabio Rosati. "We are basically an outsourcing solution for small businesses. We have small businesses online that would normally be paying $50,000 for [the right person or company for the right project], but we allow them to do it for $3,000, $4,000, or $5,000."

Elance has moved into another area. In 2001, the company realized that there was a significant opportunity to help large companies improve their service procurement and management processes. As a result, in 2002, the company introduced its Elance 3 application suite, which the company claims reduces the costs and improves the quality of service that businesses typically purchase by automating the entire services procurement and management processes—including the sourcing, contract management, procurement, and supplier management.

In 2003, Elance Inc. acquired one of its main competitors in the services procurement and management (SPM) enterprise software market, further consolidating Elance's position as the leader in the SPM market.

> ### Smart Tip
>
> If it can be sold by phone or by mail, it can be sold, probably better, on the web. E-commerce may never completely replace face-to-face selling (who wants to rent an office space over the web?), but it sure will take a huge bite out of telemarketing and direct-mail sales.

# Bulbs.com

Steve Rothschild is passionate about bulbs—lightbulbs, that is. He sometimes even closes his e-mail messages with "Have A Bright Day!" Perhaps that's why his privately held company bulbs.com (www.bulbs.com) is thriving. What is bulbs.com? "We are a B2B e-commerce company that specializes in lighting and drives sales through direct marketing," says Rothschild, founder and CEO of bulbs.com. "We are pursuing a share of the $12 billion domestic commercial/industrial lighting market." The company has a straightforward business model in which customers—85 percent of which are businesses—order lightbulbs directly from the company's web site.

Bulbs.com has distribution agreements with Philips Lighting and a host of other manufacturers. Since its launch in August 1999, bulbs.com has received orders from more than 9,000 companies, and 65 percent of its business clients have reordered.

Major customers include Central Parking Systems, Samsonite Stores, Best Western, Work 'n Gear, Perfumania, House of Blues, Verizon Wireless, and Leath Furniture, as well as the U.S. Military and the National Park Service.

Why did Rothschild decide to set up a web site that sold lightbulbs? "I was searching for my next opportunity, which I knew was going to be e-commerce related, and I knew that for it to be successful, I had to find a product that would be identifiable via the web, had to be replaced on a regular basis, and its cost-to-freight ratio had to be viable," says Rothschild. "Lightbulbs were the obvious choice for me." Rothschild also says there was a need for this business in the marketplace.

> **Smart Tip** Tip...
>
> No medium has ever been as fast at moving time-sensitive merchandise as the web. If it will rot or become terribly dated if it doesn't sell fast, the web is the best sales agent there could be. What besides produce can you think of that's extremely time-sensitive? Come up with possibilities, and then search Yahoo! to see if that niche already has players. Maybe you'll hit upon a real gusher of a new B2B play.

Last year, bulbs.com completed a $1 million round of debt and equity financing. The management team contributed 50 percent of the round in cash and debt financing, while previous investors Arbor Partners LLC, Hexagon Investments, and Grand Haven showed continued support with their 50 percent participation in the round. Rothschild says the additional funding will provide working capital for continued growth of receivables and inventory.

The business, which grows at an annual rate of more than 100 percent, is "break-even and cash-flow-neutral," says Rothschild. "Our intentional reinvestment for growth has temporarily kept us from being profitable."

As these examples show, there are many small B2B web companies thriving despite the current economy. And there is more good news: Venture capitalists are also more interested in B2B companies than in B2C companies nowadays, says IDC's Rosenthal. "The deals aren't as lucrative as they used to be [before the dotcom bust], but they are getting done in the B2B arena," says Rosenthal. "Companies are looking to invest in dotcoms that are less consumer-oriented and more B2B-focused, such as companies that provide tools for large companies or products for large companies." Why? "Because many VCs got burned investing in B2C companies, and most of the good ideas in the B2C segment are already taken, in my opinion," he says.

Some traditional B2C companies are also entering the B2B e-commerce fray. Consider eBay. Hoping to extend its popularity into the small and midsize-business arena, eBay launched a section on its site called eBay Business Marketplace (http://pages.ebay.com/businessmarketplace/index.html). Rather than hunting through more than 500,000 business items listed for sale each week on its consumer site, the business-oriented site brings together all eBay's business and industry listings under one easy-to-browse web destination. Currently more than 500,000 product listings are featured, focusing heavily on office technology products, such as computers and networking devices, as well as wholesale lots of consumer goods and services, such as insurance and shipping. EBay recently said that on an annual basis, the site is already selling $1 billion worth of goods, and about 7 percent of $14.8 billion worth of merchandise sold on eBay in 2002 was B2B sales.

## Smart Tip

The best news about B2B e-commerce? Launching a B2B site is significantly less expensive than trying to create a winning consumer site. Usually it's cheaper to target an audience and pursue it in B2B. If you have narrowed down a business niche and know how to cost-effectively target it, a B2B site can gain traction fast and on a minimal budget.

## A Slam Dunk?

Hold on, however, because the sailing for new B2B entrants won't be entirely smooth. In key respects, the bar may be higher in B2B e-commerce than it is in B2C, and the requirements for succeeding will likely be stiffer. "B2B is different from B2C," says John J. Sviokla, vice chairman of Diamond-Cluster International Inc., a global management firm that helps companies develop and implement growth strategies. "To succeed in this space, you will need deep domain knowledge," says Sviokla. You don't need to know much about farming to successfully peddle peaches to consumers, but to build an exchange for farmers, you have to grasp the fundamental issues in that industry. Lack that, and there will be no trust on the part of your target audience.

Another hitch: B2B involves long selling cycles, and, likely as not, before big deals are nailed down, you'll need to do face-to-face selling. It is one thing to buy a $10 book with a mouse click. It's an entirely different matter to buy $100,000 worth of coffee mugs. "A web site won't close deals for you," stresses eCompanyStore.com's Geer. "To make B2B deals, often you've still got to put feet on the street."

And there are times when a B2B model doesn't work. Consider Winery Exchange, which was founded by Peter Byck in 1999 in Novato, California. The company now offers private-label wine brands for large, global wine retailers and creates and delivers strategic information to assist wineries and spirits companies in building, growing, and managing their brands.

But when it started, its web site allowed suppliers of wine, grapes, equipment and services to sell their wares in bulk to wine growers, wineries, and retailers in a secure, user-friendly environment. "We are not trading online anymore," says Byck. "That didn't really work because there are a lot of relationships in the business, and people want to deal with people when they are buying these products. Also, some exchange models may work, but if you are trading bulk wine and grapes, it's just not a big enough industry with enough buyers and sellers to make a big business."

The company switched its focus to the private-label wine brand and strategic information sides of the business "because at the end of the day, you have to go where the growth and opportunities are," says Byck. "There were demands for those products, so we followed those paths."

Some analysts are somewhat suspicious of pure-play B2B e-commerce companies in general (these "pure plays" are purely online—they don't sell out of storefronts, etc.). "I know there are probably some successful ones out there, but I think that is the minority," says Christopher Dallas-Feeney, a New York-based vice president with management consultancy Booz Allen Hamilton. "I think all businesses need to be able to reach and service their customers in a variety of channels, both online and offline. In my mind, unless they reach out to their customers in a variety of channels, they become incomplete solutions for large or middle-market customers." He also says that some large companies perceive working with pure-play B2B companies as a risk. "Many of these companies fold, they go away, and vendor risk is a large corporate concern today."

But not everyone agrees. In general, it's a great time to be in B2B e-commerce if you are a small company, says IDC's Rosenthal. "You can reach buyers all over the country, all over the world, and because of the technology and service available," he says, "it's easier to appear to have the resources to deal with a big company."

# e-Chat with
## Autobytel's Jeffrey Schwartz

## Autobytel Inc.

**Jeffrey Schwartz, president and CEO**
**Location: Irvine, California**
**Year Started: 1995**

Do you wish you could get a glimpse into the mind of a successful dotcom CEO and find out what he's thinking? Read on. Next, Jeffrey Schwartz, president and CEO of Autobytel Inc., offers an in-depth look at the dotcom world. Autobytel Inc. is the world's largest internet automotive marketing services company. It helps retailers sell cars and manufacturers build brands through marketing and customer relationship management(CRM) tools and programs. Autobytel Inc. owns and operates popular web sites Auto bytel.com, Autoweb.com, CarSmart.com, and Autosite.com, as well as Automotive Information Center (AIC), a leading provider of automotive marketing data and technology. Autobytel Inc. generates an estimated 4 percent of all domestic new vehicle sales—$17 billion in car sales annually—for dealers through its web sites and is the largest syndicated car-buying content network. In essence, Autobytel is a middleman in car buying—but in a way that benefits consumers and dealers. In the beginning, the company saw the telephone ("Auto-By-Tel") as a big part of its selling process, but, almost immediately, the computer took over. Log onto Autobytel, tell it what you want—say, a 2001 Camry with a six-cylinder engine, dark green, ABS, no sunroof—and it routes your request to a dealer in your area. The dealer gets back to you with a firm quote that's usually far below the sticker price. The dealer makes money here because its advertising/marketing costs—a big spend for dealerships—plummet since Autobytel brings in the customers. And Autobytel gets paid flat fees by participating dealers that are far lower than dealers would otherwise spend to market. So it's win-win-win for Autobytel, the dealer, and the consumer.

Jeffrey Schwartz joined Autobytel Inc. in August 2001 as vice chair after its merger with Autoweb, where he was president and CEO. Schwartz led the successful integration of the two companies, reducing expenses and headcount by nearly 50 percent, which set the stage for three consecutive quarters of profitability. Since December 2001, Schwartz has led the combined company. Under Schwartz's leadership, Autobytel has expanded its customer list to include every major automotive manufacturer and thousands of automotive retailers. This expansion has been bolstered by Schwartz's attention to operations, which has improved many of the company's key financial operations, as well as increased shareholder value: The company's markct capitalization has more than doubled since Schwartz became CEO.

**Melissa Campanelli:** *What was your goal for the company when you joined?*

**Jeffrey Schwartz:** I was named president and CEO in December 2001, at the height of the dotcom shakeout that forced most of our competitors to close shop. So the most pressing goal was to usher Autobytel through the storm and put the company on a course for solid, long-term growth. My first exercise was to step back and ask myself what we should be doing and what we shouldn't—in other words, what is Autobytel's core value proposition? The answer was simple: We help dealers and manufacturers sell more cars for less. So I decided, in guiding present and future actions, to use the following filter: Does it improve the car-buying experience for our consumers while at the same time improving the quantity and quality of the marketing services we provide to manufacturers and dealers? As a result of this test, I eliminated many of what I felt were our nonessential ventures and focused on improving our service and value to the industry. On the dealer front, this meant elevating the quantity and quality of the consumer leads we provide. Our concerted efforts in this area have since paid off with dramatically improved core business operating systems.

On the manufacturer front, my strategy was to make sure that the company was fulfilling its enormous potential as an automotive marketing services company. I had always felt that Autobytel Inc.'s success was built, fundamentally, on marketing—that the company was, at its core, a uniquely efficient, dynamic auto marketing medium. So in addition to improving our core marketing business of helping dealers sell cars efficiently and cost-effectively, one of

> ## Smart Tip
>
> **Tip...**
>
> One reason Autobytel is a market leader is that the company hasn't fallen in love with how it does things. As market conditions change, Autobytel quickly adapts. That way of thinking and acting is essential for any dotcom, so once you've launched a site, prepare to change its basic approaches a week after launch ... and the next week ... and the next. That's the only way to survive on the web.

my biggest goals was to leverage the company's web traffic and internet exposure to address what I recognized as a "marketing disconnect" in the auto industry. By "marketing disconnect," I'm referring to the fact that at the time, only 3 percent of original equipment manufacturer marketing budgets were devoted to online initiatives, even though 60 percent of all car buyers were shopping or researching on the internet prior to purchase. Another goal, then, was for Autobytel to provide smart, dynamic, information-rich, and uniquely cost-effective marketing and technology on our web sites to help the auto industry reach those consumers where they live—online.

**Campanelli:** *How is the company different today?*

**Schwartz:** Well, one major difference is that we're profitable now, which we've accomplished by improving our core business operating systems and streamlining our own processes. Another big difference is that we've really become a leader in providing marketing and technology to OEMs, in addition to auto dealers. Today, we provide vehicle data or automotive research tools to 75 percent of the major manufacturers. We've also innovated new marketing programs on our web sites that are enabling manufacturers to provide shoppers with information about the cars they sell, based on each shopper's specific research decisions. Because of these uniquely dynamic, targeted marketing tools, and because of our huge audience of multibrand, active auto shoppers, we have the potential to be a critical, market-share-influencing platform for OEMs. Moving forward, this will become an even bigger part of our business and service mix.

**Campanelli:** *What advantage do you, as a dotcom, have over the big automakers?*

**Schwartz:** Autobytel is not in competition with automakers—in fact, we do business with every automaker. We do not make cars or sell them. Our core business model is as an automotive marketing services company that is dedicated to helping both automakers and dealers sell more while spending less. We support dealers and the major OEMs—helping automakers build brands online through innovative marketing programs that can reach millions of online consumers while sending dealers motivated, ready-to-buy customers.

After Autobytel invented online car-buying in 1995, it was not long before most automakers began launching web sites with information on their products—with some offering a customer referral buying model like Autobytel's. Unlike an automaker's site, however, Autobytel has the advantage of being a research-intensive, independent, third-party web site that features comprehensive, objective information and comparisons on every make and model for sale in the United States.

J.D. Power & Associates and other analysts concur year after year that consumers overwhelmingly prefer independent, third-party, multibrand sites like Autobytel for pricing, discounts, dealer referrals, vehicle research, etc. Similarly, Opinion Research found that online auto shoppers prefer independent sites to other sites (factory/dealer) by a three to one margin.

Autobytel has been instrumental in the car-buying revolution that now has 60 percent of all consumers using the internet during their car-shopping process. Autobytel has generated more online sales for dealers than any other auto site for four years in a row, generating over $1 billion a month in car sales for its dealers. We have always believed that making the lines of communication between factories, dealers, and consumers more efficient and effective would prove to be good business. Our philosophy that giving consumers objective information to make a smart car-buying decision is to the benefit of dealers, factories, and consumers alike, and our capacity to facilitate that has been our advantage.

**Campanelli:** *What's been the biggest surprise you've had in building Autobytel? The biggest challenge?*

**Schwartz:** Surprise: When Autobytel invented online car buying in 1995, it sparked perhaps one of the most overdue and needed retail revolutions of the late 20th century in the largest industry in the world. With its dramatically simple concept and even more basic initial web site, Autobytel helped spur an industrywide shakeup that has transformed the way cars are bought and sold far beyond what the company could have initially predicted. Manufacturers and auto retailers quickly scrambled to experiment with new selling models, finally acknowledging that consumers were sick of high-pressure buying experiences and opaque vehicle pricing. In the dark ages of car buying just eight years ago, consumers faced a dearth of objective pricing and comparative information to research vehicle purchases, a confusing and adversarial sales process, and a fragmented dealer network.

Autobytel's initial business philosophy seems deceptively simple: Put information and a more consumer-friendly sales process in the hands of consumers, and provide dealers with training, technology, and a cost-efficient way to acquire more customers and generate more sales. This consumer and dealer win-win has permanently altered the world's largest industry. By 2002, in eight short years, over 60 percent of all American consumers are now turning to the internet in their car-shopping process. When one thinks of the incremental adoption of television, cable TV, all forms of new media—it is hard to cite a more powerful, more rapid adoption. Car buyers were ready, and Autobytel has proved that the internet's unprecedented informational and transactional efficiencies were a brilliant fit for the auto industry.

Challenges: The two most significant challenges were transforming a technologically backward auto industry and continually battling misinformation in the press and industry about what Autobytel is and does. The automotive industry, and in particular the nation's dealer body, was one of the most technologically backward industries in the country when the inter-

> **Beware!**
> Jeffrey Schwartz says Autobytel's philosophy—and advantage— is that it gives consumers objective information to make a smart car buying decision, which benefits dealers, factories and consumers. Can you offer your customers a similarly unique experience? Consumers today—more than ever—are looking for unique experiences on the web. If you can't offer them a unique reason to come to your site, they probably won't.

net debuted. Still communicating by telephone and if lucky, by fax, few dealers had e-mail or online access. Most distrusted anything related to the internet, especially a program that would provide consumers with once heavily guarded pricing information. Autobytel had to convince dealers that if they embraced the internet, changed the way they did business, and better served this newly empowered customer, they would in fact ultimately prosper. To establish an extensive dealer network meant convincing many skeptical dealers, one dealer at a time.

Autobytel helped change an industry from one filled with techno-phobes to one of the more forward-thinking industries today. Currently, over 90 percent of all dealers have web sites, Autobytel boasts 20,000-plus dealer relationships, and dealers are rapidly embracing internet-driven CRM, marketing and sales processes. If, in the early days, we had to work to convince dealers to set up their own internet departments and retrain them to deliver a process satisfying to the internet-savvy consumer, we find that today, dealers are opening up the lessons learned in the internet department to their entire dealership. The distinctions between a "net car shopper" and a "traditional car shopper" are gradually diminishing; almost all car shoppers are essentially internet shoppers.

The other great challenge for Autobytel was overcoming the misperception among some dealers and industry analysts/media that Autobytel was bent on changing the factory-dealer distribution system. This, of course, was never the case; in fact, we went into business to keep dealers in business—to strengthen dealers' businesses. When consumers come to Autobytel for a no-hassle, no-haggle buying experience, they do all their research, know what the right car is at the right price—and are then linked

> **⚠ Beware!**
>
> Success breeds nearly instant imitation on the net. That's the irony: The more you prosper, the tougher you have to fight. How will you stay a step—better still, two steps—ahead of those who will follow?

with a trained Autobytel dealer that can meet their expectations. That dealer still sells the car, but the buying process has been transformed. At any rate, it took years to make our case—at least to some of the more rock-ribbed skeptics—but since the internet shakeout, the press and analysts are pretty much in agreement that the internet has positively transformed the auto industry for both dealers and automakers, and that these parties are embracing it more strongly than ever.

**Campanelli:** *What's your strategy for coming out ahead of competitors?*

**Schwartz:** One of the interesting things about the development of the automotive internet is that, due to the interdependence of automotive portals, manufacturers, third-party sites, and dealers, competitors have gradually evolved into partners. With 48 million consumers turning to the automotive internet every month, our strategy is to create productive partnerships and alliances that channel this enormous audience through the entire auto researching, buying, and owning process, and in so doing, to Autobytel. Specifically, we provide marketing and transaction services in a process that we share with many strategic, productive partners—including the auto manufacturers and dealers, Yahoo!, Priceline, and AutoTrader, to name a few. The web is no longer a "winner takes all" horse race; it's truly an interdependent "web"—we help grow our partners' businesses, and they help grow ours.

That said, the other third-party auto web sites in Autobytel's market include companies like CarsDirect.com, with mostly used-car players including AutoTrader. Autobytel has generated more online sales than any other auto site for four years in a row, by significant margins. We are the only profitable, publicly traded online new-vehicle site. In December 2002, Autobytel was rated the most-visited car-buying and research network on the web by Nielsen//NetRatings.

We have survived and remained the leader in this space by never wavering from our core business: to become a leading automotive marketing services company dedicated to helping both automakers and dealers sell more while spending less. We are an integral part of the auto industry and have never been in business to make or sell cars. Others rushed into our space, sensing opportunities in this huge market, not realizing that strong dealer relations, intensive dealer training, and technology programs would prove to be key. They are gone now. Still others rushed into the space thinking they could buck the century-old franchising retailing system, and somehow magically sell cars to consumers "direct," with a click of the mouse. They have failed. Some rushed into the space with internet and technology backgrounds and no expertise in the auto business. They have failed. Autobytel has succeeded because it has offered consumers, automakers, and dealers a clear value proposition—period.

# Cheap Tricks
## with
## AllLotto.com's
## Fred Weiss

## AllLotto.com

**Fred Weiss, founder and owner**
**Location: Ann Arbor, Michigan**
**Year Started: 1998**

Fred Weiss is a one-person web site machine. In a few years, he's erected several successful sites—AllMath.com (with flash cards, games and more for math junkies), AllWords.com (an online dictionary and language portal), and AllLotto.com (results for state lotteries nationwide). He has also launched a Canadian, German, and UK version of AllLotto. com. His goal? To launch versions of AllLotto.com all over the world. In early 2000, he also launched Lottery-Data.com (www.lottery-data.com), where he sells lottery data to other publishers, and about a dozen sites that offer gambling-related information.

Weiss says the most successful part of his business right now is his lottery business, which is a combination of the AllLotto sites, and selling data to publishers. Basically, the AllWords and AllMath sites make up 5 to 10 percent of Weiss's revenues and about 1 percent of his time, while his lottery business makes up half his revenues and takes a quarter to a third of his time. All his new ventures make up the rest. Along the way, he also mounted a site that didn't prosper (AllFree.com). But when you want insight into doing net business on the cheap, Weiss is a man you have to talk with.

**Robert McGarvey:** *What were your start-up costs?*

**Fred Weiss:** My start-up costs were minimal. Originally (during 1998), I paid about $200 per month for hosting and spent about $5,000 to license content. Between March 1998 and the end of 1999, I raised about $75,000 [from investors] and spent about $70,000 of it by the end of 1999. In early 1999, I began to host my own sites and spent money on office space, internet connectivity, hardware and software.

In 2000, I raised another $30,000, and then we closed the office in early 2001, and I moved my hosting over to other business associates in town, so I still have control over it, but I don't have an office, and I don't have to do all the dirty work.

Now I spend about $800 per month on an internet connection and web hosting, $400 per month on advertising, and $300 per month on contracted services. I also spend a couple hundred dollars a month on phones and internet service since I now work out of my home.

Also, while the AllMath.com site is still on a Microsoft NT server, we've moved everything over to a Linux server, and we don't buy software anymore. I pay a couple hundred dollars a year to Red Hat (a provider of Linux services) for update service. I went from a model where I had to pay for software and updates, and now I don't. As for hardware, last year I spent less than $1,000. And I don't spend money for licensed services anymore. We dropped one vendor because of the cost, and the other vendor has become a partner with us.

**McGarvey:** *How do you accumulate content?*

**Weiss:** As for content on AllWords, we have set up a link system so there is a Yahoo!-like directory of language sites. On AllMath, we create tools, such as flash cards, a metric converter and a magic square game. I am also in the process of form- ing a joint venture with a company called Crystal Reference, which is based in the United Kingdom. Among other things, Crystal supplies the biographies for our All- Math site and dictionaries for the AllWords site. Eventually, we will take the AllWords and AllMath sites and create new web sites. One will be called AllFacts.com, which will be an encyclopedia site, and another will be AllBiographies.com, featuring 30,000 biographies of people throughout history.

Right now we sell ad-free subscriptions to the AllWords site, and we'll continue doing things like that for this site. We will also offer e-mail subscriptions, where for about $5 per year, people could get a biography every day.

For the AllLotto site, the content we create is basically the gathering and distribution of lottery information. We also generate lucky numbers on the site with a computer program I wrote.

**McGarvey:** *How successful are your sites?*

**Weiss:** For AllWords, AllMath and AllLotto, we have generated about 230,000 to 240,000 unique visitors [statistically identifiable individuals who visit a site; for instance a site may have five page views by one visitor or by five unique visitors], 2.5 million page views per month, and $1,000 in revenue in March 2000.

**McGarvey:** *Some of your revenue comes from advertising. How do you sell it?*

**Weiss:** I am a member of a number of ad networks, including Burst! Media (www.burstmedia.com) and 24/7 Real Media (www.247realmedia.com), which, among other things, pays sites to display third-party advertising banners. When I first started,

# Ad It Up

**C**an you generate cash by putting third-party advertisements on your Web site? You bet. Smarter than chasing down individual advertisers (and trying to collect!) is to join a net ad network, an intermediary that brings web sites and advertisers together. Cases in point:

- *Burst! Media:* www.burstmedia.com
- *24/7 Real Media:* www.247realmedia.com
- *MaxWorldwide:* www.maxworldwide.com
- *ValueClick:* www.valueclick.com
- *Advertising.com:* www.advertising.com

Find many more by going to Yahoo!.com and clicking on "Business and Economy," "B2B," "Marketing and Advertising," "Internet," and then "Advertising." Also, check out MediaPost's Ad Network Watch at http//www.mediapost.com/signin.com.

Literally dozens of companies want your business. Before signing any deals, check references, asking the following questions: Is payment prompt? Are advertisers as promised? Can you ban certain kinds of ads from your site? And keep in mind Fred Weiss' story: The model doesn't always work. So be careful!

I was averaging $2 for every 1,000 impressions [the number of pages the banner ad is displayed on]. But these days, you average about 25 cents per thousand impressions, or less. That advertising model is really pretty bad, I'm afraid. I'm probably bringing in less than $1,000 a month from ad network advertising. I also receive advertising from several agencies that cater to online casinos for our lottery-related sites only or sell directly to interested parties. We also rely on getting listed high in the major search engines, especially Google and Yahoo!. A big part of my business is also the business-to-business side, or the lottery data that we sell to other publishers.

**McGarvey:** *Where did you get the idea for the sites?*

**Weiss:** In January 1998, I was working as a programmer when a colleague mentioned how useful it would be if the *CRC Handbook* [an engineering reference guide] was available via the web. This gave me the idea of developing automated, reference-focused sites. The first idea was for AllMath.com, which I felt could be developed over time

---

**Smart Tip**

Don't be discouraged by the fact that the internet bubble burst. That didn't stop Fred Weiss from expanding his business. As he said, when the dotcoms crashed in 2000 and advertising revenues plunged, he began to look for new areas of the internet business to go into. What did he choose to do? Gather, package and sell lottery results data to publishers and internet providers. It was the easiest business for him to enter since he was already gathering and verifying the data. So if your business is not getting the revenues you want from the start, think outside the box and figure out how to make money in another way without losing the focus of your main business. There are limitless opportunities once you sit down and think about it.

---

while still providing useful tools as development continued. AllMath launched in September 1998. I also launched AllFree.com as a political magazine but stopped updating that site in January 1999 due to lack of traffic.

**McGarvey:** *Why did you build other sites?*

**Weiss:** I built AllWords.com and AllLotto.com based on a serendipitous event and my belief that they could be developed at a low cost ($5,000 to $10,000 or less) and operated at a profit. When looking for math biographies for AllMath.com, I found that the same publisher had a dictionary available for licensing. This looked like a simple task to implement, so I registered AllWords.com and launched the site in January 1999.

I had also registered as many "All" domains as I could think of, and one happened to be AllLotto.com. I met a salesman from Flycast [a now-defunct ad network] who had a friend who ran a lottery site. He put us in contact with each other. I eventually contracted with this gentleman to host my site using his software. Some months later, in spring 1999, I wrote my own software and relaunched the site using my own hosting facility. I also arranged to resell the result data to other web site publishers as another leg to my business. Now, however, I sell my own lottery data to publishers.

As the internet bubble burst in 2000 and advertising revenues plunged, I began to look for new areas of the internet business to go into. It was clear that to keep the business alive, we needed new sources of revenue. Gathering, packaging, and selling lottery results data to publishers and internet providers was the easiest business for us to enter. We already were gathering and verifying the data; we just needed to deliver it to others. In general, all my new ventures are designed to leverage some combination of the data, software, or audience that we already have to generate additional revenue streams. You see TV ads and business articles that continue to remind us that businesses must adapt and grow to thrive and survive. We survived the dot-com implosion and feel well-positioned to thrive in the next few years by combining our existing business with new web ventures.

# 13

# The Secrets of
# Venture Capital
# Funding

As 1997 drew to a close, Jed Smith—a Boston-area computer entrepreneur who had founded CyberSmith, a chain of computer retail stores—began looking into e-commerce. "What categories haven't been taken?" Smith asked himself.

"I first looked at the grocery space," Smith recalls. "But the model didn't work. The gross margin-to-cost-of-shipping ratio was unattractive: You're shipping bulky, heavy products with low margins. Then I looked at the health and beauty aisle. Good margins and small, easy-to-ship products. A lot of this is regular, repeat purchases that don't need to be touched. To me, this category worked well, much better than books, because this is a $158 billion market. That's six times bigger than the book market. I realized this was a big opportunity. And I knew I needed to move fast."

First on Smith's list of must-haves: money. "I knew I needed money because this space was going to get crowded, fast," he says. "And I needed smart money that would help my company get more competitive."

> ### Smart Tip
>
> Tip...
>
> Don't assume that you will have to have all your ducks in a neat row to win venture funding. Quite the contrary. In many cases, VCs like helping to shape a business idea, to put their marks on a plan. And as they get more involved, their willingness to fund increases. You still need to be savvy—and to have good answers for questions—but keep your ears open to VC suggestions, and be ready to incorporate the good ones.

That meant one thing. Smith needed some of the venture capital that's ponied up by hundreds of firms—mainly around cities such as San Francisco; Austin, Texas; Boston; Seattle; and New York—that specialize in putting cash into untested businesses. How much venture capital is there? Not as much as there used to be. Just look at the statistics: While more than $36 billion was invested in start-ups by venture capital firms during 1999—and around 3,000 start-ups divvied up that money—about $20 billion was invested in venture-backed start-ups during 2002, and a little fewer than 2,000 start-ups shared the cash, according to San Francisco-based research firm VentureOne, a division of VisionOne worldwide Group.

And remember, for every firm that wins venture funding, about 100 go away empty-handed—and probably another 100, maybe more, did not even get their foot in the door.

And the news is worse for dotcom start-ups, according to Tami Zemel, a spokeswoman for VentureOne. "At its peak in 2000, the e-commerce sector attracted $4 billion in venture capital investment," she says. "But in 2002, that statistic was $120 million. The primary drivers of the decline were the lack of sustainable profitability associated with this business model and the public market failure of many companies in the sector."

What's more, while in 2000 there were more than 1,000 deals completed between e-commerce technology and internet e-commerce content or services companies, that number dropped to 61 in 2002, according to a joint study conducted by PricewaterhouseCoopers, Venture Economics, National Venture Capital Association, and Money Tree.

In short, venture capitalists are not feeling very adventurous about small e-commerce companies.

# Making Connections

Just getting in front of a major VC firm is an accomplishment, but that's where Smith had an edge. About 10 years earlier, he had worked at Oracle—one of the globe's biggest software companies—and as luck would have it, a co-worker had a roommate with whom Smith got along well. In the intervening years, Smith had kept in touch with that roomie, Dave Wharton. When Smith had his nascent idea for a cyberdrugstore, he bounced it off Wharton, who was by then an associate at Kleiner Perkins Caufield & Byers, the Silicon Valley VC firm that is well-known in internet circles because it put early money into Netscape (now owned by Time Warner), Healtheon (later merged with WebMD), Amazon, and many more major successes.

"I didn't even know who Kleiner Perkins was when I first talked to Dave," Smith says. "Call me somewhere between naive and lucky, but maybe that's why I was so successful. I didn't grovel. I just thought I had a really neat idea. What I said to Kleiner was: "I have an idea. It's yours to invest in if you want. I'm not shopping it around. Let's work on it together and create something big." I didn't say, "You want to invest? I got other guys who want to." I asked Kleiner to collaborate with me."

Kleiner Perkins liked what it was hearing, and Kleiner partner John Doerr was particularly interested. If any Kleiner Perkins partner likes an internet idea, the entrepreneur with that idea has a golden future to look forward to. Doerr is the partner who jumped into Netscape, Healtheon (WebMD), and Amazon—most of the firm's big web plays—so if he climbs on board, it's tantamount to the kiss of a god.

But Smith hadn't been kissed yet, not by a long shot. He presented his concept to Kleiner in January 1998, but they weren't ready to put money into the idea quite yet. "They asked me to come out to the [San Francisco] Bay area, spend some time working on my plan and meeting people like [Amazon founder] Jeff Bezos," Smith recalls. So he did, and a few weeks later, Kleiner said, "Stay a bit longer and flesh out your idea more." Weeks went by, Smith kept tinkering with his plan . . . and then, bingo: "In April, Kleiner put up seed money, and by June they funded it."

That is how Smith's idea became drug store.com (www.drugstore.com)—but there's

## ⚠ Beware!

Bring in VC money, and you will probably lose control of your business. That's just a reality. For every Jeff Bezos who stays on top, there are several entrepreneurs with ideas that are good enough to get funded who don't personally inspire confidence—and they get pushed aside. Ironically, it happened to probably the most fertile tech idea man of the past 15 years, Jim Clark, the founder of Netscape (now owned by AOL Time Warner) and Healtheon (later merged with WebMD). Before starting those two companies, he had the idea that gave birth to Silicon Graphics, a maker of high-performance computers, but he got nudged aside. It happens.

## Smart Tip

Who do you know? If you want a hearing at a VC firm, find a way in via friends and friends of friends. The "six degrees of separation" theory claims we all know everybody else—or at least we know somebody who knows somebody who knows somebody. Check it out: When a friend told me about this idea, I scoffed and said, "No way I'm within six degrees of the Pope." She told me: "You know me, and the father of a good friend of mine has met the Pope many times." The lesson: If you really want VC money, find out whom you know who knows somebody. That's the way in the door.

still more to this story. Kleiner, with its connections throughout the tech industry, soon persuaded Microsoft vice president Peter Neupert to leave that company and become CEO of the new drugstore.com. "I told John Doerr 'no,' and I told him 'no' again, but eventually I said 'yes,'" Neupert recalls. (For an interview with Peter Neupert, turn to Chapter 23.)

How did that sit with Smith? "My perspective is, what's best for the business is what we should do," he says. "Controlling every piece of this company is not the most important thing to me." That's a shrewd position to take because once VC money comes aboard, much of the control usually begins to slip away from the founder. Neupert had run much of Microsoft's online operations and, as a vice president, also had experience managing a large staff. That made him perfect for running an online drugstore that aimed to be the biggest in its huge sector.

And Neupert inspired confidence in outsiders, too. A major investment from Amazon followed, as did more money from Microsoft co-founder Paul Allen's Vulcan Ventures. Drugstore.com went from idea to heavily funded company in the space of a year. And, for the fiscal year ending December 29, 2002, revenues rose 33 percent to $193.9 million.

One footnote: In mid-1999, Smith left drugstore.com and has since founded Catamount Ventures, a San Francsico-based venture funding company with a focus on early-stage technology companies.

# Looking Good

Landing VC funding is not just about money. It's also about where the money comes from, and many believe nothing beats money from a well-established VC firm such as Kleiner Perkins, Benchmark Capital, Flatiron Partners, and a handful of other firms. What makes VC money better than money from angel investors, family members, and wealthy individuals is that when a major VC signs on, it adds intangibles such as class and prestige.

Talk to a start-up, and an early question is usually "What's your funding?" And the person who asks the question wants to hear names he recognizes. While it's true that many VCs that were well-known for working with dotcom companies before the dotcom crash are not really focusing on this area anymore, they will still do deals occasionally with dotcom start-ups, so "the bigger the name, the better" still holds.

VCs also like to leverage their contacts—witness Amazon, a Kleiner Perkins-funded company, joining as an investor in drugstore.com. That is no fluke. Kleiner Perkins, for instance, talks about its keiretsu—a linking of companies it's funded—and members include Amazon.com, freelance marketplace Elance.com, home improvement site Homestore.com, health information provider Healtheon (WebMD), search engine Google, women's site iVillage.com, financial manager myCFO.com, retailer OnSale.com, and dozens more. Cross-pollination (where members make deals with each other and exchange ideas) is common. That is a big boost for a net start-up. Not anybody can pick up the phone and call Amazon's Bezos with a business question—but members of the Kleiner Perkins keiretsu know that's doable.

Other VC firms do much the same, and the upshot is that smart internet entrepreneurs look for prestige VC money even when they don't really need it. Ten million dollars from Kleiner Perkins is worth a whole lot more than the same amount from your rich uncle, and that is a dotcom reality.

# Funding in Hard Times

There's no doubt about it: Left behind in the rubble caused by the dotcom bust in 2000, venture capitalists are taking a more critical look at these types of start-ups.

But some dotcom companies are still managing to get venture funding. Which ones are winning? The ones that are already successful and exhibit a focus on the bottom line.

Consider Fandango Inc. (www.fandango.com), the Los Angeles-based online movie ticketing company that was founded in March 2000 by a consortium of major movie exhibitor companies and two VC firms. It secured $15.3 million in additional funding in late 2002 from VC firm Technology Crossover Ventures (TCV), a Palo Alto, California, $2.5 billion fund and provider of growth capital to technology companies.

The company was able to secure this round of funding because it was a proven success. According to Fandango president and CEO Art Levitt III, "We had proof. We had more than three times year-over-year growth; we were cash flow-positive; we were exceeding all our expectations, and showed giant growth potential. Venture capitalists took notice, and several actually pursued us for investment."

Levitt adds that Fandango wasn't even looking for money but that the opportunity to work with TCV, a firm that has invested heavily in online ticketing company Expedia.com, along with the online DVD rental company NetFlix, was one not to be missed. He says the financing will fuel Fandango's continued growth, helping it facilitate market expansion, extend alliances with studios and exhibitors, and develop and enhance new products and services such as print-at-home ticketing, priority seating, express concessions, and other value-added services that make the moviegoing experience more convenient and fun.

## Smart Tip

Tip...

Sometimes companies bring in VC money even when none is needed. EBay, for instance, brought in Benchmark Capital because the founders believed the sanction of a leading Silicon Valley firm would be a big boost in recruiting a name-brand CEO who, in turn, would be a major asset to a future IPO. EBay was right: Benchmark helped recruit Meg Whitman to run the company—and eBay's stock offering scored a home run for all involved.

"Investors today are obviously concerned about reality vs. fantasy," says Levitt. "If you have good business fundamentals and you have a track record you can prove, there is plenty of money out there. But if you are highly speculative and haven't proven yourself, you're not going to be able to raise money right now."

Levitt says that many of today's dotcoms start-ups are starting out with very light costs and very light infrastructure, so they can show proof of concept to potential VC backers.

It's true: VCs want dotcom companies to show them the money: No longer do they back dotcoms based on the number of visitors to their sites and their potential for generating sales revenue and advertising dollars.

Instead, they want to see revenue models, P&L statements and projected P&L statements. In short, they want to make sure the businesses they are investing in are already viable.

Even the term "dotcom" could have a negative connotation to potential VC backers right now. While Levitt confirms this, he says, "The world is always waiting for great ideas to be discovered. And if you've got a great idea that's got great fundamentals, of course there is opportunity in any medium."

Another plus for Fandango: VCs are also looking for strong transaction-based dotcoms that can persuade hordes of people to pay regularly for a service or product, such as tickets or online games. This just happens to be what Fandango does.

Fandango is not the only company that received venture funding after the dotcom bust. RedEnvelope Inc. (www.redenvelope.com), a San Francisco-based company that specializes in last-minute gifts, also attracted $13.8 million in funding from various VC firms last year. And SmartBargains (www.smartbargains.com), the online bargain retailer in Boston, received a $9 million cash infusion from Seattle-based VC firm Maveron LLC, whose portfolio includes companies such as eBay and eStyle. It's no surprise that both RedEnvelope and SmartBargains had already received venture funding before and were already viable companies.

On paper, scoring VC funding looks simple. You write a business plan wherein you pay very close attention to the possible payday ahead (typically this is made vivid with charts that forecast revenue and profits). VCs do not want to hit singles. They swing for the bleachers, and to win funding, an idea has to have the clear potential to be a major winner.

Why do VCs want big winners? Simple. They're realists who know that out of every ten ventures they fund, maybe eight will vanish without a trace; one will be a modest success, but that one home run will generate so much cash, it will make all the losses forgettable as it propels the firm deep into black ink. So don't be conservative. Think big.

Also think of the exit strategy. That's key. VCs don't invest to hold; they want a way to translate a business success into an economic success. Usually, that means the company gets bought by a big fish—as, for instance, San Francisco-based internet loan site GetSmart.com was purchased by Providian Financial Corporation for around $33 million—or it goes public. Either way, early investors want to know how they will get out of this deal before they go into it.

Once you have your plan in hand—with an exit strategy and a payday spelled out—you look for every way possible to get it (and yourself) in front of VCs. It isn't easy.

## Read All About It

**V**Cs are not kindly money sources—they're in business to make piles of cash. It's an unwary (read: dumb) entrepreneur who doesn't approach VCs cautiously. Read about VC greed in Charles Ferguson's *High Stakes, No Prisoners* (Times Books), a book that tells how Ferguson took an idea and transformed it into FrontPage, the ubiquitous hypertext editor now owned by Microsoft. Also worth a read is Michael Wolff's *Burn Rate* (Touchstone Books), a brutally funny book, and Michael Lewis' *The New New Thing* (W.W. Norton & Co.), a vivid recounting of how Jim Clark—co-founder of Silicon Graphics, Netscape (now owned by AOL Time Warner), and Healtheon (later merged with WebMD)—utterly rewrote the rules of venture funding to put more power in the hands of entrepreneurs.

Maybe the best book of all about VCs is Randall Stross' *eBoys* (The Ballantine Publishing Group), because Stross won access to partner meetings at VC powerhouse Benchmark Capital, the funder of eBags, eBay, Art.com, and many others. In the book, Stross gives readers a behind-the-scenes look at the decision-making process as Benchmark decides to put cash into start-ups or to decline investing. It's a well-told story, full of useful insights.

So often internet entrepreneurs complain, "I have a great business plan, and nobody will fund it." Maybe the plan is great, maybe it isn't, but step one in proving you've got what it takes to prosper in the rugged internet economy is finding a way to get in front of VCs.

You've tried and can't seem to land VC money? Take what cash you can from anybody, of course. Get the business afloat and then maybe VCs will come calling with cash in their hands. Even better, once a business is prospering, you can usually get much more favorable terms from VCs. The earlier they come in, the bigger piece of the company they want, which means second-stage VC financing may actually be more desirable.

The moral: When the idea is good, the money will follow.

# Inside Information

Don't get discouraged about finding VC money. Garage Technology Ventures, a venture capital investment bank for emerging technology companies, encourages submissions of business plans at its web site (www.garage.com). Here, its co-founder and CEO, Guy Kawasaki (a onetime Apple Computer marketer), eagerly tells how to win funding from Garage Technology Ventures. Kawasaki's trademark is irreverence—his wit is quick and pointed—but read between the lines in this Q&A, and you'll discover he's telling you what your chances are and how to make them better.

**Robert McGarvey:** *What does an entrepreneur need to get venture funding?*

**Guy Kawasaki:** Circa 2003, the single most important factor was to show traction—that is, that someone is already paying you for your product. If not traction, then at least you need to show that someone is testing your product and will/might pay for the product soon.

**McGarvey:** *What's your ballpark estimate of the percentage of business plans that get funded?*

**Kawasaki:** Half a percent [Note: That's 0.5 percent—meaning 1 in 200].

**McGarvey:** *How many plans do you look at in an average week?*

**Kawasaki:** Our company gets 50 to 100 per week. This number is much lower than during the 1997 to 1999 time frame, but the quality is much higher.

**McGarvey:** *A typical complaint is "I know nobody—where do I start looking?" What's your answer?*

**Kawasaki:** Raising capital today is very challenging. You can't leave any stone unturned. This means friends, fools, family, and potential customers . . . not to mention your own pocket. The days of raising a few million with a sketch on a napkin are gone—maybe not forever, but for a few years.

**McGarvey:** *What's the minimum [realistic] funding for launching a B2B site? A B2C site?*

**Kawasaki:** This is tough to answer because you can't glom all B2B- or B2C-type businesses together. You could start a company with $250,000 or $250 million. It all depends. Having said this, too much money is worse than too little [because people are usually less disciplined about the way they spend when funds are plentiful].

**McGarvey:** *What's the one thing an entrepreneur can do that's sure to turn you off?*

**Kawasaki:** Ask me to sign an NDA [nondisclosure agreement].

**McGarvey:** *What's the one thing an entrepreneur can do that's sure to catch your interest?*

**Kawasaki:** Tell us that in the last 12 months they did $1 million or more in business.

What has Kawasaki told you? Develop a plan that emphasizes your strengths—the reasons to fund it—keep it short, don't ask for too much money, and never ask potential funders to sign an NDA. Why the last point? NDAs—which bind the signer not to reveal what you show or tell him about your plan—are unenforceable in many cases, and, just as bad, a busy investor probably has heard much the same idea from multiple sources already.

On the other hand, complaints that investors sometimes steal good ideas are epidemic. Are the beefs founded? Hard to say—but a Silicon Valley legend is that when Sabeer Bhatia shopped his idea for what became Hotmail, he lied to would-be funders in initial meetings, telling them about a totally different business idea. Only when they passed some kind of test for Bhatia did he lay out his real idea. Paranoid? Bhatia became a very rich man when Microsoft bought Hotmail—proof that, at least in his case, caution pays.

Do you need to be as cautious as Bhatia? Quite probably, most entrepreneurs who take that closed-mouth route will simply strike out with funders. A better route is to tell what you need to tell to spark interest and then keep offering more details as investor interest looks ever more genuine. Besides, if you treat people sincerely and honestly, more often than not, you'll get much the same in return. Sure, there are crooks in Silicon Valley—but most folks are decent, well-meaning and well-intentioned. So play things straight, and usually you'll get the results you deserve.

# Financial Angels Explain
## Why They Fund Start-Ups

D o you believe in angels? After you read this chapter, you just might. With a little luck and lots of persistence on your part, angels—of the flesh-and-blood variety—may fund your internet venture. Want to know more? Keep reading.

Today, most dotcom companies take the following four-step funding track. Step one: The entrepreneur bootstraps the business using his own resources (usually savings and credit cards). Step two: The entrepreneur seeks angel funding from seasoned professionals, who typically put in not only money but also expertise, mentoring and guidance. Step three: The business pursues venture capital. Step four: After several years of profitability, the company may go public or merge with another company.

In the fast-paced internet world of days gone by, angels may have been overlooked, as companies without any track record and no profits (nor much in the way of revenue) went public and venture capitalists took on a mentoring role. Today, there are far fewer dotcom companies going public or getting VC funding, so angel investors are a very important part of the funding mix and are looked to not only for money, but also for expertise, mentoring, and guidance.

And there are many of them. According to research conducted by Jeffrey E. Sohl at the University of New Hampshire's Center for Venture Research in Durham, there were approximately 50 formal business angel groups in the United States in 1997. He now estimates that there may be as many as 170 formal and informal organizations located throughout leading technology and business regions in the United States and Canada.

Where do you find angels? Usually through personal connections, because angels are generally friends of friends or parents of friends. Why do they invest? For many angels it's a thrill to get involved in a start-up. Maybe they don't want to personally run one, but they are nonetheless excited about being on the periphery and offering advice in addition to capital. Of course, there is also the real possibility of hitting a major home run.

Just ask Kevin O'Donnell and Reed Slatkin. Entrepreneur Sky Dayton had approached O'Donnell and Slatkin in the early 1990s with his hopes of creating an easy-to-use internet service provider that would deliver high levels of customer service. They liked what they heard and invested in Dayton's idea early on. That was in '94, and since then, O'Donnell and Slatkin have watched their investment multiply in value many, many times as Dayton's EarthLink rose to become the premier independent ISP. O'Donnell and Slatkin are still on EarthLink's board of directors and are major shareholders, with stock worth upwards of $30 million apiece.

How do you hook up with an angel? What can you reasonably ask of an angel— and what are you likely to get? We found two angels who readily agreed to provide insight into what they do: Susan Preston is currently a member and former chair of the board and president of an angel network called Seraph Capital Forum, a Seattle-area group of female tech executives who hunt for promising start-ups to fund; John May is managing partner of the New Vantage Group, a Washington, DC-based company that manages next-generation early-stage venture funds for active angel investors. Their methods and approaches differ, but that's the norm: No two angels have exactly the same motivations. But if you understand who angels are and how to persuade them, you just might get one to put cash into your company.

*Susan Preston has worn many hats during her business career. Besides being a current member and the former chair and president of Seraph Capital Forum, she has been the COO of a public company, the CEO of a private start-up company, a lawyer, and a founding partner of the Seattle office of Cooley Godward LLP, a Silicon Valley-based law firm that made a name for itself during the internet bubble. Currently, she is an entrepreneur-in-residence at the Ewing Marion Kauffman Foundation, a Kansas City, Missouri-based operating and grant-making foundation focused on entrepreneurship and education. There she works on initiatives aimed at advancing women entrepreneurs. She also does strategic planning and practice development at a law firm based in Seattle.*

**Melissa Campanelli:** *Why are you an angel investor?*

**Susan Preston:** I am drawn to the enjoyment of being an early investor with an entrepreneur or founder who is excited and committed to what appears to be a very good idea, product or service. It's also a gamble—of course you try to minimize your [risk] by doing due diligence—but there is a fun, thrilling part of being in at the ground floor and helping a young entrepreneur and hopefully growing the company and having some type of return. That's what we all are really in this for—having some type of terrific returns. We know that many will not make it, but we hope a couple of them will. It's also a great feeling to guide and help and support that entrepreneur.

**Campanelli:** *What do you see as the difference between an angel and a VC?*

**Preston:** There are some definitive differences. A venture capitalist is a very risk-averse investor, from the standpoint that they have limited partners to answer to. It's not their dollars, and so the requirements of what they go through for consideration for investment are much more rigorous, and the basis upon which investments are made can be completely different than the criteria angels use to determine what to invest in. Angels use their own money, and if they lose the money, the only people they have to answer to are themselves, not a bunch of limited partners who may not be real happy if they find out that there wasn't adequate due diligence or that they were playing out of an area that wasn't in their forte. There is a difference in risk between them, a difference in reason for investing, and a difference in results of failure or success. Venture capitalists are professional investors—they are investing for others. They may get a percentage of the carry, but really, the only reason venture capitalists exist is to invest money from someone else. An angel investor, on the other hand, has the financial wherewithal and the ability to risk a certain

### Smart Tip

Practice, practice, practice. Before you go into any meetings with VCs or angels, really hone your presentation on your business—this can prove a lot more crucial than your business plan in the funding decision. Why? Investors invest in people who inspire them. Go in with a pitch that wows listeners, and you may walk out with a big check.

percentage of their capital from their portfolio in what is probably considered the most high-risk and potentially problematic area [unproven start-ups in general] because of the uncertainties of future, no track record, etc. It's done much more from a basis of being part of a company process or having the opportunity to get in on the ground floor of a company. I think [angel investors] have much more personal reasons to invest as opposed to why VCs invest.

**Campanelli:** *How many plans does Seraph look at in a typical month?*

**Preston:** The number of applications we get varies considerably from month to month. There is a screening committee that actually screens all the applications. Some months there could be zero that look like we would even want to screen them, and other months,

> ## Smart Tip
>
> Sky Dayton, the story goes, got in touch with angels Kevin O'Donnell and Reed Slatkin through mutual friends who all belonged to the same church. Are you a churchgoer? A member of the American Legion? In the PTA? Share a background, and angels are much more likely to give your idea a listen. In Silicon Valley, there's an active group of angels from India who seek out young Indian techies with bright ideas. Connections and roots do matter.

there might be 15 or 20 that we want to review. Then the committee chooses three to four companies to present at each meeting. Many times, the companies that present come in through recommendations from members. We've seen some pretty diverse presentations. There were a lot of entrepreneurs starting purely online companies back in 1999 or 2000, such as online training programs or B2B or B2C software companies that were completely online plays. The number of [these types of presentations] has definitely decreased on a percentage basis.

**Campanelli:** *What's a typical investment?*

**Preston:** A typical investment is $25,000 to $50,000 per angel, and in most cases, more than one Seraph member will invest in a presenting company.

**Campanelli:** *How can an entrepreneur find his or her angels?*

**Preston:** A lot of angels are migrating to angel organizations because there is an opportunity for better deal flow and an opportunity for joint due diligence. So if entrepreneurs are looking for angels, they need to look to those angel organizations as a good starting point. They also need to apply and try to participate in a lot of the investment forums [that are out there]. They can find out about these forums or angel organizations through their professional service providers, such as lawyers and accountants. There are also entrepreneurial networks and forums in all cities that support entrepreneurs and that are another good source of information regarding potential sources of financing.

In fact, participating in training programs or business plan development programs that many of the entrepreneur networks offer are good things for entrepreneurs to do before they even go out to seek funding. These things will help them learn whether or not they have the kind of company that should be taking in investors. [The Ewing Marion Kauffman Foundation, where Preston is an entrepreneur-in-residence, has a nationwide program called FastTrac, which is a business development program designed to help entrepreneurs hone the skills needed to create, manage, and grow successful businesses. Kauffman also boasts a portal of information for entrepreneurs at EntreWorld (www.entreworld.org).]

**Campanelli:** *What can an entrepreneur do to win a "yes" from angels? What's sure to win a "no thanks"?*

**Preston:** We'll start with the "no" first. A sure "no" for any investor is coming unprepared with an ill-defined business plan or presentation, not knowing your company from the inside out, not understanding your financial projections or where your capitalization is, not clearly understanding your market and all your competitors, or saying you have no competition—that will never get you money. To win a "yes," an entrepreneur must have an excellent grasp of the company, its marketing, sales and operational approach, its cash flow, and its realistic financial needs. Knowing yourself and your limitations is a good way to win a "yes."

Investors also want to know that you are building a good advisory board. They want to know from whom you've sought advice and who has already said "I like this person. I like what they're doing." And remember: Now, more so than three years ago, angel investors want to see that your company has progressed or moved forward. Essentially, you need to have already done with your company what you are asking them for the money to do. I would never invest in [just] an idea anymore.

**John May** *is not only the managing partner and co-founder of the New Vantage Group, but he has extensive experience as a venture fund manager, advisor and angel. He has been a partner or consultant to five venture funds and has been at the forefront of the angel investing movement since 1996, when he co-founded and became executive director of the Private Investors Network, an angel network sponsored by the Mid-Atlantic Venture Association, which has grown to more than 120 investor members.*

*May is also managing general partner of Calvert Social Venture Partners LP, a Washington, DC-based venture capital firm founded in 1989. The company specializes in providing capital and assistance to emerging growth companies that also provide a social and environmental dividend.*

*May has spoken extensively on angel and early-stage equity investing and is the co-author of a book on angel investing,* Every Business Needs an Angel *(Crown Business).*

*He readily talks about the business of angel financing. The New Vantage Group offers a program called "Dancing with the Angels," which provides guidance in searching for and working with seasoned backers—business angels.*

**Melissa Campanelli:** *What's the difference between an angel and a VC?*

**John May:** The main difference is that angels consider psychic reward as one of their major criteria [in deciding what to invest in]. They get an emotional, or personal,

▲

## Smart Tip

Tip...

Don't delay. Check out www.nvst.com. If you are based in the Washington, DC, or Seattle area, check out both Seraph Capital Forum (www.seraphcapital. com) and the New Vantage Group (www.newvantage group.com) and see if there's anything there for you. Don't submit material too early—wait until it's polished. But once your business plan is solid, get a move on!

benefit from it, as opposed to venture capitalists, who get more of a financial benefit from the transaction.

**Campanelli:** *What's the biggest mistake entrepreneurs make in approaching angels?*

**May:** Being fixated on their evaluation and not being flexible. An angel might be willing to have a negotiation about their role and their money, but if entrepreneurs assume that an angel is fixated on a high rate of return only, they will be shooting themselves in the foot.

**Campanelli:** *What's the one thing entrepreneurs can do to make their case stronger?*

**May:** Network through friends and trusted advisors. Also, if you are planning to be a high-growth company and you plan to raise outside money—which not every entrepreneur plans to do—it's probably a good idea to also have sophisticated counsel, accountants, and an advisory board.

**Campanelli:** *How many business plans come through your door monthly? How many do you think get funded by anybody?*

**May:** We generally look at about 50 to 100 plans per month. Most entrepreneurs submit through the web; most angel groups have application forms on their web sites, and entrepreneurs either fill it out there or they send an executive summary attached to an e-mail. This seems to be the dominant entry point for entrepreneurs. Out of 100 plans, 10 will most likely be presented to our group, and one or two of those may get funded. But keep in mind, there are far more angel transactions per year than venture capitalist transactions. Last year, I believe there were only 2,500 venture transactions, and there were 20,000 to 40,000 angel transactions in the United States. Sure, they may have been only $50,000 transactions—which is a lot less than what venture transactions cost—but there are a lot of opportunities out there. There are angel investors in all 50 states, and every major metropolitan area has an angel group, while venture capital is heavily concentrated in California and New England.

**Campanelli:** *What are investors looking for in start-ups?*

**May:** Today, they are looking for mature management rather than wide-eyed ideas.

# e-Chat with
# WorldRes.com's Eric Christensen

## WorldRes.com

**Eric Christensen, president and co-founder**
**Location: San Mateo, California**
**Year Started: 1995**

When you travel, you need a place to lay your head at night, right? While the big online travel agencies (Expedia, Travelocity) have aggressively sold airline tickets, they have been less successful in selling hotel rooms—even though the global hotel market is a $220 billion business. Why the disparity? Many reasons, but mainly it's that only a tiny percentage of hotels have real-time, online booking capabilities, according to Eric Christensen, president and co-founder of San Mateo, California-based WorldRes.com, an online reservations service that includes hotels in its offerings.

"While the number is growing, the vast majority of hotels are not online anywhere—around 35,000 out of 220,000 properties worldwide," estimates Christensen. That's good news for Christensen, whose aim—after receiving a $30 million financing round in 1998 that included funding from online reservations system architect Sabre and industry giant Starwood Hotels—is to sell those hotels a back-end system that will get them online fast. Basically, WorldRes.com brings hotels on through its extranet. It charges an upfront fee but waives it if the hotel can generate a minimum level of reservations. For reservations, WorldRes.com charges hotels on a pay-as-you-go basis, with a transaction fee collected whenever a room is booked through the WorldRes.com system. Going forward, it will start selling more rooms via the "merchant model," where the hotel gives WorldRes.com one rate, and then WorldRes.com marks up that price to consumers and keeps the difference. The industry has gradually been moving in this direction. Sound good? You bet, and that's why Christensen's WorldRes is a B2B e-commerce star.

**Melissa Campanelli:** *What's been your biggest surprise at WorldRes?*

**Eric Christensen:** The internet roller coaster was all of a sudden too rewarding for our business, and then very quickly, too punishing for our business. Also, the poor hotel economy has led hotels to sell rooms at any price, and this has been difficult for us because we're focused on making online sales cost-efficient for the hotels. Lately, hotels have been more interested in sheer volume than obtaining selective volume at the right price.

**Campanelli:** *How hard has it been to raise money? What did you do right in approaching investors?*

**Christensen:** It was hard in the early years, before the dotcom boom. Starting in 1998, it became all too easy to raise funding and spend it too quickly. Since mid-2000, it has been almost impossible to raise [money].

In approaching investors, I think we correctly [characterized] the hotel industry as one where the internet would make a difference and where investors could make money. We also pointed out the need for infrastructure and our capability of providing it.

**Campanelli:** *How is building a B2B site different from building a B2C site?*

**Christensen:** One doesn't really build a B2B site—we develop and implement B2B infrastructure, including many web sites, interfaces, payment mechanisms, etc. It's not very different: You have to pay attention to solving your customers' problems; it's just a different set of customers.

**Campanelli:** *Is there a potentially bigger payout in B2B? Why?*

**Christensen:** We think so, over the long-term. When the consumer market grows incrementally, that only puts increasing pressure on the B2B business to develop and implement the solutions to support the consumer growth. Then you have all the nonconsumer markets, which are also moving online just as fast as the consumer market. However, being successful in B2B requires significant credibility in your industry, and it takes more investment in infrastructure than B2C over a longer period.

**Campanelli:** *What advantage do you have against the many competitors in your space?*

**Beware!**
Seventy VCs! That's how many the executives at WorldRes visited—and even with a winning idea in hand, the company still got vastly more turndowns than acceptances. You absolutely have to be thick-skinned when hunting for outside funding because you will get rejected—often, and coldly. Pain is just part of the game.

**Christensen:** Most of our employees come out of the hotel industry. We think our technology people understand hotels best, and we think our hotel people understand technology best. We are also supplier-focused: We've aligned our interests with the owners and managers of hotel rooms, and in the end they call the shots on how they will sell their rooms online.

# Cheap Tricks with RedWagons.com's Tony Roeder

## RedWagons.com

**Tony Roeder, president and founder**
**Location: Oak Park, Illinois**
**Year Started: 1998**

Tony Roeder is one of the internet's biggest success stories. In 1998, with virtually no experience, capital, or programming skills, he launched RedWagons.com, a site that originally sold

Radio Flyer wagons but now sells other specialty toys—such as bikes, strollers, and swing sets—for kids up to 8 years old. The company, which has had 20-fold growth over its first year, sells upwards of 1,000 different products.

How did Roeder, a former handyman, get the idea to launch the site?

About five years ago, he was on a customer's porch assembling a Radio Flyer wagon when he was struck by the look and feel of the wagon. He had lots of memories of Radio Flyer products growing up and started thinking about what a great company Radio Flyer was. Says Roeder, "Radio Flyer has been a part of my earliest childhood memories—from the Radio Flyer wagon we had careening down our suburban driveway to the old rusty wagon I pulled my children around in at the time I was sitting on that porch."

> ## Smart Tip
>
> An opportunity to start a successful business can happen when you least expect it. For Tony Roeder, a chance meeting with someone from Radio Flyer, the red-wagon company, was the catalyst that prompted him to start his company, RedWagons.com. Always keep an open mind—you never know where or when a chance to start a business will pop up.

He was also looking for another line of work and wondered about e-tailing, since he worked regularly with a hardware store that had started selling Weber grills online. Roeder realized there was a lot of opportunity in this arena.

Then, by chance, he ran into a person who worked for Radio Flyer and had a casual conversation with the employee about putting a wagon together for one of his customers. When he learned that Radio Flyer was not selling its products online—despite its online presence—he jumped at the chance to do just that, despite the fact that he had no internet experience at the time.

Here, Roeder offers his insights into starting a successful dotcom company.

**Melissa Campanelli:** *How did you start your web site?*

**Tony Roeder:** I first hired a web designer for $4,000 who worked for Radio Flyer's informational web site, but he had never done an e-commerce site before and basically could not get the site up in a reasonable [amount of time]. I had to fire him. I then contacted Yahoo! and built my site on the Yahoo! Store system. Their costs were pay as you go, and back then, it was about $200 or $300 per month, which was less than what the designer was going to charge me for monthly maintenance.

Yahoo! made it possible for me to be my own web designer and store builder virtually overnight. The site went live in November 1998, just in time for the holiday season.

**Campanelli:** *How do you handle fulfillment?*

**Roeder:** We ship. There are some products we drop-ship, but we warehouse and ship the majority of our products. The advantage of this, we believe, is that we can control our customer service in the sense that there is less runaround. If an order is placed before noon Central time, it's shipped that day.

**Campanelli:** *What are the secrets to your success?*

**Roeder:** The combination of the Yahoo! exposure, good search engine placement, and good links put us on the map.

For the search engines, I made sure my web site came up for the words "Radio Flyer," and "Radio Flyer wagons" on the search sites. At the time, I found that many web sites were only worried about their company names coming up on the search engine sites, not the names of the products they were selling. For example, in 1998, Amazon.com was only worried about Amazon.com coming up first—their name, not their products. Instead of leveraging our name, we leveraged our products. As for the links, we had a link from the Radio Flyer informational site, which helped direct people to our site.

Technology has also been very important to our company. Most of our challenges have been met by judiciously applying technology to our processes.

**Campanelli:** *What are your plans for the future? Your goals and objectives?*

**Roeder:** In September 2003, we opened a brick-and-mortar store. We'd been kicking around the idea for a while, because we knew we had to change our business model. The competitors who are coming on—expecting to do as well as we have done—are going after a model that worked five years ago, and they are getting a smaller and smaller piece of a very small pie. We still have the biggest piece, but our piece is getting smaller, and they are all getting little bites. Until now, we really didn't have the location to do it. Our warehouse is on a farmer's highway in Iowa, which is not a really hot retail site, and our office isn't really set up for retail. We then learned that a space was available nearby in River Fort, Illinois, and it was perfect. It's in a shopping center and had the three elements needed: location, location, location.

In general, our objective is to maintain profitability and to be innovative. Our birth, growth and explosion were due to being at the right place at the right time. Those types of opportunities don't exist today, but there may be some tomorrow. We are always alert to what is happening with them. We are also constantly refining our processes, our marketing and our communication—and we try to always be aware of our competition so we can continue to grow as a company.

# Cashing In
## on Affiliate
## Programs

**W**ant to generate cash, now, from your web site? Even sites that aren't e-commerce-enabled—meaning they retail nothing—can put money in your pocket through the many affiliate programs now found on the web. From Amazon to OfficeMax, leading online retailers are eager to pay you for driving sales their way. How? By putting their link—such as a banner or text—on your site. For every click-through that results in a sale, you will earn a commission, anywhere from 1 percent to 15 percent.

In some cases, you can get commission on all sales that take place up to ten days after you send someone to a site. For example, if a customer visits your site and clicks on the leading online company's banner ad and doesn't buy anything right away but purchases something a few days later, you still get credit for the sale.

In some cases, you are compensated even if the visitor doesn't buy anything, just for having driven traffic to the merchant's site. This is not as popular as the former examples, however. The affiliate's reward varies from merchant to merchant and program to program, depending on the terms of the merchant's offer.

# It All Clicks

Supposedly, the idea for affiliate programs—where big merchants enlist small sites as a de facto sales force—got its start when a woman talking with Amazon.com founder Jeff Bezos at a cocktail party in 1996 asked how she might sell books about divorce on her web site. Bezos noodled the idea, and a lightbulb went on. He realized the opportunities for both to benefit were great, and the upshot was the launch of Amazon's affiliate program, one of the industry's most successful.

What's the appeal of affiliate programs? "The primary appeal lies in the fact that affiliate marketing is always tied to performance," says Wayne Porter, vice president of product development at AffTrack, an affiliate data analyzer. "Marketers are not paying for relationships or placements that don't work. It is not without risk, nor is it always the most cost-effective in the long term, but dollar for dollar, it is usually a good investment."

How much money is involved? Forrester Research, a company that tracks web trends, interviewed 50 leading online retailers and discovered that, on average, they have more than 10,000 affiliates apiece that collectively generate 13 percent of these retailers' online revenue. What's more, big growth is anticipated, with the leading merchants expecting affiliate programs to produce more than 20 percent of their revenue by 2003, according to Forrester.

For you, getting a share is simple. You put up a few links on your site (to any of the thousands of e-tailers that offer commissions to affiliates), and, as surfers click from your site into your affiliated site, you earn money. All

> **Smart Tip** *Tip...*
>
> Once you've pasted in an affiliate code, always preview the revised page before going live. Often the placement won't be where you'd thought it would be (centering a logo can be downright tricky—just use trial and error), and sometimes the link is dead (usually because a tiny bit of code got cut off during copying and pasting).

this sounds so new, but think about it. Basically, you're getting paid for leads, a practice as old as selling that makes sense for everyone involved.

## Adding It Up

Sound good? Understand that affiliate programs rarely generate big bucks for small web site owners. In many cases, they generate no money at all, even when sales occur. Why? Amazon's affiliate program, for instance, pays up to 15 percent commissions, with most sales generating at least a 5 percent commission. But Amazon won't issue a check until commissions hit $100. Do the math: At 5 percent, you'd have to sell $2,000 in books to see a check. That's a lot of dead trees.

At Priceline.com, affiliates get $1 for a lead they generate if the lead posts "a qualified bid" at Priceline, with checks issued once your balance reaches $50. PCConnection.com pays its affiliates 4 percent on every computer and peripheral sale they generate, which means you sell a $1,500 computer and get only $45—and checks aren't cut until you hit $100.

The inescapable conclusion: You need brisk traffic for any affiliate program—no matter how generous—to actually send you checks. And don't believe the affiliate proponents who promise that somehow, just by signing up with an affiliate program, you'll see a jump in traffic. It won't happen—the web is awash with places to buy just about everything imaginable.

## Solid Links

How hard is it to create an affiliate link? The job is simple, and you'll have it done within a minute or three. It works like this: You select the logo or link you want to show at your site (most e-tailers offer many choices, sometimes dozens, so you can get exactly the look you want). Click the logo you like, and the e-tailer will automatically generate HTML code that does two things: links to the e-tailer and includes your affiliate ID so you can earn commissions. Then you copy that code and, using any HTML editor (such as Microsoft's FrontPage), paste it into your site.

Doing all this is grunt work, not rocket science, and within a few minutes the link should look spiffy. Want to see this procedure in action? Head to Amazon's excellent resources

### Beware!

Never forget that a bad shopping experience at an affiliated site will tarnish your reputation, too. Choose affiliates cautiously, monitor them (check into their sites), and carefully heed any feedback you get from your visitors. Better still, shop at your affiliated merchants yourself and swiftly eliminate any that don't measure up. You simply can't afford links to bad affiliates.

for affiliates. One page covers the nitty-gritty in vivid detail: www.amazon.com/gp/browse.html/104-2958172-8353545?no de=3435371. Even sites with heavy traffic won't necessarily see big profits resulting from affiliate programs. To make money, you have to follow the rules.

Rule No. 1: Don't make affiliate links your content. The advice seems obvious, but the web remains cluttered with pages that consist of nothing but banners from affiliates—nobody is apt to buy anything from these sites. That's why a basic element in setting up a thriving affiliation deal is to strictly limit the number of programs you join. You don't want a blizzard of banners on your site.

Rule No. 2: "Do contextual placement; it's important," advises AffTrack's Porter. But be sparing—rarely should there be more than a single affiliate link on any page—and if you explain why you are endorsing this merchant and merchandise, you may just get visitors to check it out. A saloon owner, for instance, might recommend a cocktail recipe book; a web site design firm might endorse a web hosting service.

Rule No. 3: Seek feedback from your site visitors. Do they find the links to affiliates useful? Distracting? Annoying? Pay attention to what they tell you—and if they are not clicking through to your affiliate merchants, that, too, tells you something. Put up different banners, or take them down altogether.

## The Dark Side of Banners

You've digested the warning that, at a site with modest traffic, you're unlikely to see an affiliate check in this century, but there's more bad news to consider. For starters, whenever a visitor clicks the affiliate link, he or she clicks away from your site.

# A Touch of Class

Acouple of years ago, the secret reason many small web sites slapped on a banner from, say, Amazon was to gain a kind of legitimacy. It was hoped that the hard-won (and expensively bought) credibility of Amazon would anoint a start-up with a species of classiness. Maybe it even worked—once. But if that's what you think affiliate programs will do for you now, forget it. With so many banners out there, people will think nothing more than that you took the time to copy and paste someone's HTML code into your web page.

This strategy may even backfire. Sites festooned with affiliate banners simply look cheesy, the very opposite of legitimate. The bottom line: The only valid reason to join affiliate programs is if they put cash in your pocket.

You may make the commission, but you'll lose the visitor. Is it worth it? That's your call, but this is an issue every site—no matter how heavy or light its traffic—has to ponder. Winning traffic just isn't easy in today's cluttered internet marketplace, and justifications have to be strong for you to willingly show a visitor the way off your site.

Then why does Amazon, one of the undisputed kingpins of e-commerce, routinely do it? The Amazon front page features links to drugstore.com, but Amazon is a major investor in drugstore, which in turn has paid Amazon for this prime chunk of real estate, so the payoff is plain to see. For you, the choice is more difficult. An affiliate link might put money in your treasury, but would you make more money keeping the visitor at your site? Think hard on that.

If you choose to add a banner, remember that every banner you insert takes time to load, meaning your page will take that much longer to come into a visitor's view. Always check affiliate banners to make certain they load swiftly. Amazon banners usually pop rapidly into view, while those from lesser players sometimes can take many seconds. Ruthlessly delete slow-loading banners. You can't afford to waste your visitors' time.

And what if a site visitor clicks into an affiliated merchant and has a bad experience? Whom do you blame when your pal Joe recommends his barber, and the haircut that barber gives you makes you look old, tubby and poor? The barber, of course—but also Joe.

## Working the System

Is joining an affiliate program an instant way to get yourself discounts on the stuff you intend to buy anyway? It might seem that way. Put up an Amazon logo and, bingo, whenever you buy a book, you get a 5 percent commission (or discount, since it's you shopping).

But affiliate program owners aren't that stupid. Read the fine print and, in most programs, there's a clause that says you won't get a commission on your own purchases. End of story? Maybe not: Whispers in the industry are that few affiliate program operators enforce that exclusion. Sources insist that although the program operators know it's you when you're buying—cookies make your identity known—they pay the commission anyway because they don't want to alienate affiliates and, furthermore, are fearful of driving business to competitors.

Is that true? Try it for yourself when your next major purchase looms. Don't frivolously buy, say, a computer just to get that 3 percent discount—buy only because you need to—but if a check does come, pop a celebratory bottle of wine for us. Not only is the wine in effect free, but you've paid for this book, too. What a deal!

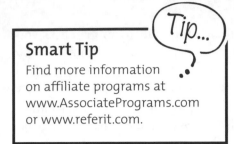

**Smart Tip**

Find more information on affiliate programs at www.AssociatePrograms.com or www.referit.com.

When affiliate programs work, they work, but when they don't, no web site owner should hesitate to take down the links and call it a noble but failed experiment. Check out affiliate programs, but don't be shy about pulling the plug if you're not seeing meaningful returns.

Want to discover more about affiliate programs? Sites that offer speedy sign-up for multiple quality programs include LinkShare (www.linkshare.com), which offers deals with The Disney Store, OfficeMax, J.C. Penney and plenty more; and Be Free (www.befree.com), which has deals with IBM, Gap and more. Other top sites are Performics (www.performics.com) and Commission Junction (www.cj.com).

Crave more obscure programs for your site? You'll find them at ClicksLink (www.clickslink.com), which provides a searchable directory plus tools for signing up with everything from astrology vendors to watchmakers.

# New Alliances

The old-fashioned approach to affiliate relationships—and still the web's most prevalent way—is to pop some HTML code onto one of your pages and hope that produces a ringing cash register for your affiliated merchant. But the drawbacks to doing e-commerce this way have prompted the creation of new styles of programs.

For example, some savvy merchants are giving private-label sites to their partners or finding more innovative ways to integrate them. Here are some examples, provided by AffTrack's Porter:

- RegNow's (www.regnow.com) affiliates can add targeted software products to their shopping carts and define style sheets so product purchases appear to be seamless on their sites.
- Smaller affiliate merchant systems like My Affiliate Program (www.myaffiliateprogram.com) allow affiliates to pick up web pages or a web catalog with products and host them in their own databases.
- Flexible tools like Website.Machine (www.w3M.com) allow merchants to produce private-label sites that can do not only commission splitting but also actual profit sharing.

# 18

# Teaming Up with Big
# Brick-and-Mortar
# Companies

**F**orming alliances with major corporations has become a common strategy for dotcom companies seeking to carve out a niche for themselves in an ever more brutally competitive marketplace. Why? Nowadays branding is crucial—it takes a name and a sizable chunk of consumer mind share to win eyeballs, and getting there is an expensive proposition.

▲

The days when a little start-up could go it alone the way Yahoo! and Amazon did are waning, and a new philosophy is taking hold. "If you're a small dotcom, you have to build alliances with bigger companies," says Phil Anderson, the Alumni Fund professor of entrepreneurship at INSEAD, a global business school in Fontainebleau, France, and director of 3i Venturelab, an academic center that seeks to become the principal source of information on European independent businesses.

"You have no choice," says Anderson. "You need to build share fast, and that means you have to leverage more resources than you can get your mitts on by yourself."

> **Smart Tip** Tip...
>
> Don't use just any lawyer to consult with when a tech marriage looms. Find one in a tech center—Silicon Valley; San Francisco; New York City; Austin, Texas—with prior experience in doing deals, and be prepared to pay fees upward of $500 per hour. Look at that money as an investment in your future, because that's exactly what it is.

Align with a big partner and you instantly get multiple pluses: cash, deep management expertise, and—when it benefits you—a name you can use to help open doors. Those are very real, very substantial benefits, and that's why partnering is epidemic (in the best possible sense of the word) among dotcoms.

A good example of a dotcom company partnering successfully with a big brick-and-mortar company is The Knot Inc. (www.TheKnot.com), a New York-based company and web site that offers products and services to couples planning their weddings. The Knot formed a strategic alliance with The May Department Stores Company, which is based in St. Louis.

In 2002, the two companies launched a strategic marketing alliance linking The Knot.com, The Knot's wedding planning web site, to the wedding-gift registry sites of May's department stores. With a $5 million strategic investment, May purchased a 19.5 percent interest in The Knot and was given a place on The Knot's board of directors.

Under the terms of the alliance, May and The Knot launched a marketing campaign to promote May's department store companies that offer wedding registry services—among them Hecht's, Strawbridge's, Foley's, Robinsons-May, Filene's, Kaufmann's, Famous-Barr, L.S. Ayres, The Jones Stores, and Meier & Frank—to the largest audience of engaged couples and wedding guests on the web and in stores. The promotions included online advertising and in-store promotions, direct-mail and e-mail campaigns, and advertisements in The Knot's publications.

When the partnership was launched, co-founder and CEO of The Knot, David Liu, said the marketing initiative with May "supports The Knot's continuing mission to enhance the quality and quantity of wedding gift services offered to today's largest audience of engaged couples and guests seeking wedding gifts on the World Wide Web."

Gene S. Kahn, May's chair and CEO, was equally excited. He said the alliance offered an unparalleled opportunity for May to team with the premier source for wedding-related information. The Knot has impressive brand recognition among today's engaged couples and is acclaimed for offering savvy, fresh ideas and great information for wedding planning," he said. "The alliance further supports our quest for the younger customer and gives us yet another opportunity to build important synergies with our department stores and introduce our home merchandise to a highly targeted audience of new customers."

This is just one example of a successful alliance. And there are plenty of them of many different kinds. For example, some turn to dotcom players because building a viable in-house dotcom operation has proved tough for old-style companies, and an alliance with a brash, youthful dotcom is a fast answer to the question "How will you succeed tomorrow?"

Over the years, alliances have changed, according to Snehal Desai, director of e-business for The Dow Chemical Company in Midland, Michigan, and chair of the board of the Association of Strategic Alliance Professionals in Wellesley, Massachusetts. "We don't have many dotcom companies coming to us anymore asking us if we want to partner with them or make an investment in their company," he says. "Companies are instead coming to us in the old context of asking us to be a beta customer for their offering. We'll receive value from this type of arrangement vs. some kind of equity."

Desai adds, "We would be less likely to just make an investment in their companies because there is little likelihood they will actually go public and we'll be able cash in. But their ability to offer us a very solid, targeted e-business software tool or service that could be integrated into the way we do business or go to market could have a lot larger impact on us."

In general, Desai says that alliances today are very reliable. "The type of alliance has changed from what might have been much more of an integrated alliance through share ownership or something like that to more of a traditional development partner, 'key client' kind of relationship. Long gone are the days when they just want me to hand them money and figure something out. It's reverted more to a transactional partnership, where I may buy their tools or software, rather than what I would consider a true strategic alliance."

# Risky Business

Good as some of the news is about the partnerships that are proliferating throughout the dotcom world, there's also a dark side. For example, big companies often put up their money but are unprepared to offer anything more. Another trouble spot is pointed out by INSEAD's Anderson: "Almost by definition, you're taking the larger brand where it hasn't been before. That's a recipe for conflict." Chew on that, because it's at the paradoxical core of small-big alliances. The big company wants the little partner for its creativity, its innovation, and its ability to plunge into terrain previously unexplored by the big fellow. But once the deal is done, the risk aversion that is at the heart of virtually all megacorporations kicks in—and suddenly the partner is counseling caution and slow forward motion.

Another problem is that today it is more difficult for young technology companies to find willing deep-pocketed partners, says Christopher O'Leary, engagement director with The Concours Group, a management consulting, research and education firm based in Kingwood, Texas. He points to several reasons for this, including the increasing scarcity of capital, the equivocal success of past alliances, and simply the fact that there are more Cinderellas looking for a ticket to the ball.

> ## ⚠ Beware!
> Are you concerned about simply being acquired—and losing all effective control? Before making any partnership deal, do research that tells you how many small companies the big company that's courting you has swallowed in the past year. If the number is high, that is not necessarily an indication that you need to back away from the deal. But it does mean you need to be aware of the possible outcomes.

Another worry to gnaw on is that a big company may acquire effective control of a little company, meaning that although a straightforward acquisition hasn't been done, by taking command of key functions—accounting, say—or by assuming multiple board seats, the big company has simply grabbed control. As a result, you absolutely need a third party to assist you.

That recommendation is seconded by Ken Burke, founder and CEO of Petaluma, California-based Multimedia Live, an e-commerce tool developer that in 1998 brought in publisher R.R. Donnelly as a sizable partner. It took eight months to negotiate the deal—which, according to Burke, left him still controlling the vast majority of the company's ownership. "Donnelly has no real decision-making power," he says. But, he says, a key for him was hiring good lawyers. "They found many things in the deal we had to get revised or deleted. You don't want to negotiate this sort of thing alone." Don't pop the cork to celebrate a business alliance too soon—60 percent of alliances fall apart within three and a half years, says business consultant Larraine Segil, author of *Intelligent Business Alliances* (Three Rivers Press) and other books. Just why do these marriages unravel? Incompatible corporate cultures were cited by a majority of the executives Segil surveyed. Seventy-three percent pointed to incompatible management cultures, 63 percent referred to incompatible management personalities, and 55 percent said business justifications contributed to the falling out. A majority of the companies surveyed felt that all three factors contributed, but some felt that one or two contributed more than others.

That's why Segil tells small companies to ask themselves: If this marriage ends in divorce, do I have the resources to recover? If you don't, get moving on developing a separation strategy. Maybe it will never be deployed, but with more than half of corporate marriages ending in quickie divorces, prudence dictates concocting a scenario for survival without the larger partner.

## Budget Watcher

Get lots of good, free information about alliances from Larraine Segil's web site, www.lsegil.com. She offers a thick sampling of freebie articles crammed with sage counsel.

There are other things companies can do to help the alliance succeed. "In order for partnerships to work, it is important that the courtship be more deliberate and involve deeper investigation than may have been required in the past," says The Concours Group's O'Leary.

He explains that enterprise strategies and operating models should be compared for compatibility and consistency. Also crucial is the development of a mutually acceptable exit strategy to protect the companies if the intended success proves elusive. "Both partners have to take the alliance or partnership very seriously and do what we call joint business planning," says Dow Chemical's Desai. "If a small business knows why they got into a partnership, and they have articulated that, and understand that, and agree upon that with their partner—and they can do what they said they were going to do—that's a huge upside."

In general, "a dedication of resources to alliances and the adoption of best practices are crucial to successful alliances," says Bill Lundberg, founding president and executive director of the Association of Strategic Alliance Professionals Inc. (ASAP) in Wellesley, Massachusetts.

## Getting Hitched

**W**ant to pursue alliances? Make up a list of potential partners, and make very sure that you see the deal from their perspective as well as yours. Then put yourself in those potential partners' faces. Talk to them at trade shows, for instance, and take every step that comes to mind that will increase their awareness of you. But let them make the first move.

In every instance of successful partnerships I've heard about, the big company made the initial suggestion. Maybe there's no jinx involved in taking a direct approach, but maybe there is. So wait to be wooed.

What are some of these best practices? "You've got to drive your alliance strategy from your corporate strategy," says Lundberg. "They have to be tied and must emerge from the specific business developments that a company has."

He also says companies need to have a clear profile of their objectives as well as what the characteristics are of a preferred partner. "What kind of resources do they have in [a particular] field? What kind of market access do they have?" asks Lundberg.

For more information about these best practices and other information about strategic alliances, visit ASAP's web site at www.strategic-alliances.org.

# Forging Ahead

Know that it won't be easy to create a partnership with a big company—no matter how good your dotcom is. How tough will it be? Here's a true story that ends with success, but the going was tough along the way.

Picture this: You have a great idea for a dotcom. You'll sell gift certificates that can be redeemed at many major retailers, and you'll make a little bit on every transaction. Sounds terrific, except there's a problem: How do you talk retailers into letting you sell their gift certificates?

Jonas Lee, former CEO of GiftCertificates. com (www.giftcertificates.com) knows—and he also knows how hard it was to do the persuading. Currently, the company has more than 300 major retailers, but "we knocked on many doors before we signed the first deals," he says. Why? Start-ups are potentially pathways to wealth, but they may also be fly-by-night concerns. Major, established businesses don't want to risk tarnishing their brand by partnering with a start-up that goes bust.

Eventually Lee got his initial commitments from a couple of name-brand shops—Barnes & Noble and The Sharper Image. "It took me two or three months of persistent calling and explaining," he says. "You may have a good idea, but you have to also convince people you are a good businessperson, and that takes time." The broader point: Partnerships can be wonderful, but persuading partners to ally with you is about as hard as building a winning web site in the first place.

## Beware!
Toysmart, the now-defunct online toy store, thought it had a primo deal when Disney acquired it in 1999 for an undisclosed amount. Those hopes turned to dust in mid-2000, when Disney simply unplugged Toysmart, shutting down the site to stop its losses. Big companies may have deep pockets, but they may also have shallow patience—and that's a real pitfall. The cruel fact is, just as they have the resources to quickly make substantial investments in a little dotcom, they can also—without a shudder or even any hesitation—afford to write off all that money and walk away.

# e-Chat with
# e-Bags.com's
# Peter Cobb

## eBags.com

**Peter Cobb, vice president of marketing and merchandising**
**Location: Greenwood Village, Colorado**
**Year Started: 1998**

Eliot and Peter Cobb, Frank Steed and Andy Young joined Jon Nordmark in spring 1998 to build a major store for shoes and accessories out of bytes, not bricks, and boy, have they pulled it off. Currently, eBags is the world's largest online retailer of bags and accessories for all lifestyles, and it has sold more than 2.1 million bags and accessories since the site launched in March 1999.

EBags has also grown 40 percent per month since its launch, and in April 2003, it announced its fourth straight positive-cash-flow quarter and its first-ever profitable quarter. The company also disclosed record holiday sales, up 101 percent in 2002 from the prior holiday period. Eliot, Frank, and Andy are no longer involved in the business, but Peter and Jon are as active as ever.

Steed was president of Samsonite USA and American Tourister prior to launching eBags. Peter Cobb, Young and Nordmark were also top executives at Samsonsite. Each has product development, merchandising and marketing experience with globally recognized consumer brands. Eliot Cobb was formerly the vice president/treasurer of The Wherehouse, a 350-store retail music chain on the West Coast. As a group, the Cobbs, Steed, Young, and Nordmark possess more than 60 years of bag and retail experience.

To start the company, each of the five founders came up with a significant amount of cash and worked without pay for eight months. Then eBags raised $8 million from angels, friends and family. The company then decided it wanted to get venture capital funding, so it carved back its angel funding to $4 million and actually sent checks back to all its angels. In 1999, financial relief came from VC firm Benchmark Capital. Other investors have followed, allowing eBags to continually improve. To date, the company has raised a total of $30 million in VC funding.

A key to the company's success? It does not overspend. For example, executives don't have golden parachutes or big bonuses. In fact, no one at the company, including its executives, makes a six-figure salary. And after 9/11, all employees, including the executives, took a 10 percent pay cut without complaint. This kind of frugal approach is one reason eBags.com is still around when so many other dotcoms aren't.

Another success secret? eBags maintains little or no inventory of its own. Instead, it relies on manufacturers to drop-ship products directly to customers. For example, 151 of the 157 brands eBags currently sells are sent by drop-shipping, including High Sierra Sport Co., Samsonite and JanSport, a unit of VF Corp. The practice has turned eBags into a luggage "category killer," offering a selection that dwarfs the several hundred items carried by the average specialty baggage store. Company executives believe this lack of inventory is one of the primary reasons eBags has survived.

Here, Peter Cobb discusses some other secrets to eBags' success.

**Melissa Campanelli:** *What made you decide to launch eBags.com?*

**Peter Cobb:** In May 1998, we saw what was going on with people starting companies selling books and music online, and there was a product we knew and loved—bags— that we knew would be a great fit for the internet. We knew from our research that many people were buying bags through catalogs, so we knew that people didn't need to feel and touch the product to make a purchase decision. They were comfortable buying bags from *Orvis, L.L. Bean, Lands' End,* and *Eddie Bauer* catalogs. We knew bags and accessories weren't like clothes or shoes, where people really needed to see the color, the size and the materials. Also, people don't really get excited about going to the mall Saturday afternoon to pick out some luggage or a backpack for their son. So with three, four, or five photographs nicely done for a product, you can really get the point across.

> **Smart Tip** Tip...
>
> Is there a niche out there that you are familiar with that isn't on the web yet—and you just know it could be a perfect fit? Then what are you waiting for? As eBags' success shows, if you have the right niche product and you do e-tailing right, you will find success on the internet.

Another key reason we started was because the retail bag market was very fragmented. If you wanted luggage, you'd probably go to a travel goods specialty store. If you wanted a ladies' handbag, you'd probably go to a department store. And if you were looking for backpacks, you'd go to a sporting goods store. There was no "Bags R Us." Because of this fragmentation, we knew there'd be a great opportunity. And there happened to be nice margins on the product—markups [average] 50 percent.

The other important thing is that in the brick-and-mortar retail world, when inventory comes in, it's there for 180 days. If somebody buys a bag, the store orders another one. What's more, these stores are limited to about 250 products because of physical space. [Because we do business on the internet, however, we can offer] more than 8,000 products, and when we take an order, we pass it on to Samsonite, for example, and Samsonite ships it to the customer. We get the sale and then, 30 to 120 days later, we pay the vendor.

**Campanelli:** *How long did it take to go from idea to funding to launch?*

**Cobb:** Idea to funding was about eight months; idea to launch was 10 months.

**Campanelli:** *What's been the biggest surprise you've had in building eBags?*

**Cobb:** There have been a few of them.

The biggest surprise is how we've been able to gain such fantastic momentum. We've shipped 1.7 million bags.

Another one probably has been watching the flameout of all the e-tailers that took in many times more money than we did and somehow spent it all. It's been a huge surprise to see companies that I thought were pretty solid companies [fail]—like eToys, Garden.com, and MotherNature.com, sites I shopped on and had great shopping experiences with. What you don't know, however, is what is going on behind the scenes. These companies were spending tens of millions of dollars on inventory in their warehouses, which we didn't have to do. They were also spending money on television advertising, which we never really did.

We have a saying at eBags: "Too much money makes you stupid." We just kept seeing that over and over again. We didn't raise nearly as much money as these guys did, and we always understood that the money we were dealing with was our money—money we put into the company with some investors' help. Every decision we made was "This is our money; how should we spend it?" as opposed to "Boy, we've got $80 million in the bank, so who cares if we spend $1 million on Super Bowl ads?"

Another surprise has been how much internet retailing has taken hold with a large percentage of the population. I think it has mainstreamed. I've heard numbers like 67 percent of the population bought something online during last year's holiday season. I think that says good things for the future of internet retailing for those who are doing it right.

**Campanelli:** *What's been your biggest challenge?*

**Cobb:** I think the biggest challenge is managing your cash properly while continuing to grow.

**Campanelli:** *How many VCs did you meet with before you got a funding commitment?*

**Cobb:** We met with well over 50 VC companies.

**Campanelli:** *What's your strategy in coming out ahead of competitors?*

**Cobb:** Our competition is really brick-and-mortar stores. Online shopping isn't for everybody. Some people want to feel and touch and taste and smell before they buy a product, and that's OK. But a large majority of shoppers value convenience and selection, and that's why online shopping is experiencing explosive growth. Bags and accessories is a $30 billion market. Our strategy is just to continue to offer the ultimate shopping experience on eBags.com.

# Cheap Tricks with No Brainer Blinds' Jay Steinfeld

## No Brainer Blinds

**Jay Steinfeld, founder and CEO
Location: Houston
Year Started: 1996**

**W**ho likes buying window coverings? Probably nobody, a fact that Jay Steinfeld—founder and CEO of No Brainer Blinds (www.nobrainerblinds.com)—has turned into a thriving web-based business that was started with just $3,000 and has been profitable from day one. Steinfeld tells his story here:

**Robert McGarvey:** *Where did you get the idea for the site? When did the site go live?*

**Jay Steinfeld:** My wife and I owned a full-service brick-and-mortar window coverings store [in Houston]. We owned the store for about 14 years, so we knew the window coverings business inside and out. But we wanted to expand into a different niche—the price-sensitive do-it-yourself market. As of March 2001, we went full-time online. With the internet, I have a web site working 24 hours a day. I'm able to do so much more volume online than what I could have done in a 1,000-square-foot store. Last year, by the way, our business almost doubled over the year before. Why? Because people are becoming more comfortable with the internet, and even in a bad economy, people are trying to get good deals, and they naturally associate the internet with a good deal. No Brainer Blinds has been live for seven years, which is two years longer than the web has been a proven entity. We figured if we hustled and used the same service-first, high-touch philosophy; kept our personality present on the site; and made it fun, then customers would react favorably.

We wanted to make it easy, too—a no-brainer. So we called it No Brainer Blinds. That name occurred to me in about two minutes. As soon as I said it, I knew it would work. It made sense, it's descriptive of our mission, and people get it.

**McGarvey:** *Have you sought outside funding?*

**Steinfeld:** We did get some financing from some local angel investors in February 2001, and it enabled us to buy our biggest competitor, Blindswholesale.com, two years ago. This was a fantastic acquisition, and it let us have access to the technology we needed to expand our business. This acquisition tripled the size of our business, and we've doubled again [since then]. When we bought Blindswholesale.com, we also created No Brainer Enterprises as a parent company. No Brainer Enterprises is going to use its experience to create a third site called Blinds.com. The site will have more products, better help, be faster, and have better navigational experiences than the No Brainer Blinds site has.

Lately, we've been barraged by requests from other sites that want us to sell blinds for them. As a result, we have also launched Blinds.net, which is a business-to-business site that allows like-minded or home-related businesses to have their own web sites mirroring our new Blinds.com site. Basically, it is an offline affiliate program. We provide local people, businesses or homeowners' associations with free web sites, but we supply all the products. They have an elegant interface into a web site with prices that they could not get on their own. It also has an Avon-type approach, where these people can hand out business cards and send their customers to their free sites, and every month we send them a commission check of about 5 percent [of sales that result from those web site visits]. Once those deals are inked, our valuation will go up significantly. We will have distribution all over the United States, and we will have volume that is unheard of.

There are some blinds factories that have hinted they want to buy us, so who knows? This is my baby, so it would be hard to sell. On the other hand, I suppose everything is for sale.

**McGarvey:** *How do you attract visitors to your site?*

**Steinfeld:** We use all the guerrilla tactics—newsgroups, link building, search engine optimization. We have about 12,000 sites linking to us. We also encourage our existing customers to tell their friends. These days, 45 percent of our volume is either repeat customers or referrals. We also do paid advertising, such as keyword buys [a type of advertising that entails paying for high placement in search engine results for pre-selected keywords and keyword phrases]. For Blinds.com, we also intend to advertise on radio and television

**McGarvey:** *What's your look-to-buy ratio?*

**Steinfeld:** About 5 to 10 percent.

**McGarvey:** *How big is the average purchase?*

**Steinfeld:** When we were just No Brainer Blinds, the average order size was about $460, but now it's about $400 because we added lower-priced products from the Blindswholesale site. We attracted customers, but we attracted customers at the lower end of the scale. But as long as we make money, that's fine. Four hundred dollars is still about three times the industry average, which is $150.

**McGarvey:** *For the consumer, what's the advantage of buying online?*

**Steinfeld:** They save a bunch of money, and they can read up on the options/products at their own pace. No pressure. We have created our own private-label product line, too. Most of those products are custom-made in just one day, and all have lifetime warranties.

**McGarvey:** *What challenge do you face in making this site grow?*

**Steinfeld:** Our challenge right now is to make sure that our success doesn't cause us to implode. We now have to start looking at the company in a different way. We now have to start thinking of things in terms of systems, procedures, control and—God forbid—coming up with an organizational chart. We will have to write memos now and then and have meetings. We're going to have to get organized.

## Budget Watcher

Do you have $3,000 and a decent idea? Check out what No Brainer Blinds did with just that. Its web site isn't likely to win prizes for spiffy or artsy design, but it's functional, fast, and helps buyers get in and out quickly. And it's profitable. What can you sell on the web? Look for products that aren't being sold very well (or maybe not at all), get your budget together, and start working. No Brainer Blinds is real proof that if you dream it, you can make it real, with very little money or technical know-how.

# Web Site
# Traffic Builders

**H**ere's the bad news: Inktomi, a wholly owned subsidiary of Yahoo! and a provider of web search and paid inclusion services, recently surveyed the web and reported that it had counted more than three billion web pages. Wow! Just a decade ago, the web didn't exist. And even six years ago, it remained a playpen for supernerds. No more. Now every business needs a web site—but just because you build it doesn't mean a soul will ever visit. "Putting up a web site is just like opening an antiques store down a country road," says Larry Chase, publisher of *Web Digest for Marketers*, a weekly e-mail newsletter that delivers short reviews of marketing-oriented web sites. "Unless you tack up signs on better-traveled routes, you won't get any visitors." What's more, traditional marketing campaigns don't necessarily produce results for web sites, warns Mark DiMassimo, CEO of DiMassimo Brand Advertising, an agency that has handled many dotcom clients. A case in point: "Generally, television advertising for dotcoms, although expensive, has been very ineffective," says DiMassimo, whose agency at one time surveyed consumers and discovered that only 6 percent of heavy web users said they had ever visited a site due to a TV ad. "Offline advertising hasn't always worked as well as the dotcoms have hoped."

That's because at the beginning of the dotcom boom, many companies were ignoring the cardinal rule of web site marketing: "Put your dollars where your customers will be." Seem basic? Not to the dotcom companies that plunked down tens of millions of dollars to buy Super Bowl ads. "Having money is no excuse for spending like a drunken sailor," says DiMassimo, who adds that the critical test always has to be "Will my potential customers see the material?"

# Baiting Your Hook

What will lure visitors to a site? Although heavily funded internet companies can make seven- and eight-figure deals to buy prime advertising real estate on the major internet portals and online services like Yahoo! and AOL, you're likely to be priced out of that race. So winning visitors becomes a matter of creative, persistent marketing. And the good news is that it's still the little things that will bring plenty of traffic your way.

There are fundamental steps that too many businesses neglect. For instance? "You should always put your URL and a reason to visit your web site on your business cards," says Chase. "I call this cyber-bait. For example, you should mention what people will get when they visit the site, such as a newsletter or a list of 'Top 10 Tips' or something. That substantially increases visitors and eventually customers or subscribers."

A few years ago, Chase says, "You could get away with just putting a URL on your

**Budget Watcher**

Get your current visitors to recommend your site to their friends and colleagues—and don't pay a cent for this clever marketing ploy when you sign up with Recommend-It (www. recommend-it.com). It's a clever concept that just might up your visitor counts.

business card, because the novelty of that URL was enough to draw people to the site. Nowadays it's just like just putting up a fax number. People are not going to fax you just to see how your fax machine works." An e-mail signature is also an especially powerful—and absolutely free—tool. Create a signature with a link to your web site in it and have it automatically attached to every one of your outgoing e-mails. If your e-mail recipients click on the link, they'll be taken to your site. It only takes a few seconds to create an e-mail signature, and it'll bring in visitors to your site every day.

Another low-cost traffic builder: "Get active in online discussion groups and chats,

> **Tip...**
>
> ## Smart Tip
> Ever wish you could use your handwritten signature in your e-mail? Check out Signature e-mail (www.signature-mail.com), which offers Signature-mail Version 2.0, an easy-to-use graphics program that allows you to sign your e-mail and personalize computer documents with your own handwriting. Currently, the beta version can be downloaded for free.

and, where appropriate, give out your URL," says Shannon Kinnard, author of *Marketing with E-mail* (Maximum Press). Sell bird toys? Scout out the many groups that focus on birds and get active. A good place to find groups is at Google Groups (http://groups.google.com), which archives discussion lists. Getting active in these groups spreads the word about you and your site. "You'll get traffic coming to you," says Kinnard.

## The Most Bang for Your Buck

Another big-time traffic builder for any web site that retails is posting items for sale on the major auction sites, such as eBay, Yahoo!, and Amazon. Those sites let you identify yourself to viewers, and a few dollars spent on putting out merchandise to bid may just bring in lots of traffic from surfers seeking more information. Many small e-tailers tell me their entire advertising budget consists of less than $100 monthly spent on eBay, but they nonetheless are seeing traffic counts above 500 daily, with most of those viewers coming via eBay. My advice: Put up a few items for bid on each of the leading auction sites and then track traffic. Even if you sell the auctioned goods at no profit, the traffic jams your site may experience could well justify your efforts.

Classified ads offer more possibilities for traffic generation on the cheap. Check out Yahoo!, for example. Classified ads there are pretty low-cost and vary depending on what you are selling. Listing is simple—just follow the steps at the site—and, again, you can insert your URL so readers who want more information can get it with a click. There are also many web sites that let you run ads for free. The best way to find these is to search the web.

For my money, classified ads—at least the freebies—represent one of the very top ways to generate no-cost traffic, yet many businesses ignore them. Why? The complaint is that classified ad sites have too many listings—hundreds of thousands—but don't let that stop you. Put up some ads, and watch your hit count climb.

Should you buy ads on other web sites? That depends. While this model is not very popular anymore, there are a few ways you may get results. Consider Microsoft's bCentral (www.bcentral.com). For $249, it offers a package of 60,000 banner ad exposures on the Microsoft bCentral Banner Network, formerly known as LinkExchange. Is that money well spent? If you have a quality banner ad and a large number of exposures on premium sites, you may see a traffic jump. But many experts warn against this type of advertising nowadays, so beware.

With any ad campaign you purchase, closely monitor results. Renew only the deals that are generating traffic to your site, and know that net advertisers have a big plus over advertisers in offline media, such as magazines, because on the Net it is very easy to track—via your log files (see Chapter 31)—which ads are producing which results. That takes the guesswork out of decisions to renew media buys.

What's a fair payback? If small businesses goof, it's in wildly overestimating the results they can anticipate from a media purchase. If you spend $100 on ads that bring in sales that produce $110 in profits, consider it money well spent. Expecting more than that is just fantasy.

---

# Snazzy Signatures

Pretty much every e-mail program offers the ability to include a signature that goes out with every e-mail. Think of a signature—"sig" in techspeak—as a teaser, a fast ad for your Web site. How do you create a signature? In Microsoft Outlook, go to "Tools/Options/Mail Format/Signatures." In AOL, click "AOL Mail" and when you are about to send a message, select "Create a Signature." On Yahoo Mail, click "Mail Options" and then "Signature."

Some advice: Short is better than long with signatures. Rarely should you use more than six short lines, and three or four are better.

What to include? If your Web site sells foreign language tapes, for instance, you might use this sig:

*John Smith*
*President, TapesRUs.com*
*"Learn Languages by Tape"*
*www.tapesrus.com*

Once you've set it up, that signature will appear on every e-mail you send out (unless you override the default). If you send out 20 e-mails in a day, that's 20 repetitions of a fast ad message. It's one of the Net's best marketing bargains.

When it comes to offline advertising, expert opinion is mixed. Some pros advocate big investments in traditional media, while others tell you to fish where the fish are, and that means advertising online to promote an online store. I split the difference here, and my advice is to incorporate your URL prominently into all offline advertising you're doing—never overlook a chance to plug your web site—but don't launch an offline campaign for an online-only property. Sure, many of the big guys, such as Priceline.com (www.priceline.com) and E-Trade Financial Corp. (www.etrade.com), extensively advertise in offline media, but these are businesses with heavy venture capital backing and the dollars to experiment with. When money is tighter, go where you know you'll find surfers—and that means hunting online.

> **⚠ Beware!**
> A strong bias against overt advertising remains on the net's newsgroups. Sigs are OK with postings, but be careful to use a sig that's informational. "Best parrot seeds on the net" is out. "Seeds for parrots" is fine. The lines seem blurry? They are. But if you cross them, hostile postings from anti-ad folks will tell you the difference.

# A Direct Approach

For many businesses, direct mail—good old e-mail—may be the surest and certainly the cheapest tool for building traffic. "E-mail still gets results," says Hans Peter Brondmo, senior vice president of strategy and corporate development at Digital Impact, a San Mateo, California-based direct marketing solutions provider for companies such as Dell Computer Corp., Citibank, and MasterCard. Who reads spam? Nobody, says Brondmo, but well-constructed e-mail is "informative and personal, and people will look forward to getting it and reading it."

Brondmo, whose recent book, *The Engaged Customer* (HarperCollins), is a national bestseller and widely recognized as the bible of e-mail relationship marketing, adds that spam is "unwanted and unsolicited, by definition. But customized e-mail can generate response rates upwards of 6 percent—sometimes as high as 30 percent. No reputable company would send out spam, but we're seeing more companies using individualized e-mail in their marketing campaigns."

## News Flash

A key to making e-mail effective: Use "opt-in" sign-ups, in which web site visitors are asked to indicate if they want to receive e-mail from you. How to get sign-ups? "Offer a free monthly newsletter," says e-mail expert Shannon Kinnard. "The key is to give really good information."

## Budget Watcher

Want more pointers about traffic building and promotion on the cheap? Check out *Cheap Web Tricks! Build and Promote a Successful Web Site Without Spending a Dime* (McGraw-Hill), by Anne Martinez. Head to "Drumming Up Web Traffic On the Cheap" (http://hotwired.lycos. com/webmonkey/97/32/index3a. html?tw=e-business), which offers great information about low-cost promotion strategies. Understand, however, that there are no magic formulas. No-money promotion can work if you work at it, and that means consistent, solid effort. Do that, and you'll see the results in a rising daily visitor count.

About what? Content is wide open, but effective newsletters usually mix news about trends in your field with tips and updates on sales or special pricing. Whatever you do, "keep it short," says Kinnard, who advises that 600 words is probably the maximum length. "The rule is, the shorter, the better." Another key: Include hyperlinks so that interested readers can, with a single mouse click, go directly to your site and find out more about a topic of interest.

How often should you mail? Often enough to build a relationship with your readers, but not so frequently you become a pest. "Monthly works for most mailing lists," says Kinnard, but she notes that every other week is OK for some businesses.

Daily updates are a big mistake, and weekly ones are probably ill-advised, too. The reason: Recipients will ask to be deleted from the list or, worse, they'll simply delete each of your e-mails, unread, as soon as they come in. I am personally on a couple lists whose daily incoming e-mail goes straight into the trash, unopened. Don't make that mistake.

Some mailing list drawbacks: Maintaining a list can be time-consuming. Worse, most ISPs put limits on the size of outgoing mailings (a maximum of 50 recipients is common) to keep spammers away, so mailing to a large list can be an aggravation involving the use of many small lists. When I recently mailed to a charity's list of 1,000 as a do-good deed, I had to break the master list into about 25 mini-lists. When I tried to use more than, say, 50 names at a crack, the server rejected the whole mailing.

## Special Delivery

A solution to common mailing hassles is to "use a mailing service," says Kinnard, who suggests Yahoo! Groups (http://groups.yahoo.com) and Topica (www.topica.com), services that provide free list hosting, meaning they maintain the mailing list and, on your schedule, send out the mailings you provide. Mailings go out with a little third-party advertisement.

A lot of the grunt work involved in mailings is handled by these services, which leaves you free to focus on the fun part: your message. Keep it simple, keep it sharp, and always use e-mail to drive traffic to your site. Don't make the big mistake of trying to cram your web site's entire message into every e-mail. Nobody has the patience for that. E-mail should stick to "headline news," with the full story residing on your web site.

Is your list succeeding? There's no reason to guess at the answer. Just track site traffic for a few days before a mailing and a few days afterwards. Effective e-mail ought to produce a sharp upward spike in visitors. How big a spike? That answer hinges on your usual traffic, the size of your list, and your personal goals. A good target, though, is the 6 percent response rate mentioned earlier by Brondmo.

> **Smart Tip** Tip...
>
> Always give e-mail recipients an easy way to "opt out" of future mailings—and whenever anybody asks to be removed from your list, honor that request immediately.

If you don't see an increase in traffic, take a hard look at what you're mailing. Is it succinct? Focused? Does it encourage readers to click through for more information? If not, odds are you need to hone your message to encourage recipients to click through.

Another possible reason for less-than-desirable results: Your mailing list is bad. Send a vegan mailing to a list of self-proclaimed steak lovers, and you're knocking on the wrong door.

The best way to build a targeted mailing list is to make it simple for site visitors to sign up to receive it. By doing that, they show they are interested in your message— enough to indicate they want to hear more from you. Those are the folks who should be stimulated by your e-mail newsletter to click through for more info, at least sometimes. Keep working on both your newsletter and your list, and it will happen for you, too!

# Stick It to Me

"Sticky" is the dream that keeps web site builders going. When your site is sticky, visitors hang around, and that means they're reading and buying—and you can bet that every minute a surfer sticks to your site translates into greater brand awareness for you. Whether you're in a mall or your site is stand-alone, sticky is the Holy Grail—but making your site sticky doesn't have to be that elusive. "When the information—the content—is there, people will stick to your site," says Bill Razzouck, former CEO of online health-care and pharmacy company PlanetRx, which is now Paragon Financial Corp. and a specialty pharmacy business.

Is he right? For a measuring stick, just look at the following statistics: Nielsen/NetRatings (www.nielsen-netratings.com), a firm that offers internet audience measurement and analysis, published a chart called "Top 25 Brands" for the week ending March 30, 2003 that measured, among other things, how long people at home stayed on the top sites. In a recent week, AOL.com held each visitor for more than two hours! When the exit is just a mouse click away, that is amazing. In second place,

Yahoo!.com held its visitors more than 49 minutes. Other sites weren't quite so lucky. MSN.com, for example, kept visitors for more than 37 minutes, and Microsoft.com kept visitors a little longer than 11 minutes.

Still, even 11 minutes merits a big "Wow!" because most sites I know are happy when visitors stay longer than three. So what do the winning sites have in common? Good content and a site that is easy to navigate. Of course, content is lots easier to say than it is to deliver. The following are concrete building blocks for making any sites stickier:

> **Tip...**
>
> ## Smart Tip
> Don't want to take on the task of producing a regular e-mail newsletter? Contact a local college or university. There you'll find plenty of students in communications or journalism departments who would be glad to write up your newsletter for a small monthly fee. But make sure you give the student plenty of direction—it still has to be your newsletter.

- *Fast loading time.* Surfers are impatient. Force them to watch a stagnant screen as dense images or fancy Java applets load, and they will be out of there before your cool bells and whistles ever come into sight. It's tempting to use these gizmos—you might think they'd increase your visitor stays because just watching them load eats up minutes—but in most cases, forget it. When you force surfers to wait until meaningful stuff happens, they won't. They will simply leave—often in a huff—and that means they won't be bookmarking your site for future visits.

  Keep in mind, however, that more and more people are using broadband services, such as cable modems or DSL, to access the internet, which means they can get a faster connection. But it's still important that you don't overload your site with too much "stuff."

- *Good copy.* "The web is still about text, words," says Motley Fool co-founder David Gardner, and he's spot on. You're not a writer? That doesn't necessarily matter—not when you stick to your field of expertise. Are you a criminal lawyer? Put up a list of the "Ten Dumbest Mistakes Defendants Make." An accountant could do likewise. An electrician could put up a list of dangerous goofs made by do-it-yourselfers. Think snappy and useful, and try to provide info readers can't easily find at thousands of other web sites.

- *Free content.* Surfers love free information, and they'll keep coming back if you offer them targeted free information that they can use, such as white papers (consumer reviews of products or services you may be selling). This will allow you to get qualified, targeted people, with whom you can build a relationship, coming back to your site. It's not just about getting visitors for the sake of visitors anymore; you want targeted visitors who will become customers.

  Some experts wonder whether this technique confuses people. For example, if you have a white paper on your web site that discusses the SOHO market, they may not realize that your main goal is to sell printer toners or printer cartridges. They may not buy anything. So make sure your main goal is clearly defined on the web page.

- *Loyalty programs.* Another way to get targeted customers coming back for more is by using online incentive marketing, such as setting up loyalty programs on your site. In a recent study by market research firm NFO Interactive, about 53 percent of online consumers surveyed said they'd go back to shop at a specific web site if it offered incentives. There are numerous such programs out there. You could do something as simple as offering customers the ability to earn gifts—like T-shirts emblazoned with your logo—if they buy enough merchandise on your site. Or you could go with the most popular option, known as a frequent-buyer or points program. This choice gives customers the opportunity to receive discounts or points toward the purchase of merchandise by buying products on your site. The more your customers spend—which can also mean the more times they come back to your site—the bigger the discounts or the more points they receive.

- *Lists of favorite links.* Surfers come to you for information in your field of expertise, so think about whether there are related sites you can point them to for more information. Sure, showing a surfer the way out of your site might seem a misguided tool for upping stickiness, but ask sites to give you a reciprocal link, and you'll get traffic from them. Besides, what's Yahoo!—the web's second stickiest site—but a collection of links? There are many much bigger search databases on the web than Yahoo! offers, but its visitors prize the editing that's gone into its listings.

Your visitors, too, will appreciate a concise, intelligent listing of "Sites for More Information," and they may bookmark your site just because they know you offer intelligent links. Note: Keep your links current, relevant to your business, and fresh—because how good they are will shape how good visitors think you are.

- *Easy navigation.* Every pro webmaster has a few "favorite" awful sites that offer great content but which nobody will ever see because it's too hard to find. Simplicity has to be a byword for any site builder, because the price of boring or confusing a visitor is that surfer's quick exit.

## Budget Watcher

Worried that your copy won't be up to snuff? You may be right. A sure way to make a site look amateurish is to post stuff that's riddled with misspellings, bad grammar and worse. The good news: The leading word processing applications (Microsoft Word and Corel WordPerfect) will meticulously check your copy. Use these tools! Doing so takes a few minutes, but the improvements in writing are well worth the time.

# 22

# Secrets of
# Search Engines

It's simple: If your site isn't listed in the major search engines, web surfers won't find it. Research shows that almost 90 percent of web users find sites through search engines.

What's more, online search is a rapidly growing and profitable segment of the internet and is expected to be a $47 billion industry worldwide by 2007, according to a recent survey from U.S. Bancorp Piper Jaffray Inc., an investment products, services, and research firm.

While search engines are great marketing tools, getting your site listed where consumers are sure to see it isn't always easy. With more than three billion pages on the web, how do you win a high ranking in search engine results? "It's hard to boil it down to one simple thing," says Noel McMichael, president of San Francisco-based Marketleap, an internet marketing and consulting firm that specializes in search engine optimization.

The inside scoop is that many engines use algorithms—mathematical formulas—to rank sites. Not only do they all use different algorithms, but they don't reveal them, and worse still, "they change frequently," says McMichael.

Should you just shrug your shoulders and give up? You can't. Experts agree that search engines have to figure largely in any web site's marketing plan because they are where users hunt for the information they want. So hunker down and follow these steps.

> **Smart Tip**      *Tip...*
>
> Usually, the "Add URL" or "Add Site" button is at the bottom of the page, sometimes in tiny print. A few engines hide theirs. At Google, for instance, it's under "All About Google." Some engines do not even offer this option and instead rely on their own spiders (search tools that automatically move from site to site, following all available links) to add listings. Find out more about spiders in "Spider Webs" on page 136. Keep in mind, however, that following Help links will usually bring up submission details.

# Getting Listed

Just about every search engine provides tools for easy registration of new sites. Just look for an "Add URL" or "Add Site" button, and then follow the directions (ordinarily no more complex than typing in the address and hitting "Send").

There are hundreds of search engines to choose from. For-hire site registration services typically say they submit to more than 100 engines. But there's little value in being on an index no one uses, which is why e-tailers should focus on a handful of high-traffic engines. According to U.S. Bancorp Piper Jaffray Inc., the leading search destinations are Google (www.google.com), Yahoo! (www.yahoo.com), MSN (www.msn.com), and AOL (www.aol.com). Together they have more than 80 percent of the market share.

Want to know which engines have the heaviest traffic? Nielsen//NetRatings (www.nielsen-netratings.com), a firm that offers internet audience measurement and analysis, found that during the month of March 2003, the top engines accessed from home and work were Google, Yahoo! Search, MSN Search, AOL Search, and Ask Jeeves (www.askjeeves.com).

Do you use Dogpile (www.dogpile.com), which is owned and operated by Info Space Inc., or Mamma, the Mother of All Search Engines (www.mamma.com)? Don't try to list with them. These are "parallel engines" (also known as meta engines) that query various search engines with your question. They don't index sites; they aggregate information from other sites. Dogpile, for instance, queries Ask Jeeves, Google, and About.com (www.about.com)—a web directory—along with many other sites. These parallel engines are handy to use when searching, but put them out of mind when seeking to get listed.

## Engine Trouble

One hitch in the listing process: Don't expect immediate results. It can take a month or so for the major crawlers to index your pages. Engines list new sites in their own time frames, and because they've been hit with a multitude of new web pages, queues of "to be added" sites have grown long. Yahoo!, however, offers an expedited entry option. (For more on this option, see "Express Delivery" below.) What's more, paid inclusion programs can speed up the process, while paid placement programs will even guarantee that you are listed for a particular word. (For more about these types of programs, read on.)

## Rank and File

Getting listed is the easy part. Scoring high in the ranking is another story, but that's also where the money gets made. It does little good to be the 212th business plan writer in the rankings at Yahoo!. Who will wade through 21 screens to find you?

## Express Delivery

You want a listing in Yahoo! now? Pay $299, and you'll qualify for Yahoo! Express. The hitch is, payment does not guarantee entry into the index. What the money buys is priority handling: Yahoo! guarantees you'll hear a verdict within seven business days of filing. Get more information at https://ecom.yahoo.com/dir/express/intro.

Is this a good deal? If you get into the directory, yes, because you'll be weeks ahead of the game (in many cases, perfectly good sites simply get overlooked in the crush of applicants). But it's a risk—you may not get in and will have wasted the money. My advice: Pay the money to Yahoo!. It remains far and away the most trafficked search engine. It's hard to win heavy visitor counts if you're not in Yahoo!.

▲

Nobody is likely to read that many pages of information. You only look at perhaps 30 results from a given search, maybe 50 or 100 if the query is proving elusive. Patience runs only so deep, and a surfer's attention span isn't infinite.

Can you do some of this yourself? You bet. The best way to score high in search engines is to have good, solid content, especially with regard to the terms you want to use to deliver surfers to your site. "Focus on good quality that makes your users enjoy your site, and become informed about your products and services, and search engines will recognize it," says Marketleap's McMichael, who also says it's important to continually add new content to your site.

According to Danny Sullivan, editor of SearchEngineWatch.com, a leading web site about all things relating to search engines, good page titles are also extremely helpful, as are "meta tags," an HTML expression that defines a web site's content, to be read by search engines and crawlers. Sound tricky? It's not. When constructing

# Spider Webs

User submissions aren't the only—or even the main—way search engines compile their indexes. A popular tool used by the engines in scoping out the lay of the web are spiders—also called crawlers—which meander from site to site, following links, and reporting findings back to the search engine. Has your web site been spidered? Check your log file (see Chapter 31 for more on logs), and you'll easily see a spider's trail.

A recent look at the log for www.mcgarvey.net revealed that AltaVista, which was purchased by Overture, had paid a visit. I knew that because this showed up on the log: scooter.pa.alta-vista.net. "Scooter" is the nickname used by AltaVista's spider. (Cute names are the norm for spiders; Inktomi, for example, calls its spider "Slurp.") In this sweep, it took in about one-third of the pages at mcgarvey.net. That can be a sign that it needs to be reminded about the other pages. Whenever you see a spider has missed key pages, resubmit them to that engine. Maybe the engine already knows them, maybe it doesn't. Either way, resubmitting is good policy.

A sure tip-off that a spider has come is when the log file reveals a request for the "robots.txt" file—a file that tells a visiting spider what parts of a web site are off-limits. If you don't have one, that request is put in the "errors" bins. Do you need a robots.txt file? Probably not. If you have nothing that's meant to be strictly private stored on your web site—and you shouldn't, because if a file is on the web, it's in the public domain—there's no need to tell a spider "hands off."

any web page, just insert simple meta tags high on the page. For example, a computer discounter might insert the following tags: <META name="description" content="discount prices on name-brand computers"> and <META name="keywords" content="discount computers, computers for sale">.

Many search engines use keywords and relevance—how directly a site relates to particular keywords—to determine how high you show up in the ratings, and meta tags let search engines know what you're about. Sullivan warns that while meta tags can be valuable, they are not a magic bullet. "Meta tags are mainly helpful in giving your pages good descriptions," he says.

Another good tip from Sullivan: If you have links on your site from good sites about topics you wish to be found for, that can help you rank better.

# Directory Assistance

There's another way to get your site in front of users' eyes: directories at Yahoo!, LookSmart, and the Open Directory Project (ODP) (http://dmoz.org), which is run by AOL Time Warner-owned Netscape. They are not search engines but rather directories compiled by human editors. ODP, which launched in June 1998 under the name NewHoo, uses about 210,000 volunteer editors to catalog the web, many of whom are search engine marketers.

Should you submit your site to these types of directories? By all means. When you submit your site to these indexes, keep in mind that the tweaks the pros use to maximize search engine placement will not work with these human-edited directories. What's especially important about getting listed here? Good, relevant content and design are the secrets with the human-edited directories.

Getting into any directory is tough. But don't dwell too much on the complicated nuances involved in getting ever-higher rankings. Put that energy into building a spiffier, more user-friendly site, and odds are you'll get a payoff.

How do you get listed in a human-edited directory? You can go to the sites and—as with search engines—look for an "Add URL" tab. Then cross your fingers, and you just may show up in that directory. "Getting listed in these directories provides important links that may help you rank better with crawlers," says SearchEngineWatch's Sullivan.

## Smart Tip

*Tip...*

Want to know more about search engines and rankings in general? Head to SearchEngineWatch.com (www.searchenginewatch.com), where all the ins and outs are explored. Other sites worth a look include Understanding and Comparing Web Search Tools (http://Web.hamline.edu/administration/libraries/search/comparisons.html) and Search Engine Showdown (http://searchengineshowdown.com).

# Paid Placement

What are paid placement and paid inclusion programs?

Paid placement—or paid search or pay-per-click—programs guarantee your site will appear in the top results of search engines for the terms you are interested in within a day or less. Basically, every major search engine accepts paid listings, and they are usually marked as "Sponsored Links" on the web sites.

The leaders in paid search right now are Overture Services Inc. (www.overture.com), which was acquired by Yahoo! (the transaction is expected to close by the fourth quarter of 2003—Overture will operate as a wholly owned Yahoo! subsidiary), and Google Technology Inc. (www.google.com).

> ## ⚠ Beware!
> Don't put the names of big competitors in your meta tags. Some small companies have tried to boost traffic this way, but big companies get annoyed with this and are starting to sue. Even if they don't ultimately win in court, who has the time and resources to fight back against a Fortune 500 behemoth? Be scrupulously honest about content in your meta tags, and you'll do fine.

Overture allows sites to bid on the terms they wish to appear for you, and then you agree to pay a certain amount each time someone clicks on your listing.

For example, if you wanted to appear in the top listings for "clocks," you might agree to pay 25 cents per click. If no one agrees to pay more than this, then you would be in the No. 1 spot. If someone later decides to pay 26 cents, then you fall into the No. 2 position. You could then bid 27 cents and move back on top, if you wanted to.

While some people go directly to the Overture web site to search, most people see Overture's paid listings via other search engines, such as MSN, Yahoo!, and Lycos. For example, the very top listings for "clocks" at Overture would also appear in the "Sponsor Results" section at the top of Yahoo! Search results pages. With Overture, there is a one-time service fee of $199 to join the program, an account requires a $50 minimum deposit, and you must spend at least $20 per month. There is also a minimum bid requirement of 10 cents. SearchEngine Watch's Sullivan says that by carefully selecting targeted terms, you can stretch that money out for one or two months and get quality traffic. You can sign up for Overture's paid listings by visiting http://www.content.overture.com/d/USm/about/advertisers.

Google also sells paid listings that appear above and to the side of its regular results, and on its partner sites. Since it may take time for a new site to appear within Google, "these advertising opportunities offer a fast way to get listed with the service," says Sullivan.

Google's self-service "AdWords" program has a $5 activation fee. After that, you tell Google how much you are willing to pay per click and per day. You can choose a maximum cost-per-click from 5 cents to $50 and set a daily budget as low as 5 cents or as high as you want.

Paid inclusion, on the other hand, is slightly different. Paid inclusion programs mean that, in exchange for a payment, a search engine will guarantee to list pages from a web site. These programs typically do not guarantee that the pages will rank well for particular queries, however. Whether a page ranks well still depends on the search engine's underlying relevance algorithms.

**Tip...**

**Smart Tip**

Get the scoop on meta tags, content and links on the Search Engine Placement Tips page at Search Engine Watch: http://www.searchenginewatch watch.com/webmasters/ article.php/ 2168021.

Yahoo! recently unveiled a new paid inclusion program—Overture Site Match. Site Match ties together Inktomi's, FAST's, and AltaVista's paid inclusion programs into a single point of submission for Yahoo!'s index. Review of the first URL is $49. There is also a category-based cost-per-click of 15 cents. Some Site Match categories cost 30 cents.

What's one of the key benefits of paid inclusion? According to Sullivan, even the best crawler-based search engine is unlikely to get all your pages. So "if a page absolutely must get in and isn't picked up naturally, consider paid inclusion programs," he says.

# e-Chat with
## Drugstore.com's Peter Neupert

## Drugstore.com

**Peter Neupert, chair
Location: Bellevue, Washington
Year Started: 1998**

What would it take to lure a high-powered Microsoft millionaire to quit Gates & Co. and join a brand-new net start-up? Money clearly won't do it. Listen up as Peter Neupert—onetime vice president of online services at Microsoft—explains what prompted him to plunge into the role of chair of drugstore.com and what he believes it will take to succeed in the crowded online drugstore niche.

**Robert McGarvey:** *Why did you quit Microsoft to join a start-up?*

**Peter Neupert:** John Doerr [a legendary venture capitalist with Kleiner, Perkins] called and said, "I have a great opportunity." I told him, "I'm not interested." He kept calling, and it took about a month, but I became convinced and I took the position. The opportunity to run my own show in a big category of e-commerce was too good to pass up.

**McGarvey:** *How big will the drugstore category be?*

**Neupert:** This market is huge, around $250 billion in annual sales. But the web can really change how people shop by empowering them with information. This literally is a way to revolutionize how people purchase healthcare products.

> ### Smart Tip
>
> How do you persuade wary consumers to buy? For drugstore.com's Peter Neupert, the answer is information—and that's an area where the net can excel. Pick up a bottle of vitamins in a drugstore, for instance, and what do you know about it? Only what's printed—usually in microscopic type—on the bottle. On the web, an e-tailer can offer detailed information at very little cost, and this is the fast track to gaining a leg up on traditional retailers. Whenever you encounter customer resistance, try informing them into making a purchase. It just may be the key that opens sales.

**McGarvey:** *What's your major competition?*

**Neupert:** Customer inertia. While drugstore.com is the only pure-play survivor and now clearly the largest—even when including the click-and-mortar players—there are hundreds of thousands of places that buy what we sell—drugstores, grocers, Wal-Mart. People get into patterns. We want people to understand that shopping with us will save them both time and money. Our value proposition is this: Shop with us, and I will give you 20 minutes back a week because you no longer have to do this chore. It's much easier to click a mouse and get this merchandise delivered to your door.

**McGarvey:** *Hasn't the online drugstore space taken off more slowly than many expected?*

**Neupert:** The category is growing rapidly online, which is much faster growth than in the brick-and-mortar world, and faster than some mature online categories, such as books. However, we still have the challenge of communicating how the prescription process works online, which takes time.

**McGarvey:** *How will you beat competitors?*

**Neupert:** Our focus is on the customer experience. Our product assortment is better than competitors', and we've made it easier for customers to buy. We provide deep, detailed product information. We believe those will be the most important factors to users. We have also added a number of specialty stores to improve the "shopability" of our large assortment [of products], such as household, sexual well-being, and natural stores. In addition, we have evolved to emphasize our value, offering customers drugstore.com dollars, diamond deals, free shipping over $49, etc. We also recognize that relevant information goes beyond product information and includes community content, such as customer ratings; current information, such as what is new and why; and safety information, like what we offer with our eMedAlert service.

> **Smart Tip** Tip...
>
> Closely scan your product sales reports—and don't be thrown for a loop if there are a few surprises in the mix. Audiences you never expected can find you on the web. However, when you see unanticipated sales trends, react fast—that's a key edge of the web over other kinds of retailing. Adjust product mix to meet customer needs, and redo pages to point to what customers are looking for.

**McGarvey:** *Where will your profits come from—prescription drugs or other merchandise?*

**Neupert:** Our revenue mix won't be dissimilar from traditional retail drugstores—about 50–50 prescription drugs and other merchandise. We see more profits coming from the nonprescription side. The profitability of prescriptions has been squeezed, but I do think there are profits to be made there as well.

**McGarvey:** *Have there been any surprises in your mix of products sold?*

**Neupert:** We have found that anonymity—the ability to buy without embarrassment—is an appealing aspect of shopping at our site. We sell a lot of K-Y Jelly [a lubricant], and initially I couldn't figure out why. We also sell a lot more condoms than we expected. Privacy products have been an important part of our product mix, which is why we opened the sexual well-being specialty store—so that customers could explore and shop in private from a reputable source.

**McGarvey:** *Critics say online drugstores will sell drugs to kids—is this a worry?*

**Neupert:** If I were a kid and I wanted Valium, I'd take a prescription pad from a doctor's office, then pay cash at a local pharmacy. To do it on the internet, you need a credit card and a shipping address. If you were breaking the law, why would you leave that trail? That said, we spend a lot of time, money, and effort to ensure that prescriptions are legitimate. In addition, our incidence of this kind of fraud is almost nonexistent.

**McGarvey:** *What will e-commerce look like in a few years?*

**Neupert:** E-commerce will look very different ten years from now than it does today—and it will be fun to be a part of that. I believe we are in the early phases of the growth of e-commerce. More and more, people are using the internet every day, and as it becomes a more integral part of everyday living, I believe we will continue to see dramatic evolution of the services available to consumers that will make their lives easier and better.

# Cheap Tricks with

## eHolster.com's Tom Traeger

### eHolster.com

**Tom Traeger, founder and CEO**
**Location: Norcross, Georgia**
**Year Started: 1999**

Who hasn't lost a PalmPilot or a cell phone? There's never anyplace to comfortably tuck them, and that is why they are so easy to leave behind in restaurants, airplane seats and such. But that also meant a big business opportunity for Tom Traeger, founder of eHolster.com (www.eholster.com), where the product is a shoulder holster for personal electronics gadgets. E-Holster cases are unique because they are modular by design and can be worn on a shoulder harness one day and then easily moved to your belt or across your chest another day. The costs range from less than $40 to $195, depending on the number of cases you purchase and the material of the cases.

The web is ideal for launching an innovative product because there aren't dozens of other sites all selling essentially the same product. On the other hand, it takes work, time, money and even luck to build public awareness that this new gizmo exists. As Traeger learned, it can be done, but it's not enough to simply come up with a clever product idea.

Here, Traeger tells how he designed the product, arranged for its manufacture, and built his web site—all on a thin budget.

**Robert McGarvey:** *What were your start-up costs?*

**Tom Traeger:** Total costs to date have been less than $25,000 to develop the e-Holster product, create the electronic storefront, and complete the trademark searches and the LLC, etc.

**McGarvey:** *How long did it take you to build the site?*

**Traeger:** First, I had to fully design the product, which has taken me nine months. Then it was on to the web site, which has taken a solid six months.

**McGarvey:** *Other than the conventional steps, are you doing anything new to bring in site visitors?*

**Traeger:** Every e-Holster has a "branding label" on the back with the URL eHolster.com, so every customer is a walking billboard. I [also] sent a sample to the costume designer for HBO's *The Sopranos*, suggesting that an actor wear an e-Holster to symbolize the transition from wearing a shoulder holster for old-fashioned weapons to wearing an e-Holster for cell phones/PDAs, [today's] weapons. I am always trying to get e-Holster in the movies or on TV. The sample that we sent to HBO's costume designer was never worn by the actors in the show. We wish it was, but it didn't work out.

# Accepting
# Credit Cards

The number one question on the minds of most new web site builders is "How do I arrange to accept credit cards for payment?" Once upon a time (which means last year in internet time), getting merchant account status for an online storefront was tough because credit card companies were suspicious about vendors who lacked brick-and-mortar storefronts. No more.

Even bankers have awakened to the reality that the net is creating a revolution in how commercial transactions are completed, and credit card issuers nowadays truly "get it"—they understand that the net is a legitimate retail channel, and they are rushing to set up merchant accounts with online stores.

But that doesn't mean it's suddenly easy. Issuers still want proof that yours is a real business and not a fly-by-night con game. Patiently answer all their questions and show the requested documents, and you're likely to get the status you crave.

## Taking Credit

A good place to start your search for merchant status is your own bank. Most issue credit cards, and if you have a long-term relationship with the institution, that's a big plus. What if your bank says no? Try a few other local banks—offer to move all your accounts there—and you just may be rewarded with merchant status.

You may also try other companies that specialize in issuing accounts to online merchants, including:

- *Cardservice International:* www.cardservice.com
- *VeriSign:* www.verisign.com
- *Credit Card Processing Services:* www.mcvisa.com
- *The Processing Network:* www.processing.net
- *21st Century Resources:* www. merchant-account-4u.com

Or log onto Yahoo! and search for credit card processing. You'll find dozens of outfits, large and small, that are on the prowl for start-ups seeking merchant accounts.

Credit cards aren't processed cheaply, however, at least not for a start-up. A typical fee schedule for a small-volume account (fewer than 1,000 transactions monthly) would include start-up fees amounting to around $200 and monthly processing fees of around $20.

Is that money you need to spend? Absolutely. It's simply impossible to run a real electronic storefront without credit card processing capabilities. In very special cases, yes, you can go online and ask customers to mail checks, but when your aim is to build a volume storefront, you've got to take credit cards. Customers expect it, and it will make transactions easier for everyone involved.

## Secure Horizons

The one must-have for online credit card processing: secure, encrypted connections. You've seen this many times yourself. Go to virtually any major e-tailer, commence a purchase, and you are put into a "secure server" environment, where transaction data is scrambled to provide a measure of safety against hackers. Truth is, worries about credit card theft from nonsecure sites are generally unfounded—the odds of a hacker grabbing an unencrypted credit card number from a nonsecure web site are pretty slender—but buyers by now feel reassured when they see they're entering a secure site, and that means you need to provide it.

Is this a technical hassle for you? It shouldn't be. Whatever vendor sells you your credit card processing services should also, as part of the package, provide a secure transaction environment. If they don't, look elsewhere.

It may sound daunting to arrange for online credit card processing, a secure server, etc., but nowadays, you can have all of this in place in a matter of minutes. Sign up for a Yahoo! Store, for instance, and it's simple to tack on an application for credit card processing through Paymentech (which charges no setup fees, a $22.95 monthly service fee, 20 cents per transaction, and 2.52 percent for Visa and MasterCard).

## Beware!

Plenty of shady outfits are bent on getting rich offering bogus merchant accounts to gullible online beginners. Before shelling out any cash, make sure you're setting up an account that will handle industry-standard cards (such as MasterCard and Visa, not "Big Bob's Lollapalooza Credit Card" or some specialty card). A stop at the Better Business Bureau—www.bbbonline. com—would be good policy before inking any costly deal with an unknown vendor.

The Yahoo! Store program also doesn't charge extra fees for online processing; those fees are included in the regular monthly fees. That's a pretty good deal—especially since it only takes one to three business days to process your application, and if your application is accepted, that's all you have to do. Your new merchant

## You'd Better Shop Around

**M**y hunt for online credit card processing services revealed wide variations in fees and pricing menus. Start-up fees ranged from free to more than $500, with monthly fees ranging from free to more than $100. Volume is a key factor—sites anticipating fewer than 1,000 transactions monthly can often arrange low-cost credit card deals—but a lot of this seems to be Wild West pricing.

Should you go with the lowest price? Not necessarily. My advice is to go with companies you trust. If there's a premium involved, pay it if you can. Always do business with your local bank, if it will accept you as a customer, even if the rate schedules are higher than those charged by online credit card processing specialists. There have been many, many crooked operators, and caution in this realm can pay off big time.

account will be automatically hooked up to your Yahoo! Store, and you'll be ready to process orders online.

Once approved, you're set to take Visa, MasterCard, American Express, and Diner's Club—nothing more has to happen. You may hear how hard and time-consuming setting up an online merchant account is, but that was yesteryear. Now it's one of the easiest parts of setting up your dotcom.

# e-Chat with
# Buy.com's Scott Blum

## Buy.com Inc.

**Scott Blum, founder and CEO
Location: Aliso Viejo, California
Year Started: 1997**

Scott Blum, founder and CEO of Buy.com Inc. founded what was originally called Buycomp.com in 1997. The company currently offers more than 5 million customers 1.5 million-plus products in a range of categories, including computer hardware and software, electronics, cellular products and services, music, DVDs, books, and more. Buy.com, however, is not the first company Blum has started, nor will it be his last.

Blum is a serial entrepreneur and technology visionary who has founded several successful technology companies. At the age of 19, Blum, a college dropout, started MicroBanks, a company that manufactured technology enhancement products for IBM PS/2 and Macintosh personal computers.

By age 21, Blum sold MicroBanks, which provided him with the capital to start Pinnacle Micro, a leader and pioneer in the optical and recordable CD industries. He sold his stock in Pinnacle Micro in October 1995. Blum launched Buycomp. com in 1997. In fall 1998, Softbank invested $60 million in Buycomp.com. In November 1998, the company name changed to Buy.com. Then, in September 1999, Buy.com received a landmark $165 million investment from Softbank. In October 1999, Buy.com filed for an IPO, and in February 2000, its stock soared to $37.50. That same month, Blum left the company. In November 2001, however, he bought the company back, took it private, and began rebuilding it and repositioning it into a multichannel retailer.

> ### Smart Tip
>
> **Tip...**
>
> Got an idea for a web business? It's never too early to start living your dream. Scott Blum founded his first company at age 19 and sold it for $2.5 million when he was 21—the same age he was when he started his next company. What are the secrets to his success? Blum says he always tries to do something that no one else is doing—in essence, to be the first one on the block with a new concept. If an idea is already taken, he still runs with it but just makes sure to do it better than anyone else. Do you have an idea for a completely new type of company, or do you think you could improve on a company that is currently out there? If so, take the plunge and realize your dream—you just may be as successful as Blum.

In 2002, Buy.com launched *BuyMagazine*, a monthly direct-response magazine providing access to "cool products, the latest reviews, special offers, and discounts." In 2003, it changed its format and now the magazine is all digital.

What's next on the agenda? Buy.com is currently planning a foray into television. It will soon produce television programming that will combine talk show-like interviews with artists, authors, and movie stars, and it will also feature product mentions and sales pitches. The programming will run on cable networks.

Buy.com is now also part of a holding company—also created by Blum—called DRN, which stands for Direct Response Network. The five companies comprising DRN are Buy.com, BuyMagazine, BuyTV, United Commerce Service (UCS), and Thinkbig Media.

Here, Blum gives us a peek into his past and his future.

**Melissa Campanelli:** *What was your goal when starting Buycomp.com?*

**Scott Blum:** Our goal was to be the leader in intelligent technology, or more specifically, computer equipment, over the internet. We came up with the name Buy comp.com by taking two names from well-known computer equipment companies— Best Buy, and CompUSA. When we were starting out, however, these companies did not have a web presence. I got the idea for the company in early 1995, and at that time, the only real web company out there was Amazon.com.

**Campanelli:** *What challenges did you face when you were starting up Buycomp.com?*

**Blum:** It took about 17 months to actually launch the company, and the main reason for that was because there was no e-commerce software available to build the kind of company and web site that we wanted. So we spent a ton of time just writing code and eventually launched the company in November 1997.

**Campanelli:** *After the company went public, you bought it back, and now it's privately held. Why did you buy it back?*

**Blum:** I didn't buy it back to get back into the internet. In my opinion, I had already achieved what I wanted to achieve there and was really ahead of the curve. I bought it back because someone had invested a lot of money into the company and its infrastructure, and I wanted to take that infrastructure and go to the next wave.

**Campanelli:** *What is the next wave?*

**Blum:** I believe the next wave is direct response. We have positioned the company—through our web presence, our magazine, and the TV show that we are producing called *BuyTV*—to be the leader in the direct-response industry. We are really focused on direct response vs. just the internet.

The name of the game in our business is eyeballs, and we will be able to get those eyeballs by having the magazine on newsstands, having the TV show on cable, and having the web site.

We will also be able to cross-market our properties. The magazine, for example, will promote the TV show, and the web site will promote both the show and the magazine. This strategy will also offer our vendors cross-marketing opportunities. Sony, for example, would be able to market its products across all three channels.

**Campanelli:** *Will Buy.com still be your flagship brand?*

**Blum:** Right now, Buy.com is the anchor brand, and most of our sales come from the internet site, but long term, I think most of our sales will not come from this channel.

**Campanelli:** *Who do you perceive as your biggest competitor today?*

**Blum:** I think our main competitor today would be Amazon.com. They pretty much dominate the sector in terms of online retailers. But, again, we are trying not to follow in their footsteps but actually go in a different direction.

# Cheap Tricks with Bowling Connection.com's Gary Forrester

## BowlingConnection.com

**Gary Forrester, owner**
**Location: Tucson, Arizona**
**Year Started: 1999**

Turned on by pink retro bowling shirts? How about bowling jackets and T-shirts? If bowling is your passion, you want to know about BowlingConnection, where pretty much everything a bowler craves is on sale.

Site owner Gary Forrester pegs his start-up costs at "just about zero," but he's managed to mount a handsome, fast-moving site with plenty of functionality, including secure online ordering. How? He built the site using an e-business solution that is no longer available.

Forrester found creating the site so simple that after BowlingConnection, he soon launched two more sites, www.southwest-gifts. com and www.usatiles.com. However, a lot has changed since those early days. Forrester's business is now called Creative Productions, and the domain name is www.CPstore.com. The company combined www.BowlingConnection.com and another one of its sites—www.RockinRetro. com—and renamed itself Creative Productions in August 2001. In March 2002, Forrester also combined www.southwest-gifts.com and www.usa tiles.com into one site, www.TeissedreDesigns. com. That same month, the company put all its web sites on a new server at www.Bekker-Studios.com, which can handle unlimited products.

Forrester made these changes for a number of reasons: The server that was hosting his web sites could only handle 100 products for each web site, which was too few. Some of the prod-

## Smart Tip

J. Peterman built a hugely successful business starting from one item—a duster-type raincoat that he happened to discover in the West. It was a cool coat, different, and he began running little ads selling it. Orders came in, and he expanded. Yes, he eventually filed for bankruptcy, but that doesn't mean there wasn't a good business in that duster, or in Forrester's retro bowling shirts. Think about it: It cost Peterman big bucks to buy even little ads in places like *The New York Times*. A web site's cost is mere pennies by comparison. What cool products can you build a site around? Think unusual, easy to ship, and good profit margins. For every product you can think of, there's a thriving web business that's waiting to happen.

ucts the company was offering crossed over on different web sites, and he also wanted a company name that was more generic.

In addition, Forrester says it's much easier and less time-consuming and costly to manage one web site than to manage several. The servers that its web sites were on (US West's Sitematic) were starting to run very slowly, orders weren't coming through, and customers were complaining every day. It got to the point where the company's web sites were down more than up. Forrester says the company was losing money, and it was getting worse every day. At one time, all the sites were down for four days straight, and that's when he decided to make a change.

**Robert McGarvey:** *What were your start-up costs?*

**Gary Forrester:** My start-up costs were almost zero. I already owned the computer, and U.S. West Sitematic made it so easy to build the web site, I didn't have to employ any outside sources at all. One of my web sites costs $49.95 per month, and the other two sites are $79.95 per month because the catalogs are bigger. I look at that cost as my "rent" payment. Where can you have a store that is open to the world 24 hours a day, and you don't even have to pay employees to take care of your customers? You actually make money while you sleep.

**McGarvey:** *How long did it take you to build the initial site?*

**Forrester:** The initial site only took a few minutes to get up. I knew nothing (and I stress *nothing*) about building a web site. Sitematic has many templates to choose from. You fill in your company information and then choose how your site will be presented to the world. You just keep clicking on the templates to view your site in many different formats and then select the one you like best. I am constantly making changes to make the sites better, and I'm always adding new products to my catalogs.

**McGarvey:** *What is your monthly revenue?*

**Forrester:** More than I ever imagined. We put an addition on the house to run the business, [bought] a pickup truck, [took] a vacation to Jamaica, [and bought] a John Lennon Collector Series guitar—the one I had only dreamed of owning. Among other things, all were paid for in cash. In addition, our gross sales increased by 90 percent after we changed to the new servers. We could offer many more products and more services.

**McGarvey:** *What has been the biggest surprise?*

**Forrester:** The [1999] Christmas season was our biggest surprise. I expected business to pick up a little more than usual. I didn't expect it to get crazy. We worked day, night and weekends to fill the orders. It was a challenge, but we did it—all our customers received their orders by Christmas.

Christmas time is still crazy. But now our best month is October. With the unlimited space on the new servers, we started selling a lot of costumes and related items. In October 2002, because of Halloween, our gross sales were 94 percent more than in December 2002. [During] our biggest day in October, we shipped out 81 orders. Other days in October we were shipping out 30 to 60 orders per day. My wife/business partner had to leave her job as a medical transcriptionist in June 2002 to dedicate her time strictly to our business.

**McGarvey:** *How do you promote the site?*

**Forrester:** There is a helpful site called www.selfpromotion.com that makes it easy to list your site with all the search engines. When we started, we promoted our BowlingConnection web site by passing out fliers at bowling tournaments. We promoted our other two web sites by opening a temporary gift store in Las Vegas. We passed out a lot of fliers and business cards to tourists from all over the world.

Another way we promoted on an ongoing basis was by putting items up for auction on eBay. It was not only another source of income; it drove people right to our web site to order more of our products. And it only cost 25 cents to list each item.

This has probably been the most cost-effective advertising I have ever seen. We no longer pass out fliers and business cards, and we don't promote our web site on eBay anymore. In fact, eBay no longer allows you to promote your own web site. Because of that, very seldom do we put anything up for auction on eBay. Now, the only form of paid advertising that we use is the pay-per-click search engines—Overture.com and Google.com. Of course, we do get repeat business, and word-of-mouth is still the cheapest form of advertising. We have sold to Bon Jovi, Campbell Soup, Merrill Lynch, PricewaterhouseCoopers, Disneyland, and many more.

**McGarvey:** *How do you handle online purchasing?*

**Forrester:** Our web site is still very secure, and customers can feel confident when they order from us. We do not sell, trade or give away any information about any of our customers whatsoever. Due to changes in our product line and because our customers have "must have" dates, 25 percent of the orders are made by phone. If they need their order by a certain date because of a company event, they feel more confident talking to a real person instead of just sending the order through the web site. We don't mind at all when our customers call on the phone. Imagine sitting in your home office talking on the telephone to Bon Jovi's marketing manager.

# 28

# Tapping
# International
# Markets

One of the lures of the web is that once your site is up, you are open for business around the world 24 hours a day. But don't be too quick to take the hype at face value. Yep, you are open 24/7, but international sales may prove elusive, and even when you land orders from abroad, you may wonder if they're worth the bother. Shocked?

There are excellent reasons for many e-tailers to aggressively pursue global business, but before you let yourself get dazzled by the upside, chew on the negatives. Then, once you have seen that foreign customers represent their own hassles, but you still want them, you will find the information you need to grab plenty of international sales.

## Foreign Affairs

Here's the root of the problem with selling internationally: Whenever you ship abroad, you enter into a complicated maze of the other country's laws. Let's assume you're in the United States. You know Uncle Sam's laws, and you know that one neat thing about doing business in the United States is that barriers against inter-state commerce are few. For a Nevada e-tailer to ship to California is no more complicated than putting the gizmo in a box and dropping it off at the post office. With some exceptions, few e-tailers collect sales tax on interstate sales.

Sell abroad, however, and it's a quick step into a maze of complexities, including customs, for instance. Generally, it's up to the buyer (not you) to pay any customs owed, but make sure your buyers know that additional charges—imposed by their home countries and payable directly to them—may be owed. You can pick up the forms you'll need at any U.S. post office.

> **⚠ Beware!**
> It's tempting: Declare that an item is an unsolicited gift, and the recipient often doesn't have to pay any customs charges. The amount that can be exempted varies from country to country; usually it's $50 to $100. But don't make that declaration even if a buyer asks (and savvy ones frequently will)—they are asking you to break the law.

Some countries also charge a national sales tax, or a value-added tax (around 20 percent on many items in many European countries). Again, as a small foreign retailer, you can pretty safely not worry about collecting these monies, but your buyers may (and probably will) be asked to pay, and they need to understand this is not a charge on your end.

Mailing costs, too, escalate for foreign shipments. Airmail is the best way to go for just about any package, and that gets pricey. A 1-pound parcel post shipment to Europe costs more than $10, for instance. Insurance, too, is a must for most shipments abroad, mainly because the more miles a package travels, the more chance of damage or loss. Costs are low (insuring a $100 item costs about $2.50 via the U.S. Postal Service), but they still add to the charges you've got to pass on to the customer. Add up the many fees—customs, value-added taxes, postage, insurance—and what might initially seem a bargain price to a buyer can easily be nudged into the stratosphere.

Getting authorization on foreign credit cards can also be time-consuming. Although many major U.S. cards are well-entrenched abroad (especially American Express and Diner's Club), and validating them for a foreign cardholder is frequently not difficult, as a rule, this process is fraught with risks for the merchant, so be careful.

# All Aboard

If you're still not discouraged, do one more reality check to make sure international sales make sense for you. Is what you are selling readily available outside your country? Will what you sell ship reasonably easily and at a favorable price? Even with the costs of shipping factored in, will buying from you rather than from domestic sellers be a benefit to your customers? If you pass these tests, you are ready to get down to business.

Step one in getting more global business is to make your site as friendly as possible to foreign customers. Does this mean you need to offer the site in multiple languages? For very large companies, yes (American Express, for instance, offers its site, www.americanexpress.com, in six languages). But the costs of doing a good translation are steep and, worse, whenever you modify pages—which ought to be regularly—you'll need to get the new material translated, too.

Small sites can usually get away with using English only and still be able to prosper abroad. Consider this: Search for homes for sale on Greek islands, and you'll find as many sites in English as in Greek. Why English? Because it's emerged as an international language. A merchant in Athens will probably know English because it lets him talk with French, German, Dutch, Turkish, and Italian customers. An English-only web site will find fluent readers in many nations. (But keep the English on your site as simple and as traditional as possible. The latest slang may not have made its way to English-speakers in Istanbul or Tokyo.)

To make your site more friendly to foreign customers, put up a page—clearly marked—filled with tips especially for them. If you have the budget, get this one page translated into various key languages. (A local college student might do a one-page translation for around $20.) Use this space to explain the complexities involved in buying abroad. Cover many of the hassles we just discussed, but rephrase the material so that it looks at matters through the buyer's eyes. By all means, include the benefits, too, but don't leave anything out, because the more clear a customer's thinking before pressing the "Buy" button, the more likely he is to complete the transaction.

In the meantime, routinely scan your log files in a hunt for any patterns of international activity. If you notice that, say, Norway is producing a stream of visitors and no orders, that may prompt you to search for ways to coax Norwegians into buying. Try including a daily special

## Smart Tip

*Tip...*

When is a foreign customer not a foreign customer? When he or she wants you to ship to a U.S. address (perhaps an Edinburgh father sending a birthday gift to his daughter at a Boston college), or when the customer is an American in the military or diplomatic corps (shipping to their addresses is no different from mailing to a domestic address). Don't judge an e-mail address by its domain. The address may end in "it" (Italy) or "de" (Germany), but it can still be a U.S. order.

## Budget Watcher

Want a no-cost translation of your site? Offer a link to AltaVista's Babel Fish, an automatic, free online translation service (http://babelfish.altavista.com). Before putting this up, however, ask friends—or pay an expert—to take a look at the translation. Babel Fish's translations are often very good, but you don't want your site's translation to be the embarrassing exception.

"for Norwegian mailing addresses only" or perhaps running a poll directed at Norwegians.

Clues about foreign visitors will also help you select places to advertise your site. While an ad campaign on Yahoo! may be beyond your budget, it's entirely realistic to explore, say, ads on Yahoo! Sweden. If you notice an increase in visitors (or buyers!) from a specific country, explore the cost of mounting a marketing campaign that explicitly targets them.

At the end of the day, whether you reap substantial foreign orders or not is up to you. If you want them, they can be grabbed, because the promise of the web is true in the sense that it wipes out time zones, borders and other barriers to commerce. That doesn't mean these transactions are easy—they can be challenging, as you've seen—but for the e-tailer determined to sell globally, there is no better tool than the web.

# e-Chat with
# Proflowers Inc.'s
# Jared Polis

## Proflowers Inc.

**Jared Polis, founder**
**Location: San Diego**
**Year Started: 1997**

When Jared Polis launched Proflowers Inc. (www.pro flowers.com) in 1997, his vision for the venture was to provide customers with a fast, easy, reliable way to send the freshest-quality cut flowers and plants—shipped directly from growers—at a competitive price to and from anywhere in the world. (In 2003, Proflowers changed its corporate name to Provide Commerce Inc., reflecting its broader mission to be the leading e-commerce marketplace for the delivery of perishable products direct from supplier to customer. It still operates its floral web site at www.proflowers.com. In addition, in November 2004, Provide Commerce announced the launch of two new web sites—Uptown Prime at www.uptownprime. com and Cherry Moon Farms at www.cherrymoonfarms.com—each offering high-quality products shipped direct from the supplier to the consumer at competitive prices.)

Polis knows a little something about growing a business: Since its launch, Proflowers has become the largest domestic direct-from-the-grower internet flower company. Proflowers also announced that it had a 25 percent increase in net revenue during 2003's Valentine's Day season (February 1 to 14), growing from $16 million in 2002 to $20 million in 2003. During the week of February 11 to 14, 2003, Proflowers shipped approximately 2.6 million rose stems and 1.4 million tulips.

The company also saw a 4 percent rise in revenue generated per order, from $55.53 in 2002 to $59.01 in 2003, as well as a 13 percent increase in orders from new customers during the 2003 Valentine's Day period, compared to the same period in 2002. The company announced that second-quarter revenues rose 19 percent to $16.4 million for the period ending December 31, 2002, compared with the same period last year.

Here, we offer a look back at Proflowers' early days—and a peek into its future.

**Melissa Campanelli:** *Why did you decide to focus on flowers on the internet?*

**Jared Polis:** I had been involved in several internet businesses before [Polis founded, funded, and/or ran several high-tech start-ups, including BlueMountain.com, American Information Systems Inc., Onesage.com, Dan's Chocolates, Lucidity Inc., and FrogMagic Inc.], and what excites me the most is introducing new efficiencies into the economy, and the way that flowers were sent to people was obsolete. Most retail floral companies buy their flowers through wholesalers and distributors, so the companies not only incur overhead along the way, but by the time they were delivered, they were very old flowers, usually between five and ten days old. So I saw the opportunity to use new technology to disintermediate the supply chain to get better flowers at better prices. Proflowers ships direct from growers to the end consumer, and they've usually been picked a day or two before they arrive, so they last a lot longer than flowers that were picked a week or two before.

> ## Smart Tip
>
> Tip...
>
> If you can't get venture capital funding, don't despair. As Jared Polis explains, Proflowers was funded with only a small amount of money from investors. In fact, Polis tried to avoid accepting venture capital. Most of the money that funded the company came from bootstrapping and from cash Polis made by selling another company. If you have a good business model and your own cash, you can go far without VC funding, as the success of Proflowers shows.

Proflowers has also developed a technology that allows us to electronically interact with the customer, shipper, and grower within minutes after a customer places an order. Without any human intervention, the system automatically transmits a shipping label, packing slip, and customer-generated gift message to the grower. Through our automated link to FedEx's shipping and billing data, e-mail notifications are sent to customers when orders are confirmed, shipped, and delivered. The system is entirely automated, expediting the order and delivery process and allowing us to deliver superior customer service in a cost-effective manner.

**Campanelli:** *Do you ever have problems with your growers where they're not able to provide what your customers want?*

**Polis:** Actually, that's another competitive advantage of our business model. We can guarantee what each bouquet consists of. The legacy model used by companies such as FTD.com and 1-800-Flowers relies on whatever a local florist has in inventory. For example, they can say that they have a spring bouquet, but they cannot say that it has three mums, two tulips and one red rose in it, for example, because it depends on what the local florist has. We can tell our customers exactly what each bouquet consists of because we get the flowers from the source, and we design the bouquets ourselves so we know what goes in them.

**Campanelli:** *How did you fund the company?*

**Polis:** In a variety of ways. We bootstrapped it for a while, and then I sold one of my companies—American Information Systems—and I put some of that money back into Proflowers. We also raised the minimum amount of money that we thought we could to build the company. We didn't raise significant outside capital. Among our many investors, there were some venture capital firms that offered small amounts, but I'm not a big fan of venture capital, so we tried to avoid venture capital wherever possible. We haven't raised any capital since 1999, and we don't have any plans to get more funding to expand. We generate cash flow from our business to expand.

**Campanelli:** *Tell me about your marketing techniques.*

**Polis:** Flowers are a very marketing-intense category, so we do a variety of marketing. The key metric we look at is cost of customer acquisition. So we look at the cost of acquiring a customer across different channels like radio, TV, print, online, etc. With any [advertising or marketing] deal where we can acquire customers at the right price, we will take it.

**Campanelli:** *How do you ensure good customer service, which is essential with gift items like flowers?*

**Polis:** Maintaining the quality of product is a key part of our long-term success. Every week, we survey by telephone hundreds of recipients so we can quickly identify which bouquets—and which growers—are delivering the best value to our customers.

# Cheap Tricks with
# Fridgedoor Inc.'s Chris Gwynn

## Fridgedoor Inc.

**Chris Gwynn, president and founder**
**Location: Quincy, Massachusetts**
**Year Started: 1997**

Fridgedoor Inc. (www.fridgedoor.com) has one primary goal: to be the single largest stop for all things magnetic—novelty magnets, custom magnets, and magnetic supplies.

The company, founded in May 1997 and located outside Boston, is a retailer of novelty magnets for consumers, custom magnets for businesses, and magnetic supplies for consumers and businesses. The items are purchased at wholesale from more than 100 suppliers around the world. The company stocks close to 2,000 items for immediate shipment. Visit www. fridgedoor.com and you're greeted by lists of dozens and dozens of magnets—everything from Elvis Presley magnets to U.S. Postal Service state stamp magnets. Products include humorous magnets sets, such as the popular Cat Butts set, custom-imprinted business-card-size magnets, attractive magnetic bulletin boards, and sheets of magnet material.

> **Budget Watcher**
>
> Do you make something unique or special? Put up a web site, submit the URL to all the main search engines, and see if traffic comes in. Chris Gwynn suggests building traffic on the cheap. His is not the kind of site that's likely to become a gazillion-dollar business, but it's a site that can easily generate a nice, steady cash flow, month in and month out.

Fridgedoor was founded and is operated by Chris Gwynn, whose online experience dates from early 1994 and encompasses marketing and e-commerce positions with Ziff-Davis' ZDNet, the AT&T Business Network, and Industry.net (an internet-based marketplace for industrial supplies that's now a part of Techsavvy.com) and as a business-to-business internet commerce analyst for the Yankee Group. Gwynn started Fridgedoor as a part-time endeavor in May 1997 while employed as the product marketing manager for Industry.net. Revenue had reached a point by the end of 1999 that Gwynn felt comfortable enough about the company's future to quit his day job.

**Melissa Campanelli:** *What were your start-up costs?*

**Chris Gwynn:** The start-up costs came to approximately $20,000. The most significant expenses were inventory and a software program to handle all back-end order processing, credit card payments, and inventory management functions. Smaller expenses, such as hosting fees, domain name registration, telephones, etc., collectively get expensive.

**Campanelli:** *Is this do-it-yourself, or did you hire a programmer?*

**Gwynn:** I created the site myself using a template-based store builder and hosting solution designed for nontechnical users like myself. I wanted to avoid a situation where I was beholden to a programmer to make changes and maintain the site. Creating a basic site took less than a day. The time-consuming part is determining the products you want to offer, and creating product images and descriptive copy. Creating the site is the easy part.

**Campanelli:** *What are your monthly revenues?*

**Gwynn:** Our monthly revenues are in the low six figures.

**Campanelli:** *What are your monthly visitor counts?*

**Gwynn:** Fridgedoor [has] approximately 125,000 unique visitors per month.

**Campanelli:** *Where did you get the idea for the site?*

**Gwynn:** I had always wanted to start my own businesses and thought the web was a unique opportunity for someone with a limited budget. I also felt I had an understanding of how people buy online that I developed by working in marketing for an online service and later at web-based companies. I looked for a "low touch" product that was easily displayed online, easy to ship and relatively hard to find. I hit on magnets, which I personally like, and decided to give it a try. Luckily, it worked.

**Campanelli:** *How do you attract visitors?*

**Gwynn:** We rely heavily on search engines, word-of-mouth, and press [coverage]. Since we've been around for a while, we're extensively indexed by the search engines. Our market is very fragmented, making it difficult to profitably attract customers through traditional print advertising. Creating positive word-of-mouth by handling customers properly is our best advertisement.

# Knowing Your
## Customers

now thy customer. If there's a first com-
mandment of business, that's it. Run a brick-and-mortar store, and
knowing customers is easy. Talk to them, size up their clothing, hear
how they form sentences, and in a matter of seconds, a traditional
storefront owner knows a lot about who's stopping in. But the
question for companies doing business on the web is "How do we
know customers when all they amount to is a wispy cybervisitor?"

This is a key issue because knowing your visitors can help you more precisely target your web site. Suddenly notice a flood of visitors from, say, Japan, and that could lead to a decision to edit certain sections of a web site to make them more friendly for those users. See that you're a hit on a particular college campus or in a government agency, and you can post a special deal just for those people. Observe that you're getting a lot of traffic from Puerto Rico, and that's a clear signal to market there. Not making an effort to get to know your customers makes as much sense as golfing in the dark.

# Log Rolling

The good news: Every web site visitor leaves a trail that, when properly analyzed, will tell you the country of origin, the browser and platform used (Windows XP, Mac, Unix, etc.), the internet service provider, and more. This data is ordinarily collected by web hosting services in a "log file," but only hard-core techies could ever have the patience to scroll through a log because it contains a mind-numbing avalanche of details.

Want a peek at a log file? Here's a sample of the sort of information available:

we-24-130-40-120.we.mediaone.net-[08/Feb/2000:16:08:47-0700] "GET/HTTP/
1.1" 200 5867 "-" "Mozilla/4.0 (compatible; MSIE 4.01; Windows 98; Compaq)"we-24-

---

## I See You

**M**ost stats folders include a file that details the search phrases used by visitors in finding your site. Check it out regularly. In analyzing McGarvey.net traffic, I found the most common search phrase was "cosmopolitan cocktail" (there's a recipe on the site). Other cosmo-related stuff also rated high, as seen in the number of visitors who come in via AltaVista:

- ○ 40 cosmopolitan cocktail
- ○ 14 cosmopolitan martini
- ○ 14 Robert McGarvey
- ○ 14 cosmopolitan drink

So the cosmopolitan information was moved to the front of the site and a second cosmopolitan recipe was added, resulting in big traffic increases. Know what visitors want to find, and give them more of it.

130-40-120.we.mediaone.net [08/Feb/ 2000: 16:08:47-0700] "GET/indtextb.jpg HTTP/1.1" 200 959 "http://www.mcgar vey.net/" "Mozilla/4.0 (compatible; MSIE 4.01; Windows 98; Compaq)"we-24-130-40-120.we.mediaone.net-[08Feb/2000: 16: 08:48-0700] "GET /banner. gif HTTP/ 1.1" 200 27782 "http://www.mcgarvey.net/" "Mozilla/4.0 (compatible; MSIE 4.01; Windows 98; Compaq)"

Weird stuff? You bet—and that's only about 5 percent of the report on a single visitor who, on February 8, 2000, dropped in for a look at just a couple of web pages. Some interesting tidbits are that the user was running a Compaq computer with Windows 98 and he has high-speed cable access ("Media One"). But mainly this log is cluttered with details you don't need, or want, to know. There are smarter ways to measure traffic.

# Analyze This

If you're curious about your logs, go to your web hosting service and look for a directory called "Logs." Download the most recent file and have a look (any text editor should open the file). Your web hosting service probably provides—free of charge—a basic analysis of those logs. The log is run through interpretive software, and the output is tucked in a folder that's usually called "Stats." Open that folder and look at recent files.

What will you see? Here's that same visitor's trail, as reported in the stats folder. The first column is the date, followed by the time of day, amount of time spent on the web page, and the web page (or other web element, such as Java buttons) viewed.

we-24-130-40-120.we.mediaone.net

08 Feb—16:08:47—00:09—/

08 Feb—16:08:56—00:01/UAButton.class

08Feb—16:08:57—00:01—/UleadEffect  Base.class

08Fcb –16:08:58—00:20—/UleadNeon.class http://mcgarvey.net

08Feb—16:09:18—00:09—/mcgarvey.htm

Here you see the visitor (with the internet address we-24-130-40-120.we.media one.net) looked at two pages (www.mc garvey.net and www.mcgarvey.net/mcgar vey.htm), spent less than a minute, then split. How did he get there? What browser was he using? Other files in the stats folder provide those details, and sometimes they are worth a look. But ordinarily just the basics—who and how long?—are what you need to know.

The free stats file reports are good, but even better analysis is easy to come by when you use third-party software tools designed to dissect log files and automatically produce spiffy, usable reports that will tell you not only which countries are producing visitors but also their ISPs and more.

Top choices among traffic-analysis tools and services include:

- *WebTrends Log Analyzer*. This program offers dozens of reporting options plus powerful tools that measure time spent by users on particular pages, "referrer analysis" (Which external sites refer visitors to you? Which keywords lead search engine visitors to you?), and path analysis (How do visitors navigate your site?). You can also get a spiffy "geographical profiling" tool that allows for tracking visitors back to specific cities of origin. Get a trial download from www.netiq.com. Cost: $499.

- *NetTracker Professional*. Select from 42 standardized reports that provide you with detailed information about your web site visitors with just a few mouse clicks. It's a full-featured, fast, easy-to-use tool. Download a free evaluation copy at www.sane.com Cost: $495.

# Just the Stats

The building block for site analysis is the log file—but what if you don't have one? Users of free web space on sites such as AOL.com often don't. But don't despair. Sign up with STATSView (www.statsview.com), a free web-based service that lets you track many facts about visitors, including referrer stats, unique hits, browsers used, and more. Just register with STATSView and paste some HTML code (provided by STATSView) into your pages, and you're in business.

The downside? You have to put STATSView buttons on your pages, and that means not only more clutter, but the buttons can slow page loading. But when a log file isn't readily had, this is the way to go. A twist provided by this service is that it also lets visitors vote on your pages and provides you with user ratings for design, speed, and content. Painful as these votes can be to read, they're invaluable when it comes to modifying a site to maximize user-friendliness.

- *HitBox Professional.* This self-service solution requires no hardware or software and offers a real-time web traffic analysis solution. All the information is collected in real time and made available on demand through a convenient web-browser interface. The service starts at $34.95 for up to 50,000 page views per month. For more information, visit www.websidestory.com.

Which should you use? Download a trial version of WebTrends Log Analyzer and NetTracker Professional. Users can get a free 30-day trial of HitBox Professional by calling the company's sales hotline. A special link will be sent to you via e-mail with instructions for coding their web sites and taking advantage of the trial version. Put them through their paces and see what you like best. Also, before deciding to buy, ask yourself if you really need this level of analysis. Many low-traffic sites don't, and for them, the free stats files provided by the server may be sufficient. When traffic increases to the point where you need more fine-tuned analysis, buy a sophisticated tool—but certainly wait until the traffic increases to more than 100 visitors daily.

# Getting to Know You

Logs provide a step toward knowing your customer, but more can be done. Here, the big guys can clue you in on strategies you can use.

## Survey Says

A discount coupon from Amazon came in this morning's e-mail but with a string attached. If I answered a half-dozen multiple-choice questions, I would earn a $15 credit good on any electronics item sold by Amazon. Through highly specific questions about competitors and Amazon's own product offerings, prices and service, Amazon picks up valuable insight into the thinking of a customer and its competition. Wow!

Why aren't you doing likewise? Don't kick yourself too hard, because Amazon is as good as they get in e-tailing. But it amazes me: I receive an Amazon survey every few months, always with a discount coupon that's activated when I answer the survey, but I cannot remember getting anything similar from any other e-tailer, and I shop at lots.

Strip this down, and what Amazon is doing is taking its customers' e-mail addresses, firing off a survey, and, to sweeten the pot and up the percentage of respondents, offering a discount if you answer the

**Budget Watcher**

Find plenty more free analysis tools and hit counters at TheFreeSite.com, a page devoted to linking with just about every tool around (http://www.the freesite .com/Newest_Freebies.

▲

## Smart Tip

Tip...

Want to wow your cus-tomers? Respond to all e-mail the same day—and offer answers that are truly respon-sive to what the customers are writing about. One sure way for a small business to excel is with a personal touch, and e-mail gives you a power-ful weapon. Use it.

survey. The discount isn't so hefty that it would obliterate margins; it's exactly what it seems to be—a small "thank you."

Don't wait: Do a survey right now. Keep it short, and offer a tangible reward. You don't have Amazon's many millions of people to survey, so randomly choose 10 or 100 customers. Then— and this is crucial—read every answer that comes in. Trust me: Jeff Bezos isn't doing this surveying to fill slow days. The CEO of Amazon honestly wants to know what's on his customers' minds, and, for sure, every response is logged. Odds are, Bezos—a notoriously hands-on boss—personally puts in time eyeballing survey data because he knows what every CEO needs to know: If you want to find out ways to run your business better, look at it as customers do.

Surveys are also sweeping the web as "pop-ups"—screens that jump up when you surf onto a site. Pop-up windows may be popular (I've seen maybe 10 in the past week), but I don't recommend them. Surfers don't like them; complaints about pop-ups are epidemic because they often cause system crashes. They're also technically tricky to put into place—probably beyond your budget and technical know-how. And the data they produce is highly suspect, at least in my mind—I cannot recall ever com-pleting a pop-up questionnaire, mainly because the things are so annoying. Don't feel left out just because your site lacks pop-ups. Instead, rejoice!

# Going to the Polls

What tools should you use besides e-mail? Online polls can be tailored to serve many ends, and you'll find many variations. For example, check out Sparklit (www. sparklit.com). Here you'll find a free option that lets you sign up for advertising-supported web polls, or for $14.95 per month, receive "Gold Service Options," including advanced features, improved integration and no advertising. You can also try Pollwizard (www.pollwizard.com), which offers free polling.

These tools may cost you next to nothing, but, used intelligently, they can be pow-erful. "Free Polling on Your Site, Setup in Five Minutes," shouts Pollwizard on its front page, and these resources live up to that promise. How good will the data you collect be? As good as the polls you create and as good as the tools you use for ana-lyzing your responses.

Don't just put up a poll as a plaything for visitors. Oh, sometimes that's useful— polls are fun and we all like completing them, at least when they're short (never go over ten questions in a poll—five or fewer questions is ideal). But the real payoffs come when you carefully construct polls to target highly specific concerns. Do customers like your web site's speed? Your product selection? Pricing? Ask them, and watch out—they'll love telling you their answers. Big corporations pay megabucks to marketing wizards to examine customers and their motivations, but the truth is, you can get most of the payoffs from this work, free of charge, just by using the tools that are readily at hand.

And one last thing: Read and respond to as much customer e-mail as possible, because it, too, is a real window to customers and their motivations. Strangely, many small businesses, when asked, will mumble and admit that they don't read e-mail and certainly don't respond to it, but there is no faster way to make yourself obsolete than to stay aloof from customers. Sure, nine customers will write with complaints for every one who has good things to say about you, but read it, absorb it—and stay alert to trends. If one person complains about your packaging materials, big deal. If 10 do and you only sent out 12 orders last week, you have a problem—and the great thing is that now you also have the opportunity to fix it.

# Private Eyes

Now that you're excited about gathering information on your customers, know this: It all has to be done gently, respectfully and cautiously. That's because a very sensitive topic these days is web site snooping. And sensitivities are increasing as more users realize exactly how detailed a trail they leave behind when visiting web sites.

But there is a remedy—one that will let you gather the information you need while also reassuring visitors. It's simple: Develop a privacy policy. If you don't, this lack just may cost you big bucks. How big?

Consumers International, a worldwide federation of 263 consumer organizations, reviewed 750 commercial web sites in Europe and the United States and recently released a report that showed that two-thirds of these sites collected personal information from their visitors and 60 percent lacked a privacy statement. Possibly more troubling is that only 9 percent of the European sites asked permission to sell the information that the customer provided, a mere 20 percent asked for approval before adding the customer to a mailing list, and 15 percent gathered personal information in a way that was invisible to the web user. Popular U.S. sites did better in the study. About half asked for approval to sell the customers' details.

What does this mean? These web businesses may well be shooting themselves in the foot. By not winning trust—and by not safeguarding visitor privacy—these e-tailers just may be inadvertently pushing would-be customers toward the exits before the cash registers ring.

**Beware!**
Get another eyeful at BrowserSpy (www.gemal.dk/browserspy). Exactly how much this web site knows about you, instantly, is frightening. Check it out!

# Too Close for Comfort

In America, proof of consumers' sensitivity to this issue are the PR nightmares suffered by RealPlayer, Alexa and numerous other net companies that were found to surreptitiously collect information on users. The companies claimed no harm was done—that the information (mainly pertaining to a user's viewing habits) was collected so that user needs might better be served—but for a time, dark clouds hung over many net companies as users fretted about invasion of privacy.

Privacy is not a concern only for the paranoid, either. For a demonstration of just how much information is easily collected from web surfers without their knowledge or participation, go to http://privacy.net. In a minute or so, you'll probably see a long—and spooky—report on exactly how much information you surrender at every web site. Everything from your internet address to your computer's name is readily known by sites you visit. Also revealed—although not included in Privacy.net's demonstration—is your e-mail address, so this can get very personal, very quickly.

Why do web sites want this information in the first place? Mainly because it's a marketer's dream. In an era when "knowing thy customer" is seen as a path to riches, it's hard to resist collecting vast stores of customer data that tumble into your lap when

## Get Lost

**N**ever assume your online activities are private. With court orders in hand, law enforcement can track virtually all surfers in a matter of minutes. That may be no big deal to most of us, but if you're doing stuff you want kept private, think about it. One way to avoid the scrutiny is to head to a public internet cafe and pay cash for a surfing session. You might do that simply to keep competitors from knowing you're checking out their sites.

Another option: Go to Anonymizer (www.anonymizer.com), which allows anonymous surfing. A bare-bones model is free, while heavy users will opt for the subscription version ($49.99 per year).

AOL users, incidentally, can breathe easily. Many ISPs give users a fixed internet address—like a street address, it uniquely identifies the user—but AOL owns many fewer addresses than it has members, so it dynamically and randomly assigns addresses, which means no AOL address can be seen as identifying a particular user. When presented with a court order, AOL has opened its records and pinpointed which user had a specific address at a specific time—but only serious lawbreakers need to fret about that. For most people, an AOL address actually gives all the privacy they are likely to need.

you create a web site. Know where a visitor has been before—which sites he's visited earlier in this internet session, for instance—and an alert marketer can use that insight into the surfer's interests to tweak offerings to more closely match the surfer's wants.

That's so tempting that some sites dramatically up the ante by overtly collecting more detailed and personal information from visitors. Usually that occurs in tandem with an offer the visitor accepts. Before you can create a free e-mail account at Pronto Mail (www.pronto-mail.com),

> **⚠ Beware!**
>
> In some states—among them, Washington—sending spam is illegal. Granted, enforcement of anti-spam laws has been inconsistent, but the fact is plain: Smart retailers don't spam away the goodwill of customers.

for instance, you have to provide a name, geographic location, age and a few more details. This is common, and experienced web surfers have come to expect a trade-off of personal information for freebies—except the savviest surfers long ago stopped giving out accurate information. Many maintain a separate e-mail box just for use in connection with freebies and simply lie when filling out the forms.

Another dose of bad news is that, in some cases, information collected in your "cookies" has been transmitted to third-party sites—and that can strike fear in just about everybody. A cookie, theoretically, is a bit of information about you that's written to your hard drive while visiting a web site that will let that web site identify you as a repeat visitor in the future. This is how some sites greet you with "Welcome Back, Fragonard" (or whatever your name is) when you return. Cookies, their architects argue, save users time and make the surfing process more efficient. Who could complain? Well, Consumer.net has found instances where those cookies have been visible to other sites—and that's a scary thought indeed.

A last privacy breach is that, wherever you go on the net, you leave a trail. Very good hackers can hide their trails, but 99.9 percent of us leave tracks that are easy to follow. That is no big deal to most of us. But it means that your feeling of anonymity on the net is a false one: Your movements can be cataloged and associated with you.

Added up, the situation is this: Experienced surfers do their best to mock the system, while comparative newcomers—fearing privacy violations—avoid making purchases to protect their identities. This is not good for you, and it's not good for web users, either, because it is limiting their use of the medium.

## Confidence Boosters

What should you do to reassure visitors? As a rule, mainline web sites fairly openly explain their privacy policy. At the Entrepreneur.com site, for instance, at the bottom of the front page is a link that says "Privacy Policy." Click it, and you are delivered to a clear, concise statement of what information is collected from visitors, what's done

▲

with it, and if it's made available to other companies. (The answer in this case is no—"Any information collected about you will never be sold or rented to any third party for any purpose," says the Entrepreneur.com statement.)

Most other leading U.S. sites you'll visit will explain their privacy policy somewhere on their sites in much the same way. They may vary in how easy it is to find the link and how clear the statement is, but poke around and you'll probably find a policy.

Another trend: privacy promises made by third parties, such as by the Better Business Bureau Privacy Program (www.bbbonline.org/privacy) and TRUSTe (www.truste.com). Program mechanics vary a bit, but the essence is that a business site meets certain basic privacy requirements, pays a fee, and then gets to display a button on the web site touting that it fulfills the program's requirements. Some users grumble that these programs don't truly guarantee privacy so much as they promise disclosure of what happens to information surfers reveal, but pretty much everybody agrees that such programs are a step in the right direction.

Should you join? Since the cheapest TRUSTe membership was $599 annually at a recent look, it may not be the shrewdest use of sparse cash in a start-up. My advice: Keep the money in your pocket and look for do-it-yourself tactics to up visitor security.

Detailed guidance on the how-to of raising visitor confidence can be found in groundbreaking research—conducted by AT&T Labs and several universities, including

## DSL Dangers

**A**re you using high-speed net access via a cable modem or always-on DSL? If you are, you're enjoying the best web access around, but you also are exposing yourself to invasion by hackers.

Theoretically, a hacker could penetrate your system when you are connected to the net with a dial-up connection, but the likelihood is not high. Why? Usually when you're connected you are sitting at the computer. If suddenly you see that you're opening Quicken financial files—and in fact you're not—you'd know a hacker was there, and poof, you'd shut down. End of threat.

Always-on connections raise different worries. Maybe 20 hours a day your computer is sitting there, open to invasion. But antidotes are plentiful. I use Norton Internet Security (www.symantec.com/sabu/nis/nis_pe). It costs less than $100, installs in minutes and protects your system against intruders. Plenty of other packages are available. Whatever you use, if you have high-speed access, get software to protect the privacy of your computer. It's an ounce of prevention that can save many pounds of tears.

Harvard and MIT—that pinpoints exactly what internet users fear regarding the net and privacy and what steps reassure them. A key finding in "Beyond Concern: Understanding Net Users' Attitudes About Online Privacy": When an explicit privacy policy is combined with a third-party seal of approval, surfer confidence soars.

Users are especially sensitive when their data is shared with other sites or businesses. Most seem to feel that if they are interested enough in a site to want to hang around, revealing a bit about themselves is OK—but they do not want that information passed on. Another finding: Users are very, very unwilling to reveal any information about their children. Why? Who knows—just accept that as fact and don't ask. (Get your free copy of the full report at http://www.research.att.com/projects/privacystudy.

To sum up, the steps you should take are to post a link to your privacy policy in a prominent place on your site. In that policy, be clear, simple and direct. A good strategy is to say: "We sell no information that we collect about you. Never. To anybody." Don't ask questions about visitors' kids—unless there's a compelling and obvious reason to do so. And if you offer visitors free sign-up to e-mail newsletters or sales notices, be quick to remove anybody who asks—preferably on the very day you receive the request. Users grumble a lot about spam, and an easy way to win visitor confidence is to promptly remove anybody from any list upon request.

Winning—and keeping—visitor trust really isn't, and shouldn't be, rocket science. Lots of the same hurdles were overcome years ago by direct mail and catalog sellers. In the case of the net, plenty of credit card issuers (American Express, Citibank, etc.) are working overtime to encourage their cardholders to make online purchases with the full assurance that the card will protect them from fraud. And in probably the broadest, most objective look at net privacy issues, the FTC—a lead government agency in the e-commerce arena—has argued that there is no need for government intervention to offer more assurances of privacy and that, on balance, the industry is doing a satisfactory job. For most site operators, this means don't screw up, and you'll be able to develop trust on the part of visitors. And once they trust you, they will buy.

---

**Tip...**

## Smart Tip

See your visitors giving out e-mail addresses at Hotmail, Excite, and Yahoo!, and, guess what, you're probably getting their secondary addresses. Sure, some employees at big corporations use such addresses for personal e-mail, but, mainly, folks usually set up these accounts to help dodge spam. What can you do better to earn their trust—and their primary addresses?

# Customer
## Service
## for Success

E-tailers used to be innocents who thought that with web-based retailing, all customer service would be a thing of the past because the entire sales and service process would be neatly (and oh so inexpensively) automated. Ha! If there's a mantra for e-commerce players, it's this: Customers may be virtual, but their dollars are real.

"[Internet customers] expect and need the same level of service in-person customers get," says Cynthia Hollen, CEO of Knowledge Strategies Group (www.kstrat.com), a New York City-based internet consulting firm that's worked with Bloomingdale's, among others, in creating online stores. "When you don't understand that, you lose sales," she says. "Consumers now expect high levels of service from online retailers, and the better ones see it as a competitive edge and are delivering." How? Just follow the leaders:

> ## Smart Tip
>
> Do it now: Create a place for FAQs on your site ASAP. View your FAQs as a work in progress. You'll continually update and expand them as more customer concerns and needs come to light.

- *Anticipate questions.* Many e-tailers anticipate questions and then answer them in their FAQs. This will save you and your customers time. Of course, sometimes customers will e-mail you with questions, and this can be a good thing. Get lots of e-mail complaining about a certain feature that the customer has simply misunderstood or bemoaning the lack of a particular product that you know is in stock, and you are learning important things about how your site is failing to communicate to visitors. As e-mail comes in, don't ever look for how the e-mailers are wrong. Look for ways to reshape your site to eliminate user problems (even the ones they only imagine they have).

- *Stay in touch.* At Hewlett-Packard's Shopping Village (www.hpshopping.com), every customer is asked if he or she would recommend hpshopping.com to friends, and 88 percent say they would, according to Chief Operations Manager Cindi Zelanis. But the small percentage who say "no" aren't forgotten. "We contact them via e-mail or phone and ask how we can satisfy them," says Zelanis, who adds that it's usually not hard to do: "Just contacting them alone is often enough to win them back."

  Hewlett-Packard's way is cheap. Why aren't you doing likewise? A week or two after any order is filled, e-mail the customer and ask if they would recommend your shop. "No" answers will hurt, but follow up on every one because these are the people who will tell you what you need to do to build a winner of a web site. Given how awesomely powerful this simple tool is, it's stunning that more e-tailers haven't jumped on it. Don't make the same mistake!

- *Respond quickly.* The web is an instant medium—except when it comes to getting responses from many businesses that seem to route incoming e-mail into a folder labeled "Ignore Forever." Smart e-tailers know better, however. HP's Zelanis says, "Our goal is to respond to every inquiry within 24 hours." Others raise the bar higher still, with responses within four hours emerging as the new goal of many. What's right for you? With a smaller staff (and probably no staff during night hours), you might find a 24-hour standard to be enough of a challenge. But monitor customers. If they demand faster response, somehow you have to find a way to meet their needs.

To keep in touch instantly, try free, easy-to-use, off-the-shelf software, such as AOL's Instant Messenger (www.aol.com). The more accessible you are, the more sales you are likely to log.

- *Hold their hands.* "Online, not every customer knows how to shop, and you have to be ready to help them buy," says Anne Marie Blaire, director of internet brand development at Limited Brands, where she ensured the successful launch of VictoriasSecret.com and the continued growth of the Victoria's Secret brand online. No brick-and-mortar retailer has to teach customers how to buy, but online, that remains a thorny problem. Every day thousands of shoppers log on for the first time, and these newbies genuinely crave handholding as they make purchases. Understand that and be ready to help. Be patient, too. Only a very ignorant e-tailer complains about how stupid his newbie customers are. They can, in fact, become your best customers, because they will shop only where they feel comfortable—and if your site makes it on that shortlist, watch the orders tumble in.

- *Use cut and paste.* Canned responses—cut-and-paste scripts—are used by all the leading sites, which track questions, hunt for the most asked, and produce templates for their representatives. You can do likewise. As you answer customer questions, file away your responses. Odds are, you will be asked the same question within the week, and it's a great labor saver to have an answer ready.

- *Stay sensitive.* A worry with e-mail: It's easy to seem cold and unresponsive in the formality of the written word. Read and reread your responses before they go out. You want to be—and appear—interested in the customer's issues and eager to find solutions.

- *Aim higher.* In the online space, the service bar is being lifted ever higher. "Good service is expected these days for online retailers," says Ken Young, a spokesperson for 1-800-Flowers.com, a leading gift retailer and an online pioneer going back to 1992. "Only truly outstanding service will get your company noticed. And the term 'service' has been greatly expanded," Young says. "At a minimum, you must have 24/7 phone support, as well as functionality like real-time chat and personalization that enables you to better meet your customers' needs."

Office Depot is another company that has gone beyond providing great customer service. For example, its web site (www.officedepot.com) offers a free online "Business Center," which provides a "Small Business Handbook," "Free Downloadable Forms," and a complete online directory of web resources. In addition, OfficeDepot.com hosts a free online weekly "Web Cafe" with small-business experts on topics such as marketing, public relations and technology tips. "Our customers appreciate that we strive to provide them not only what they need, but also what they need to know to run their businesses," says Monica Luechtefeld, executive vice president of global e-commerce at Office Depot.

**Smart Tip**

Take a tactic used by the slick catalog companies, and when you haven't heard from a customer in a while, drop him or her an e-mail: "Have we disappointed you in any way? We would really value your feedback." Maybe the customer is indeed irked with you; maybe not. Either way, this e-mail will remind the customer that you are a store that cares.

- *Offer choices.* It's important that you offer a variety of choices that customers can use to contact you, such as e-mail and phone. The easier the online shopping experience, the more likely the customer will come back for more.

These steps will get you started delivering better customer service, but they are not enough. Successful entrepreneurs say that the only way to do online service right is to have the right attitude, really believe the customer is king, and make sure that every one of their customer service reps knows it. Many fail on this score, but when you've made customer service your top and continuing priority, success is within reach. Don't get seduced by the notion that the web sites with the best technology will inevitably win. Usable, reliable technology is a must, but where the real e-tailing battlefield will be is in service. That's the irony about e-tailing: At the end, what prevails online is what prevails off—and that's consistent, respectful, considerate service.

# e-Chat with
# Netflix's Reed Hastings

## Netflix Inc.

Reed Hastings, founder and CEO
Location: Los Gatos, California
Year Started: 1997

Netflix (www.netflix.com), the world's largest online DVD movie rental service, is a true e-business success story.

Founder and CEO Reed Hastings and his colleagues formed Netflix in 1997 and launched a subscription service in 1999 with the goal of becoming the world's largest and most influential movie supplier.

The company wanted to use the DVD format and the internet to make it easier for people to find and get movies they would appreciate. As a result, they could reliably discover and enjoy lesser-known titles and watch more films, and at the same time, filmmakers could reach a larger audience and produce more new films.

Hastings is no stranger to successful start-ups. He founded his first company, Pure Software, in 1991, took it public in 1995, completed several acquisitions, and made it one of the 50 largest public software companies in the world by 1997. Pure was acquired in 1997 by Rational Software.

> ### Smart Tip — Tip...
>
> The essence of Netflix is both very simple and very complex. Its founder, Reed Hastings, realized that the web was the perfect tool for a no-hassle, subscription-based DVD movie rental service with no late fees and free delivery. Tomorrow's billionaires are likely to come from the ranks of creative thinkers who get out of the box and see new ways to put the web to use. What new ways can you think of?

Here's how Netflix works: For $19.95 a month, members rent as many DVDs as they want and keep them as long as they want. It's this "no late fees, no due dates" online movie rental model that has eliminated the hassle involved in choosing, renting and returning movies.

Members also enjoy free shipping both ways, and currently more than 50 percent of Netflix's members receive next-day service. Netflix also operates 18 shipping centers—a key to providing overnight delivery—and plans to open more throughout the country.

Members are also encouraged to rate movies, allowing Netflix to customize its site based on a member's movie tastes. Netflix says this helps to make the more than 15,000 film titles it offers relevant and accessible. The company, which is now a cash-flow-positive public company on Nasdaq, had total revenues of $81.2 million in the fourth quarter of 2003, up 80 percent compared with $45.2 million for the fourth quarter of 2002. It also ended the fourth quarter of 2003 with approximately 1.4 million subscribers.

The company is also seeing competition from heavyweights. Last year, Wal-Mart and Blockbuster started online DVD rental services to compete with Netflix.

Can Netflix stand up to the competition? Netflix thinks so. Here, Hastings offers some secrets to his success.

**Melissa Campanelli:** *Why did you decide to start an internet company focusing on DVD movie rentals?*

**Reed Hastings:** It was a growth opportunity to improve the movie experience for consumers using the internet. An internet store can offer a very broad selection and free home delivery, and I believed there was a need for something like this—there was nothing else like this out there.

On a broad scale, the idea stemmed from the fact that consumers in general dislike the late fees, the due date, and the limited selection of the store-based video rental model.

The idea also stemmed partly from personal frustration. I had a very large late fee one day—approximately $40—and it was all my fault because I had not returned a movie that I had rented from a little independent movie rental store. After that experience, I started thinking that one could do video rental on a subscription basis with no late fee.

**Campanelli:** *You charge everyone $19.95 per month. How many DVDs does someone have to rent for this model to become unprofitable?*

**Hastings:** Some of our subscribers rent 20 movies a month, and we still love them because they tend to be very evangelistic for the Neflix service. The average number of DVDs people rent per month, however, is five to six.

**Campanelli:** *How was Netflix funded?*

**Hastings**: We raised a little over $100 million in venture capital from Technology Crossover Ventures and Foundation Capital. We received our first round of funding in 1997.

**Campanelli:** *In your opinion, what was it about your company that attracted that kind of cash from VCs?*

**Hastings:** A lot of companies attracted that kind of cash back then, but it's not the case today. They saw great potential.

**Campanelli:** *What is your marketing philosophy?*

**Hastings:** We've had very lean marketing. We did a deal back in late 1997 with Sony and Toshiba where they put a "try Netflix for free" offer in their DVD players. We do some online banners, and we do the search listings—both paid and regular search—on Google. But our biggest source of marketing is word-of-mouth, which has grown over time as we've gotten a better reputation.

**Campanelli:** *What's the biggest surprise you've had in building Netflix?*

**Hastings:** How complicated the logistics are. We ship over 1 million packages a week, and it is very complicated dealing with large volumes. There are [many] things that can go wrong, such as performance issues, mail ability—just the complexity of the whole process.

**Campanelli:** *What has been your biggest challenge?*

**Hastings:** We've grown so rapidly. We've nearly doubled every year, so scaling our operations systems to be able to ship more and more movies has been very challenging.

▲

**Campanelli:** *Whom do you consider to be your competition? What's your strategy in coming out ahead of them?*

**Hastings:** Blockbuster and Wal-Mart both have online competitive services to Netflix right now. Our strategy is to focus on our business. [Wal-Mart and Blockbuster] are spread across many different businesses, but we do one thing, and we do it extremely well.

**Campanelli:** *What is your market objective over the next five years, and how will you go about reaching that goal?*

**Hastings:** To get five million subscribers. How we get there is by continuing to improve our service by adding more titles, more availability, more local shipping centers, and an improved web site. Just improve every aspect of the business.

**Campanelli:** *What are your secrets to success?*

**Hastings:** We focus on a simple, core proposition and doing that really well, and not getting distracted by 100 gimmicks or extensions on the business model. Instead, we focus on doing the core model very, very well.

# Cheap Tricks with FrugalFun.com's Shel Horowitz

## FrugalFun.com

Shel Horowitz, founder and owner
Location: Northampton, Massachusetts
Year Started: 1996

**W**ant to see a simple site that also makes money? Check out FrugalFun.com and its sister sites—FrugalMarketing.com, launched in 2001, and PrincipledProfits.com, launched in 2002.

No doubt about it: They are frugal—really cheap, in fact—but their developer and owner, Shel Horowitz, says the sites produce a steady stream of income, mainly from sales of his books, among them *Grassroots Marketing: Getting Noticed in a Noisy World* (Chelsea Green Publishing). To keep the traffic flowing, Horowitz serves up generous portions of freebies—tip sheets on frugal living and travel tips for the frugal on the FrugalFun.com site, and reams of low-cost marketing tips on FrugalMarketing.com

PrincipledProfits.com is a business ethics web site that highlights another book Horowitz has written called *Principled Profit: Marketing That Puts People First* (AWM Books). Horowitz has two additional sites, ShelHorowitz.com, which directs visitors to the most appropriate of his web sites, and AccurateWriting.com, which promotes Shel's marketing and copywriting services. Read on to find out more about why his sites are successful.

> ### Tip...
>
> ### Smart Tip
>
> Listen up when Shel Horowitz tells you how he markets his site on the cheap. Maybe you don't have books that will win reviews, but you do have e-mail. Are you using your "sig" (signature) for maximum impact? Keep it short—two lines are twice as powerful as four. Then, as Horowitz says, get busy scouting out Internet chat groups and discussion lists where visitors might find your site to be a useful hang out. Put up your posts, sig included, and watch the traffic come in.

**Robert McGarvey:** *What were your start-up costs?*

**Shel Horowitz:** I went online in 1994 with an AOL account. When I set up [FrugalFun] in 1996, I registered a domain name [$70 for two years]. Since I went online, I have spent $60 on ads hawking the site. My first two site designs [for FrugalFun] cost me nothing—the first version was done by an intern, and the second was a barter. The site was up for over three years before I paid anything for site design. Oh, yes, and I had to renew my domain name when the time was up. I am currently paying, I think, $15 or $16 per year each to register three domains hosted and registered at Web Wizards (www.webwizards.com), a web hosting company. [The three domains are Frugal-Fun, FrugalMarketing, and AccurateWriting.] I started with a $45-per-month account covering e-mail, web hosting, web surfing, and site updating, then switched to an $18-per-month ISP/Web host. Several years ago, I outgrew that host and separated hosting from my internet access. Now I spend $36 per month to host these three sites and another $42 per month through the local cable company for high-speed internet access. I pay about $9 per year to register my ShelHorowitz.com site, which is a simple one-page site hosted at GoDaddy (www.godaddy.com), another web hosting company. Hosting the one page costs $14 or $16 per year.

PrincipledProfits is hosted at Site Build It! (www.sitebuildit.com), another web hosting company, for a flat fee of $300 per year for registration, hosting, and a number of other services.

**McGarvey:** *Where did you get the idea for the FrugalFun site?*

**Horowitz:** People started telling me in early 1995 that I needed a web site. In my field, marketing, I was shooting myself in the foot not having one. I thought for several months about what the site would contain, did a lot of preplanning, and found an intern who wanted to learn HTML. She coded the first 40 pages, which went up in April 1996. She also taught me what she'd learned. A year later, I bartered with a web site designer for the template I used for the next three years. That design, dating from 1997, became somewhat tired. In 1999, I paid a high school student to redesign the page, but it was left unfinished. So, in 2000, I hired a woman I'm still working with, who has redesigned FrugalFun twice and created FrugalMarketing using a similar design. PrincipledProfits uses a template model. I couldn't achieve the look I wanted, but a friend set up a better template for me.

**McGarvey:** *How do you attract visitors and market the site?*

**Horowitz:** I have done quite a bit to market the site. I participate actively in many discussion lists, and my sig [e-mail signature] draws people to the site. I use some 30 different sigs, depending on what I want to emphasize. I do radio talk shows as a guest about 20 times a year, and I always mention the URL and a reason to visit. For example, [I'll say], "On my site at www.FrugalFun.com, you can find out how to have a wedding for $300," or "One of my tip sheets has a really good article on trade shows. You'll find the back issues archives at www.frugalmarketing.com."

Also, for the book *Principled Profit* (AWM Books), I'm starting a reseller program, which should spread my reach to many other sites. I am hoping that resellers will account for a high percentage of sales for that title and perhaps with some spillover to sales of another one of my titles—*Grassroots Marketing: Getting Noticed in a Noisy World* (Chelsea Green Publishing).

Also, I actively solicit book reviews and editorial coverage, and most mention the URL. Search engines draw a fair amount of visitors, but they're mostly in to see a particular page of the rather diverse content. They'll find one article that interests them, and then they move on. If they're looking for marketing info, they stay a while. I've been averaging 30,000 to 35,000 visitors a month for FrugalFun.com lately. The other [sites] are much less heavily trafficked, something I'll be working to change in the coming months.

**McGarvey:** *What's your look-to-buy ratio?*

**Horowitz:** Low—but I am not real concerned about that, because the people who need what I have seek me out.

**McGarvey:** *How big is the average purchase?*

**Horowitz:** I have two kinds of buyers: those who buy books, who spend $8.50 to $35, and those who buy marketing services, who spend between $125 and several thousand dollars over time. Because of the integrated nature of my business, it's hard to separate revenues. It's not an uncommon pattern, for instance, to have someone visit the site to order my marketing book and then some weeks or months later come back to look over the pages about my marketing services—and then they buy.

**McGarvey:** *Is your site profitable?*

**Horowitz:** This site, while not bringing in megabucks, achieves a very high return on investment, in my estimation. I sell a fair number of books directly from the sites, and I also secure a number of lucrative marketing clients from the sites. I also now have more than 12,000 subscribers to three tip sheets—*Frugal Fun Tips, Frugal Marketing Tips,* and *Positive Power of Principled Profit*—so I have a way of marketing to my visitors.

How's that for a cheap, effective web site? Of course, I've written three books on cheap marketing and one on cheap fun, so I am a very good shopper—but pretty much anyone could duplicate my success.

# Security Holes,
## Fraud, and More
## Bad Stuff

It seems too simple: Put up a web site, and you're
on the road to riches. Guess what? There are plenty of potholes
in that road. Experts are eager to acknowledge the dark side of
the web—the many ways it is easy to go wrong, often before
you even suspect there's a problem.

According to Wally Bock, an author and consultant on business in the digital age, "Today 70 percent of web sites are bad. They don't answer the questions or solve the problems that visitors have. They are hard to use, and many simply don't work the way they should." Keep talking to experts, and look at any statistics on the number of dotcom companies that have failed and the fact that so few are starting up, and it's pretty clear that many dotcom companies are doomed.

"It is hard to do an online business right," says Phil Terry, CEO of Creative Good Inc., a web strategy consulting firm in New York City, "and there are so many ways to do one wrong." Fledgling e-tailers need to know the problems this industry faces, from visitors who look but never buy to wholesale theft of your most sensitive information. Keep reading, and you'll discover the obstacles e-businesses face on the way to the top.

- *Security.* "The magnitude of security fraud and theft is staggering, especially when you consider that many breaches go unreported—and just as many undetected," says Chad Grier, president and CEO of META Security Group, a tech security consulting firm in Cornelius, North Carolina. How can that be, when most web browsers and e-business server computers use encryption technology that scrambles a customer's credit card information when it's moving through the internet? Because one of the biggest problems is hackers who break into the web site's computers and steal the whole credit card database. The cure? Work with security experts. Usually, inexpensive solutions can be implemented that safeguard data.

  Need convincing that security is a worry? Chew on this: In March 2000, two teenagers in Wales were arrested on charges that they stole upwards of

> **Beware!**
> What's your vulnerability to hackers? Create a vulnerability scorecard to pinpoint exactly where your weaknesses are. One common solution: Keep credit card and customer databases on a separate computer from the one connected to the internet. This isn't the only security issue, however, so ask yourself what you would do if you were a hacker, then find ways to fend off that line of attack.

> **Smart Tip**
> **Tip...**
> How can you make your site one where people buy, not just look? Experts heatedly debate all aspects of site design, but the one area where there is clear agreement is that visitors will shop when the site is created with a firm intention to make it easy to shop. A role model is Amazon—everything is there to enhance and simplify the buying experience. You don't want your site to be a carbon copy, but if you are an e-tailer, ask yourself the following about every site feature: "Does this simplify buying?" When the answer is no, cut out that feature. It's that simple.

26,000 credit card numbers from various web sites. Even security experts were amazed by this case because the teens, far from being seasoned hackers, were amateur enough to leave a clear trail from the hacks back to their personal computers. They used none of the tactics of slick hackers, yet, seemingly with ease, the kids broke into a number of business web sites and waltzed out with credit card numbers—some 6,500 of which they reposted on various hacker web sites. And that has become a disaster for the sites that were cracked, mainly small businesses that thought they could go unnoticed by hackers. Don't delay: Start today improving your site's security features.

> ### Budget Watcher
>
> Well-funded e-tailers install system wide redundancy—if the whole Amazon setup were to collapse, for example, a carbon copy is ready to stand in and do the job. You probably don't want to incur those expenses, but you need to back up all your files. No need to get fancy here. Backups on Zip disks that are kept off-site will do. Why off-site? Losing your backup files as well as your originals in a fire, flood, or hurricane is a nightmare you'll want to avoid. If off-site storage is too much of a hassle, use a fireproof and waterproof safe.

- *No buyers.* The startling news is that 55 percent of online customers who fill shopping carts bail out before clicking the "Buy" button, according to research from e-commerce marketplace BizRate (www.bizrate.com). The news gets worse, according to Creative Good's Terry, who helps clients calculate what he calls "the conversion rate," meaning the percentage of visitors who actually buy something. "For many companies, it's still below average, and almost all companies continue to leave significant money on the table," says Terry. In other words, fight hard to get traffic, and that might not matter at all. A site can be jammed, but the cash register may never ring. "Most sites focus on the wrong thing—they seek traffic, not conversion into customers," says Terry, who adds that the remedy is to build an e-tailing site from the ground up, with the goal of enhancing and simplifying the shopping experience. "But you don't see many sites that do it."

- *Outages.* EBay has had them, and so have many of the online stock brokerages. The inevitable result is a flood of bad publicity as daily newspapers rush to slam a faltering web business. Sometimes outages are flukes—bugs that surface in software or during a site upgrade—but often the problem stems from poor planning at the beginning.

More troubling still is the fact that outages often happen exactly when a web site begins to catch on. For example, a site that works fine when there are 100 visitors a day may show strains at 1,000 and go into meltdown at 10,000 visitors. Sites need to be built to scale as traffic increases and, frankly, doing that requires nothing more than planning. Always ask, "If traffic goes up tenfold, how will we handle it?" If you don't know the answer, make sure your technical consultants do. And if you can, address the issue before launch—because when a web site catches fire, it often becomes a wildfire.

- *Fraud.* A dirty secret about the web is that crooks love it. What better place to use stolen credit cards than under the relative anonymity afforded by the internet? Jonas Lee, founder and former CEO of GiftCertificates.com (www.giftcertifcates. com), who is no longer with the company, knows something about this. "From day one, we've had problems with fraud, but every e-tailer does," Lee says. "Fraud is part of selling on the internet. We're lucky we started slow. As we grew—as public awareness of us grew— we also grew more expert at detecting fraud. Every e-tailer has to do the same."

> ## ⚠ Beware!
>
> Nobody knows how much money is lost to credit card fraud on the Internet, but conservative estimates are that the tab long ago reached the $800 million mark. The e-tailer conundrum is that you don't want to lose a sale to a valid customer due to cumbersome security clearances, but you also can't afford to get ripped off. But think about it: It's better to lose a sale than it is to become a victim. Always look for ways to improve your security as well as the customer's shopping experience, but keep an eye firmly on the till at all times.

Most e-tailers flatly refuse to talk on the record about their losses from fraud, but know that every site has had to battle with crooks.

What are some things to look out for? Experts say you should watch out for orders with different "bill to" and "ship to" addresses, as well as orders coming from countries with high cyberfraud rates, such as Ukraine, Indonesia, Yugoslavia, Lithuania, Egypt, Romania, Bulgaria, Turkey, Russia, Pakistan, Malaysia, and Israel.

For a comprehensive list of things you can do to reduce credit card fraud, check out "Nine Steps to Minimize Credit Card Fraud for Merchants," included in an e-book called *The Best of Internet Scambusters*, which you can find at www.scambusters.org. Internet ScamBusters is a web site and a free electronic newsletter designed to help people protect themselves from internet scams, misinformation, and hype.

- *Fighting off the big dogs.* Larry Cuneo, the 51-year-old CEO of Minneapolis-based CarSoup, knew he had big problems from the day he launched in 1998. The space he coveted—selling cars through dealers and connecting auto buyers with auto sellers on the net—had already been staked out by very big companies, including Microsoft (with CarPoint, now called MSN Autos) and Autobytel.com.

But Cuneo thought he had a unique twist—his site would be local, targeted strictly at nearby dealers and car buyers. Sounds good—"but we had considerable difficulty gaining credibility," says Cuneo. "That's lowered our recognition—and our revenues—from advertisers and e-commerce partners."

Small might sometimes be beautiful, but on the web, it's rarely a distinct advantage. Cuneo didn't quit, though. For one thing, he had budgeted about 50 percent of gross revenues for marketing and promotion, he says. He also invested substantial time in coming up with local promotions the big boys couldn't rival. "We'll sponsor cars in parades and little local events," says Cuneo. The upshot: Today, his site, www.carsoup.com, holds a genuine lead in its market over the national rivals. "We have 85 percent of the total local market penetration, but we've had to work hard to get here, and we'll have to work to hold this spot."

Is this dark side of the web so gloomy that you should rethink your enthusiasm for this business venue? Nope, because the upside is the potential of fantastic wealth—the payoffs scored by the founders of, say, Amazon, Yahoo!, and eBay.

### Smart Tip

*Tip...*

Thinking local remains a smart route to web wealth. Knocking heads with Amazon, drugstore.com or 1-800-Flowers.com isn't smart—the war will be expensive and painful. But stake out a well-defined local turf, offer more in-depth local knowledge than any national site could hope to provide, and you just may be onto something.

# A Tour of the Web

Sam Walton, the legendary founder of Wal-Mart, loved to shop—especially in competitors' stores. He did not necessarily buy anything, but he delighted in roaming the aisles, noting prices, and observing unique, eye-catching ways to display merchandise. Why? Every shopping trip turned into an exercise in competitive intelligence, and whenever Walton caught a competitor doing something right, he looked for ways to do it better in his Wal-Mart stores.

You would be wise to do the same, and that means routinely surfing the web, visiting pace-setting e-tailers, and learning everything you can about what people are doing right. Don't think of surfing as goofing off. When you are doing it so that you can become a better e-tailer, it's some of the best work you can do. Jeff Bezos, founder of Amazon, is known to keep his Tuesdays and Thursdays open whenever possible to give himself time to surf the web in search of cool ideas.

Here's a yardstick: You are doing valuable work when, after every surfing session, you have specific, concrete ideas for improving your site. If you're not getting ideas, you're surfing the wrong sites or not thinking hard enough. And neither will get you ahead in the competitive world of e-commerce.

Want to know how to look at web sites? On the following pages, many name-brand web sites are critiqued. Some win generous praise, but throughout, the emphasis is on what we can learn from these sites. And next time you put in a surfing session, ask yourself the kinds of questions you'll see in these site critiques.

# River of Dreams

## Amazon.com Inc.
## www.amazon.com

Amazon founder Jeff Bezos named his web site "Amazon" because that river is bigger than any other river on earth. Or so the story goes. And Bezos' aim from the get-go was to build the web's biggest store.

Bezos came up with the idea when, as an employee of a New York financial firm, he was asked to run numbers on various possible web businesses. When he hit upon books, all the lights went on—Bezos knew he had a winner. Just a couple of distributors stock pretty much every book in print, and it seemed simple to set up a business that amounted to a web site with no inventory. As orders came in, books could be bought from distributors, and whoosh—profits would roll in. Bezos took the numbers to his bosses and asked them to join in funding a start-up, but the verdict was no way. So Bezos quit, moved out to Seattle, and began building what just may rank as the web's crowning e-tailing achievement.

In internet research firm comScore Media Metrix's (www.comscore.com) February 2003 tally of the Top 25 internet properties, which tracks total unique web visitors, only one e-tailer placed in the top ten sites: Amazon sites, including its international sites, ranked eighth. Why is Amazon so successful? In part because its pages and tools are brilliantly executed, and throughout the site the emphasis is on making it as easy as possible for the buyer to make a purchase.

Case in point: "1-Click" buying. Like a book? A registered Amazon user can, with a single mouse click, buy it. It's that fast and that simple (so much so that tests showed users didn't believe it could be so easy—so afterward a screen pops up that says the deal has been done). It doesn't work only on books, however. Anything Amazon sells can be bought with a single click, and nowadays that includes TV sets, videos, CDs, power saws, toys, and more. Doesn't Bezos risk diluting Amazon's message by expanding into so many diverse product lines? Remember the company's name—from the start Bezos envisioned expanding into other product lines.

> **! Beware!**
>
> Amazon has filed patents on various bits of its site operation, and although nobody is clear about what Amazon intends to do to assert its rights, wary site designers are treading softly when it comes to closely imitating Amazon. This will not likely be a worry for you, both because your operation will be small and your technology will not be nearly as robust as Amazon's, but if you find yourself exactly duplicating the "1-Click" purchase tool, back up a few steps and try another approach.

Amazon also offers free shipping. While free shipping has been used as an online promotional tool since the internet's earliest days, the idea really picked up steam in 2002 when Amazon began experimenting with it as a full-time service. Initially, the company offered free shipping to customers whose purchases totaled $99 or more. The company later lowered the minimum to $49 and then to $25, which it currently offers. (There are some exceptions to free shipping, however, including apparel, video games and accessories, baby products, and certain oversized items.) While it may be difficult for a small company to offer this promotion, it is something to think about.

What else is cool about Amazon.com? Notice how fast the home page loads. The look is fresh and clean but is primarily text-based, with plentiful use of white space to make the page easy on the eyes. With its treasury, Amazon could well afford to put up the glitziest tech tools imaginable, but it doesn't. Cool tools—Java applets, sound effects, and so on—gobble up bandwidth and really bloat page-loading times. And rom the start Bezos has put a primacy on making it easy for a customer to buy what he or she needs, fast.

Keep looking at the home page, and you'll notice that if you've bought from Amazon in the past, the page is personalized in keeping with your prior purchases. Books, music and videos are recommended in line with an educated guess about what you'll like. Although personalization is hard for a low-budget site builder to incorporate, any site builder can insert "Bottom of the Page Deals," just as Amazon does. Amazon also offers a freebie on its front page—"Free e-Cards," says the button. Again, any site builder ought to find a useful freebie.

One exceptionally clever feature: "Help a Charity," where you put a link to Amazon on your page, and for every purchase, a charity of your choice gets a contribution from Amazon. You can find "Help a Charity" at www.amazon.com/exec/obidos/subst/associates/charity-links/charitylinks.html/102-6645523-8620169. A variation on the usual affiliate program, this charity tool is geared to bringing in computer users who might not want to bother trying to earn a few dollars for themselves but will feel good helping for instance, the American Indian College Fund or the World Wildlife Fund raise money.

Smart e-tailers bookmark Amazon, whether they shop there or not, and check in at least once a month just to look at the site. This is as good as e-commerce gets, and there are always tools, techniques, and tactics to learn from the site.

# In Full Bloom

## 1-800-Flowers.com Inc.
## www.1800flowers.com

Wall Street is ambivalent about this company. For example, its stock (Nasdaq: FLWS) sells for about half its IPO price. After reaching a high of approximately $23 within a month of its IPO in August 1999, the stock collapsed by November 2000 to a low of approximately $2.75. Currently, it is in a trading range of $7 to $8 per share, which is less than its IPO price. However, after losing millions of dollars, the company started to become profitable in the second half of 2002. In fact, for the six months ending December 29, 2002, net sales increased 19 percent to $286.7 million, and net income totaled $2.8 million.

One reason for its success? 1-800-Flowers.com seems to be on a mission to offer the perfect gift to shoppers.

In the past few years, the company's product line has been extended by the merchandise sold through its subsidiaries, including Plow & Hearth Inc. (www.plowandhearth.com), a direct marketer of home decor and garden merchandise; The Popcorn Factory Inc. (www.thepopcornfactory.com), a manufacturer and direct marketer of popcorn and specialty food gifts; and The Children's Group Inc., a direct marketer of children's gifts, operating under the HearthSong (www.hearthsong.com) and Magic Cabin (www.magiccabindolls.com) brands.

Another advantage? It's a company that truly understands and embraces net-based selling. It was also a pioneer: Its first electronic storefront opened on CompuServ in

1992, followed by an AOL store in '94. Its web site went up in 1995, which is early in internet time. 1-800-Flowers accomplished that by serving as a beta tester for what became Netscape's Commerce Server. While other leading businesses often stumbled when it came to jumping into the online world, 1-800-Flowers got it right from the start.

Does the site still work? Absolutely. And keep this in mind: Flowers are easier to sell on the visual web than they are by phone. Do you know what a "Memory Garden" bouquet looks like? Of course not. And even if you're told it has a half-dozen roses arranged along with floral favorites such as stock, alstroemeria and waxflower, you may be clueless about its looks. But at the web site you see the arrangement, which can usually be magnified.

> **Smart Tip** Tip...
>
> Always compare your site to competitors', and do this ruthlessly and without an iota of favoritism. What do your competitors do better? If you cannot list a dozen things, go back and look at their sites more closely until you come up with a dozen. The only way to make your site the best it can be is to study competitors, see what they are doing well, and then do it better yourself.

A fast-loading site that is primarily text-based (but with enough imagery to capture the visuals of the floral business), 1-800-Flowers aims to make the shopping experience easy. Flowers appropriate for an upcoming holiday are noted. Tabs offer gift suggestions for common events—birthday, get well, love, and romance. A "Best Sellers" tab tells a visitor what others are buying so it's easy to follow the pack. Still don't know what to buy? The home page offers gift suggestions—essentially pushing suggestions to visitors, many of whom come to the site not knowing what they want to buy.

The most impressive thing about 1-800-Flowers is it offers up lots of information on a page that nonetheless doesn't seem cluttered or overwhelming. That is exceptional page design, and it is a goal every site designer ought to aspire to.

Another plus: If you are truly clueless about flowers, or reach a roadblock in trying to make a purchase, a real-time live chat with a customer service representative can be had by clicking on a simple "Online help" button at the bottom of the home page. This is a well-thought-out strategy that looks at several issues from the customer's point of view, such as the slow speed of e-mail (by the time the user gets a return e-mail, he has probably already purchased elsewhere) and the inconvenience of making a telephone call (many home users have only one line, and to use it, they have to disconnect the computer from the net).

Can you implement a real-time feature? Probably not. The service is offered by a third party, eAssist Global Solutions Inc. (www.eassistglobalsolutionsinc.com), but odds are, it's beyond your ambitions and budget. Even so, what any site builder can take from this is the focus on anticipating and solving customer needs before the customers even know they have a problem.

# Pushing the Envelopes

## Staples Inc., Office Depot Inc., and OfficeMax Inc.
## www.staples.com
## www.officedepot.com
## www.officemax.com

The three office supplies chains—Staples, Office Depot, and OfficeMax—slug it out online every bit as vigorously as they do in the brick-and-mortar world. And think of the barriers to building a good office supplies site: The products are nonvisual (who wants to look at a ream of paper?) and inherently unexciting. Hardly anybody gets a tingle thinking about buying the month's toner, paper clips, and envelopes. This is boring stuff, and, as consumers, we want to get in and out as quickly as possible.

That's good news for office supplies site designers. With some kinds of retail, shoppers actually enjoy the physical shops (fine jewelers, for instance), but with office supplies, if we never have to step into a brick-and-mortar store again, likely we'll all toast our good fortune. The trick for a site designer is making it all work on the web so that it's easy to make the purchases we need.

Unsurprisingly, all three of the office supplies giants take essentially the same route. In fact, Staples and Office Depot erect pages that are stunningly similar—heavily text-oriented, scant use of graphics, with an organization that revolves around imitating the aisles in a physical store.

OfficeMax follows the same organization concept but is much more generous in the use of graphics (a chair, a box of paper, a scanner). You have to wonder exactly why OfficeMax's designers use so many graphical elements because, again, if you've seen one box of 500 No. 10 envelopes, you've seen all you ever need to see. Granted, the images have very low resolution and don't add appreciably to load time (a shot of a scanner, for instance, is a trace more than 1 KB), but this also means they have so little detail (the scanner could be a photocopier or a printer) that their inclusion adds nothing positive to the page.

### Tip...

### Smart Tip

How can you make your customers' shopping easier? Are there "ready-made lists" you can create? How about lists of the most ordered items? Face it: No matter what any tech headie says, web shopping lacks the buzz and fun of a mall (although it has other strong advantages). Build in tools that make shopping go fast, and your customers will thank you by spending more money in your store.

Which site comes out on top? For my money, it's Staples, but only by a nose. Staples wins because it builds in numerous useful shopping tools—"Favorite Items," "Feature Finder" (the site searches for specific features within categories to find exactly what the user needs), "Order History," and more. The others have similar tools, but finding them on those sites is tough. Staples puts them right in your face, and for that the designers deserve congratulations. By making it easy to replenish supplies with just a couple mouse clicks, Staples takes some of the drudgery out of this chore.

# It's In the Mail

## Stamps.com Inc.
## www.stamps.com

The biggest challenge in selling is convincing people to do something new, something they have never done before. Witness escargots. You've seen them on menus. Have you ever eaten snails? If you have, you either like them or you don't, and you know without further ado if you'll order them again. But if you have never ordered them—never tasted a snail—it's difficult to be persuaded to order one at a restaurant. A freebie may help, but probably not. What would tempt you? Tough question, with no easy answer.

What do snails have to do with the web? Quite a lot, actually. Just look at Stamps.com, a site where you can do things you have never done before. Of course you understand postage, but the way it has always worked is that you've gone to the post office with money and walked out either with a sheet of paper stamps or with credits entered into a postage meter. Stamps.com wants to change all that.

Its aim is to entice you to buy postage on the internet from a company you have never heard of and—somehow—to affix this postage to your outgoing mail in ways you do not yet understand. How could you ever be enticed

### Tip...

### Smart Tip

What can you give away? Stamps.com gives away $20 in postage—which is something visitors know the value of and will use. But if you use this tactic, keep close tabs on both your visitor counts and the numbers that take advantage of any freebies you are offering. If the visitor count dramatically exceeds the number of folks who go for the freebie, maybe you are trying to give away escargots—meaning visitors don't know if they actually want what you are offering. The remedy? Think hard about finding a way to position what you are offering as both valuable and desirable, and keep tinkering with this value proposition until a healthy percentage of visitors are jumping on your freebie.

into taking this deal? Simple: Sign up with Stamps.com, and you get $20 in free postage. Because it's free, you just might try it out.

Look closely at Stamps.com's front page. Its highest goal isn't to sell you; it's to tempt you to try out the service. For example, the first button on the page isn't "Sign up Now"; it's "Learn More." Is that putting priorities in the wrong place? No, because you won't be sold into buying Stamps.com's service until you try it, and the smartest, fastest, best way to induce you to try it is to give it away.

Everything about this front page aims at achieving that goal, and that makes this a well-designed site. It's a lesson web site designers should absorb. Sometimes the web merely offers new ways to do old things (as, for instance, Amazon adds a cybertwist to book buying), but in other cases the web is about wholly new things to do, which is the case with Stamps.com. And the only way to get customers to plunge into uncharted waters is to tempt them with freebies.

Once you're tempted, the "Learn About Stamps.com" kicks into action. In five quick steps, a visitor is guided through the how-to of the Stamps.com process, offered multiple sign-up bonuses, shown clear pricing, and then prompted to do the deed and sign up.

The jury is out on the near-term viability of Stamps.com or any of its competitors, but for now the site wins applause for doing all the right things to persuade us to, at the very least, give this newfangled way of buying and affixing postage a whirl.

# The Right Dose

## drugstore.com Inc.
## www.drugstore.com

Who likes shopping for aspirin, soap, razor blades, prescription medicines, and the rest of the stuff that takes us to drugstores? Almost nobody, and that's why an early niche targeted by trailblazing e-tailers was the drugstore category. Imagine if you could save yourself a half-hour—maybe more—weekly by eliminating those shopping trips and instead clicking a mouse a few times.

That's the value proposition put forth by drugstore.com, a leader in this category (where its prime competitor is CVS.com—formerly Soma.com, a Washington start-up bought outright by brick-and-mortar chain CVS in '99). And drugstore.com has so far managed to stay ahead of it. It has won a variety of awards and accolades over the years. It was also named one of the Top 100 e-Businesses in the United States in 2001 in *Internet Week*'s Top 100 Survey in June 2001.

Check out the drugstore.com home page, and notice it's similarity to Amazon's, right down to the use of navigational tabs at the top of the page (pharmacy, medicine cabinet, beauty & spa, etc.). That's actually unsurprising because Amazon owns a large slice of drugstore.com's equity, and the two are strategic partners who do many cross-promotions. Buy from drugstore.com, and when the box arrives, it might contain a discount coupon good at Amazon, or vice versa.

Also similar to Amazon.com: The company offers every-day free shipping. The bottom line? Spend $49 or more in eligible drugstore.com products—currently ineligible items are prescriptions, magazine subscriptions, contact lenses, gift certificates, and bulk orders—and drugstore.com will ship them out for free. No special codes or clicks needed.

Keep poking around the drugstore.com site, and there is much to admire: pages that load

> ## Smart Tip
>
> **Tip...**
>
> With whom can you forge alliances? Which companies will dress up your pages and build higher levels of visitor trust in your business? Make up a list, and start knocking on doors. For a dotcom start-up, these kinds of partnerships can spell the difference between a fast ramp-up into success or a swift plunge into failure. A few partnerships are plenty; put too many on your page, and you risk blurring your message and losing your identity.

very fast, numerous tools for personalization ("Your List"), and a well-organized store directory where you can shop by department such as "medicine cabinet," "beauty & spa," "nutrition & wellness," etc., that make browsing reasonably easy. A "Great Deals" button is highlighted on the front page, and it opens the door to many discounted items.

Also eye-catching are the deals drugstore.com has cobbled together with brick-and-mortar pharmacy Rite Aid (which enables drugstore.com to fulfill prescriptions under most medical insurance plans) and vitamin seller GNC.

Hop over to CVS.com's home page, and they are similar, which perhaps ought to be unsurprising; brick-and-mortar drugstores look much the same, too. Can you tell a Walgreens from a CVS? Certainly those companies would like to think so—and they spend big money trying to develop unique identities—but over-the-counter allergy pills look alike no matter whose shelf they're on.

So what puts drugstore.com in the lead? Two things. One, drugstore.com's page layout and design are closer to Amazon's. That's a plus because as the most-trafficked e-commerce site, Amazon is understood by millions of consumers who have acquired a comfort level in dealing with the bookseller. Drugstore.com can do this because of its financial intertwining with Amazon, but, again, other e-tailers must be careful not to copy too closely those patented features.

The other distinguishing feature about drugstore.com is that it's leveraged upon joint marketing arrangements with well-known businesses—notably Rite Aid and GNC. Both those companies have spent millions of dollars nurturing consumer awareness and comfort, and they rank high in their niches. Drugstore.com gets to parlay their investments into a powerful play for consumers' trust and shopping dollars.

That's a brilliant move because no matter how long a cyberstorefront spends trying to drive traffic to its pages, it still has to wrestle with consumer distrust. Nobody's "seen" it, nobody's been inside, nobody's touched the merchandise on its shelves. Those are high hurdles, but not the only ones faced by drugstore.com. Its products touch a customer's body, and that's a field where trust is paramount. Lack trust, and selling is simply impossible. Drugstore.com wins cheers for its attempt to bridge the trust divide through strategic alliances. That simply is first-rate marketing smarts.

# Riding the Wave

## Yahoo! Inc.
## www.yahoo.com

No web site comes close to Yahoo! in winning visitors. It was among the net's first web sites, but remained a powerhouse. In a recent count of the top 25 internet properties by visitor count from research firm comScore Media Metrix (www.comscore.com), Yahoo!'s sites had more than 105 million visitors in one month. White-hot eBay's site (www.ebay. com) managed only 53 million visitors in the same period. Yahoo!'s performance is simply amazing, especially since this is month-in, month-out leadership that has lasted for years.

Surf into Yahoo!, and what you find is a monument to an internet philosophy of less is more. Graphical elements are so few as to be almost not used at all, and the page is heavily text-based—but it somehow manages to remain both uncluttered and readable. This is as skilled as web site programming gets: Yahoo! programmers manage to make an extremely sophisticated site design somehow look simple.

Now notice how many services and options Yahoo! offers, from personalized stock quotes to e-mail, auctions—even a customized "My Yahoo!" page where registered users can select exactly the information they want to see. It's a rich array of individualized information, and since it's free, smart users tap into it.

Especially when compared with its main competitors, Yahoo! has a better-looking site. For example, head over to the MSN site. You will see a very different look, consisting of

### Smart Tip

Tip...

Surf around and visit all the portal or gateway sites that in the past eight years Yahoo! has trounced: Lycos.com, Excite.com, even Google.com, which is gaining in popularity. Keep asking, "What does Yahoo! do better, and how can I adapt it to my site?" Odds are you can't duplicate the sophisticated programming or the high level of personalization offered by Yahoo. But keep surfing, and you'll soon be jotting down concrete ideas for your site.

more visuals and, strangely, both less information and more irrelevant stuff. On a recent site visit, I found a line out of nowhere, "What to do if you regret getting married," and an even dumber line, "Find a rad pad online." Huh? Yahoo! manages to be sober and useful, compared with a kind of frivolity at MSN. Most users want to dispense with the frivolous and get down to business.

Learn from Yahoo! that less is definitely more, and information—useful, relevant information—is power. Give surfers facts, make the page load fast, and you are following in Yahoo!'s footsteps, which is an excellent path to take.

# It Takes a Village

## iVillage Inc.
## www.ivillage.com

A site aimed at women, iVillage.com recently ranked 24th in comScore Media Metrix's tally of the top 25 web properties—pretty high for a special interest site—and attracted more than 18 million visitors in a month. With the intense competition that's out there, what moved iVillage to the top of the heap?

Log into iVillage and see for yourself. It's evident that the site strives to be a portal for women, the kind of page it hopes users will set up as their start page. That's because the site offers a full range of services, everything from horoscopes to quizzes and free web-based e-mail. There are recipes, beauty tips, pointers for parents, places to chat online, and shopping in the iVillage Market. Whatever a person could want to find online is offered on this page somewhere.

One problem: The page is cluttered, and finding anything in particular isn't easy. But at the top of the front page there's a link for new visitors to iVillage. Click it, and you enter an orientation to the site's content. The tone is warm, woman-to-woman, with absolutely no techie blabbering. On many sites, you'll find a similar tool, but it's usually labeled "site navigation" or something similarly cold, and its content consists of a grid. At iVillage, the navigational aid is friendly and helpful.

The most impressive thing about iVillage is it knows its target audience and gears everything to those viewers. Many sites are unfocused or try to be all things to all people, and that

### Smart Tip

Tip...

Have you defined your target audience? The more you know about your viewers, the more closely you can match your site to their interests and needs. Get to know your viewers—run surveys, solicit e-mail feedback, and routinely seek to find out what's on people's minds—and that will make it easier for you to tailor content to them.

never works. What does work is knowing who your viewers are and gearing everything on the site to them. In this respect, iVillage excels. Looked at from a functional point of view, it is not fundamentally different from, say, the AOL start page (www.aol.com), with the major exception that iVillage has defined its audience and pursues it.

# Keeping It Fresh

## FreshDirect Inc.
## www.freshdirect.com

The odds are certainly against it, but FreshDirect Inc. (www.freshdirect.com), a New York-based online fresh-food retailer, is actually succeeding.

What is making this company succeed when other cybergrocers—such as Webvan and Kozmo.com—were two of the most well-known dotcom flops? Well, for one thing, those companies were straightforward grocery distribution companies with hubs located all over the nation. FreshDirect, on the other hand, is really a fresh food company that just happens to deliver its products to New York customers.

The company, conceived three years ago by Joe Fedele, (a New Yorker who has started gourmet supermarkets), shortens the supply chain by purchasing fresh foods direct from the source and processing orders in a manufacturing facility using batch-manufacturing processes. Then it delivers its products to customers in New York.

Its food-friendly facility lets the company do much of its own food preparation, like roasting its own green coffee beans, dry-aging its own prime beef, and baking its own breads and pastries. It also sells specialty foods and popular grocery brands. And because it doesn't have a retail location, it doesn't pay expensive rent for retail space. These factors help keep food fresh and costs low and allow the company to pass the savings on to its customers. As a result, FreshDirect says it can save customers up to 35 percent compared with local retail markets. The service is currently available throughout New York city.

FreshDirect customers can shop anytime from work or home, and the company brings everything directly to you in a FreshDirect refrigerator/freezer truck so the food is protected all the way to your door. There is a $40 minimum total per order. Delivery costs $3.95, and delivery people won't accept tips. Customers are advised to tell FreshDirect where and when they want their delivery by choosing a convenient two-hour delivery window on weekday evenings and all day weekends, seven days a week.

The formula seems to be working: According to FreshDirect, the company has currently attracted more than 50,000 customers. In addition, 75 percent of first-time customers buy from the company again. Further, more than 17 percent of households where the service is available have tried FreshDirect, and the company is attracting more than 3,000 new customers weekly. It also expects to be profitable by the end of 2003.

There are numerous reasons for the company's success. One is the concept itself—fresh food sold at low cost and delivered to your door. Another is that for several months in 2003, the company offered "$50 in free food" to web shoppers, a very successful promotion.

But another reason for its success is its easy-to-use web site. FreshDirect's online store is a cinch to use and is loaded with great information. Learn about what you're buying. Compare products by price, nutrition and flavor. Get recommendations for foods to suit your taste. When you come back, the company remembers what you ordered last time so that you can reorder in minutes.

When you visit the home page, you'll see that it highlights its delivery information, which is important, especially since it must get many calls and questions from people about this important part of its business model.

Aren't located in an area where FreshDirect delivers? No problem. When I opened the page at home, a statement written in bold type appeared at the top that said FreshDirect is not in my area at this time. It also said that it would send me an e-mail "a few weeks before we arrive in your neighborhood." In the meantime, it told me to feel free to browse around its online store. It also told me to "Click here" to see current delivery zones, or to enter a different ZIP code, click somewhere else. When I clicked to this page, it told me to enter my ZIP code and my e-mail address, and it would drop me a note "when we start delivering to your neighborhood."

The rest of the page, however is focused on fresh food. "Departments," such as "Fruit," "Dairy," and "Meat," are clearly listed, and you can either click on the word or a picture (for fruit, there is a picture of an orange, for example) to enter that department. Once you are in each department, you are treated to more graphics and details so you can easily click on the exact item you'd like. Prices are clearly listed here as well, which is a plus. As you go along, you are treated to even more details about each item. When I clicked on "Fruit," and then "Apples," and finally "Granny Smith," I was greeted with the following description: "The tartness of a Granny Smith piques your palate, but then its deep sweetness comes out to balance the flavor." I was also shown the price again. Also important: As I clicked through each page, the "$50 in free food offer" was prominently displayed.

Checking out is easy as well—almost every page has an icon that lets you view your shopping cart or check out. All in all, it's a great experience.

## Smart Tip

*Tip...*

A key to FreshDirect's success is its graphics. It shows all its products in a clear and very appetizing way. Are you selling products that would benefit from appealing graphics? If so, spend the bucks, and make sure they look good. It really makes a difference to consumers. The better, more appealing something looks, the more likely people are to buy it.

# Tech Savvy

## Dell Computer Corp.
## www.dell.com

Michael S. Dell, chair and CEO of Dell Computer Corporation, founded the company in 1984 with $1,000 and an unprecedented idea in the computer industry: Sell computer systems directly to customers. Michael, who is also the longest-tenured CEO in the computer industry, knew what he was doing.

Under Michael's direction, Dell has established itself as the world's most preferred computer systems company and is a premiere provider of products and services required for customers to build their information-technology and internet infrastructures.

Dell is also acknowledged as the largest online commercial seller of computer systems. The company is also known for redefining the role of the web in delivering faster, better and more convenient service to customers.

To see how well it is serving customers, take a look at Dell's web site. Navigation is about as "Easy as Dell," which just happens to be the tagline splashed on its home page. On the front page, online shoppers are also clearly presented with easy-to-read categories such as "Home & Home Office," "Small Business," and "Medium & Large Business."

If they'd like, visitors can also shop by type of product, and those products—servers, notebooks and desktops, or printers, for example—are clearly displayed by name and graphic image as well.

When clicking on the "Home & Home Office" button, shoppers are presented with a cleverly designed web page with specials—such as free shipping with the purchase of any Dell Home System—clearly displayed. If shoppers want to just get on with it and purchase a specific product, the categories are again clearly displayed.

Shoppers can also find a "Purchase Information" section on the page, where they can click on different buttons to receive useful information about taxes and shipping, or direct store locations. They are also presented with a "Shopping Alternatives" section, where they can find information about things such as Dell Recycling and Dell Auctions, a secure, easy, and direct way to buy and sell used and refurbished computers, peripherals, and software of any brand.

> ## Tip...
> ### Smart Tip
> Navigation is key to a web site—can users find what they're looking for on yours in a glance? Heavily monied corporations actually test and time users as they poke around rough-draft web sites. You can do the same. Ask employees, friends or neighbors to navigate your site, and listen to their feedback. It does no good if you hide your gems—they need to be readily visible, even to casual lookers.

Another thing: The site has its 800 number listed clearly on top of every page. This is an important point—many companies do not do this, making it difficult for people to do the one thing e-tailers really want: Buy something.

An important thing to remember: While Dell may have an elaborate back-end infrastructure, most of the elements on the site are pretty basic and could be done by a small e-tailer just starting out. In fact, the real beauty of the site is not anything flashy but rather how it's organized. It's user-friendly and shows that Dell really understands its customers. It understands, for example, that most of them probably want to know how much their tax and shipping is going to cost before they make their final purchase, so they give customers that information upfront, as soon as possible. This is a pretty basic—but important—concept that any e-tailer should think about before finalizing site design plans.

# If the Shoe Fits

## Shoebuy.com Inc.
## www.shoebuy.com

Shoebuy.com is yet another e-tailer that has found success despite the dotcom bust. The company, which has 13 full-time employees and generated about $10 million in sales in 2002, is the largest retailer on the internet focused on all categories of footwear and related apparel.

Shoebuy.com has partnerships with more than 200 manufacturers and represents more than 150,000 products from top brands, including Adidas, Bass, Bostonian, Dexter, Dockers, Dr. Martens, Fila, Florsheim, Hush Puppies, Keds, New Balance, Reebok, Rockport, and many more.

Simplicity is the guiding principle of the Shoebuy.com web site. There are several ways to find your shoes of choice quickly and easily, and they are clearly listed on the Shoebuy.com home page: departments for men, women, teens, and children; search by profile, including age, size, width, color, and price; or choose a brand from the "View All Brands" link.

### Budget Watcher

How can you give away shipping and not go broke? While FedEx and its competitors negotiate highly favorable rates with big shippers, they won't necessarily do the same with small businesses. But that doesn't mean only big-bucks options are left. Use UPS standard delivery or the post office. Both are cheap. A one-pound package can be shipped cross-country via the post office for around $3.85, and that buys two-to three-day Priority Mail delivery. If that gets you a buyer who becomes a repeat customer, isn't it some of the smartest money you've ever spent? Don't be too quick to say you can't afford to offer free shipping.

Shoebuy.com also offers a 30-day money-back guarantee, a printable fitting chart, and live toll-free customer service. Plus, the company has been offering free shipping on all its orders since January 2000, when its site was officially launched. This freebie is prominently displayed throughout the site.

The CEO and co-founder of the company, Scott Savitz, has said that he didn't want to enter into this business if he couldn't sell a product that offered free shipping, because he believed it was part of the whole value proposition. He felt that just because Shoebuy.com was offering a product on the internet, that alone wasn't enough for somebody to make a purchase.

Shoebuy.com, Amazon.com, drugstore.com, Dell Computer Corporation—all of these companies and many more—are using free shipping promotions to encourage people to buy online. And why not? Experts have said that they lure more mainstream buyers to the internet—such as shoppers who are more price-sensitive, have lower incomes than frequent online shoppers, and are more used to the brick-and-mortar world than surfing the internet. But there are some downsides to free shipping, and a major one would be cost. So before taking the free shipping plunge, make sure it won't have a devastating impact on your bottom line.

# Film at Eleven

## Netflix Inc.
## www.netflix.com

Here's a novel idea: Launch a movie rental service with the goal of using the DVD format and the internet to make it easier for people to find and get movies they will appreciate. This is what the founders of Netflix had in mind when they formed Netflix.com in 1997, and the site is now a success. Netflix is the world's largest online DVD movie rental service, offering more than one million members access to more than 15,000 titles. Its appeal and success are built on providing an expansive selection of DVDs, an easy way to choose movies and fast, free delivery.

The concept is pretty simple: For $19.95 a month, members can rent as many DVDs as they want and keep them as long as they want, with three movies out at a time. Netflix also

### Tip...

### Smart Tip

A key to Netflix's success is that it truly understands its audience. It knows, for example, that its customers are film buffs, so it allows them to pick and choose films from genres and collections that only true film buffs would understand and enjoy. What's more, it offers them fully personalized pages with suggestions for DVDs that they would most likely rent. While Netflix's personalization capabilities are at a level that many e-tailers might not be able to achieve, they should still make an effort to get to know their customers in general and talk to them in their own language on their web sites. It's not rocket science, just pure business sense.

provides free, prepaid return envelopes so members can just drop their movies in the mailbox to return them. Many members also receive next-day delivery.

The more you use Netflix, the more the site is tailored to your tastes. After you see a movie, for example, you can rate it by clicking on the stars that appear next to every movie's listing on the site, from one star if you hated it to up to five stars if you loved it. The more you rate, the more Netflix learns what you like, and it delivers personalized recommendations every time you log on. It also allows you to easily rent these DVDs by displaying a red "Rent" icon beside each movie description.

Besides highlighting picks especially for each member, the Netflix home page also allows you to easily search by genre ("Action Adventure," "Comedy" or "Documentary," for example), or by collections ("'70s Cinema," "Movies With Mockery," or "Tough Guys"). And it even offers a "Critic's Pick" from Netflix's own in-house film critic.

The site clearly understands its audience—film lovers—and makes ordering DVDs a very pleasant experience.

# The Future of e-Commerce

Where is e-commerce heading? Tough topic, but to gain insight into the future, I asked Bruce Weinberg, an associate professor of marketing and e-commerce at the McCallum Graduate School of Business of Bentley College for his thoughts.

▲

A writer and thinker about the net, with particular expertise in online shopping and online consumer behavior—and whose web sites, InternetShopping247.com and EcommerceAndMarketing.com, are rich resources—Weinberg is both a tough critic of present-day e-tailing and a bona fide optimist about the role of e-commerce in tomorrow's retailing mix. You may not always agree with the opinionated Weinberg, but his thoughts are well worth pondering.

**Robert McGarvey:** *What's the best e-tailing site on the web?*

**Bruce Weinberg:** At the present time, the two most dominant exclusively online retailers are eBay and Amazon. In 2002, consumers purchased approximately $15 billion and $5 billion of merchandise through eBay and Amazon, respectively. Some key aspects of their approach to constructing and operating a business are:

- Enabling customers to develop high degrees of trust in the exchange process, which, theoretically and practically, is critical for long-term success in any business. As 1972 economics Nobel Laureate Ken Arrow said, trust reduces the friction in commerce.

- They each offer great value by making it easier for customers to find a wide variety of items through a one-stop shopping process. The notion of value in a one-stop shopping process in an online environment may sound strange given the ease with which you can switch from one web site to another. However, some factors at play that make this plausible are that time is relative and loyalty is an investment that keeps on giving.

- Time is relative. If I told you that you could be physically transported to the aisles of your favorite bookstore in 5 to 10 seconds, you would be elated. Normally this could take on the order of 5 to 30 minutes. However, waiting 5 to 10 seconds for a web page to download would drive you nuts (assuming the use of a high-speed internet connection). Normally, a web page loads in one to two seconds or less with a high-speed connection. In the physical world, one to two seconds is really fast; however, in the web world, one to two seconds is not so fast—it may even be annoyingly slow to some people. So time is relative. The few seconds it may take to type in another URL or search for another online store to visit may not be perceived as quick when operating in an online state of mind (with apologies to Billy Joel). One-stop shopping saves online consumers time.

- Loyalty is an investment that keeps on giving. On average, consumers continue to view shopping online as a very risky activity. This risk is reduced when consumers find a trustworthy and reliable merchant (or merchants, in the case of eBay). Consumers believe that the majority of online purveyors are untrustworthy, so when they find one they can trust, they are surprisingly likely to stick with it. One good experience after another increases customers' trust and loyalty. Consumers are investing their shopping hearts and minds into the online merchant.

This results in a cycle that is difficult for a competitor to break. The loyal and invested customer is more likely to consider and value alternative offerings, such as those that could be offered in a one-stop shopping environment.

In general, a web site—and the processes set in motion based on customer interaction with a web site—should do the following six things:

1. Allow customers to perform some aspect of the buying process better than is possible through other means. If the purpose of the site is to provide information, then it should provide information either more effectively or more efficiently than was possible before the firm offered a web site. If the site allows customers to order products, then it should enable a better experience in some meaningful way. For example, catalog retailers should make the online ordering process either faster or more convenient than ordering via telephone.

2. Clearly describe a product so that consumers know exactly what they are considering (check out a camera review at www.Steves-Digicams.com, and you'll see an example of a site that leaves little to the imagination).

3. Put forth a sincere effort to truly understand a customer through communication and sincere interest, not exclusively based on click streams.

4. Provide full and accurate information upfront about what is being offered. For example, don't make customers go through the checkout process in order to find out whether an item is in stock or to find out the full cost of an order (which includes the costs of the product, sales tax and shipping).

5. Keep promises. Say what you mean and mean what you say. For example, deliver the next day when a customer pays for next-day service. And don't call something next-day service unless it means the product will be delivered to the customer on the next day.

6. Respect customers' privacy and security. Consumers have serious concerns about these issues. Once a person overcomes them to buy from you, do everything in your power to maintain the promised and expected levels of privacy and security.

**McGarvey:** *Do you have a personal favorite web site?*

**Weinberg:** I have several favorites, but I'll mention two here. For online shopping, my most preferred site is eBay, the online auction site. At eBay, I almost always find what I want, when I want it, at a price that I find reasonable (as I play a role in setting the price when bidding in an auction). In addition, I get a thrill from shopping at eBay; it is an affect-rich shopping and buying experience. First, there is the excitement associated with finding an item that I thought I would never find anywhere (e.g., a Rolls-Royce key case). Next, there is the delight associated with interacting with other bidders (though some would call this the rush of competition). Then, there is the agony of defeat or the thrill of victory (with apologies to the *Wide World of Sports*). Finally, I don't buy items on eBay; I win them. I love the feeling of getting a great deal when I win. But on eBay and other online auction sites, you should be careful of the winner's curse (in essence, paying too much for an item) and of the potential for addictively "chasing losses." Researchers at Harvard Medical School have observed some similarities between gambling and auction bidding with respect to human behaviors and emotions.

I also enjoy Google. It may sound strange to have a search site as a favorite. But in both my professional and personal life, I frequently find the need or desire to search for information online. Google typically leads me to information that will either solve [a problem now] or help me down the road in solving a problem. For example, I easily reconnected with a long-lost friend from Sweden by "Googling" him (i.e., entering his name into the search field—I typically place quotes around my search terms). His name appeared in a few web pages, one of which included his e-mail address.

**McGarvey:** *What's wrong with all—or virtually all—e-commerce sites today?*

**Weinberg:** Tough question. I'll stop short of saying that certain problems are associated with all e-commerce sites. But I will highlight some areas where firms should seriously reconsider the status quo.

First, I believe many sites could benefit from a greater appreciation of the consumer buying decision process. The process has been the same for centuries, and it is unlikely to change in the foreseeable future. It details precisely what consumers do when engaged in the process of buying. They: 1) recognize a problem or need, 2) may search for information to reduce the risk associated with the buying decision to be made, 3) may evaluate alternatives and come to a decision about which one may be "best," 4) make the purchase, and 5) carry out a variety of post-purchase activities, such as consuming the product, spreading negative or positive word-of-mouth, returning the item and so forth. For more details, see my report at www.InternetShopping247.com.

Second, firms should realize that humans engage in exchange and that the internet, the web, computers and other technologies are exchange tools for humans—not the other way around. Model your approach for exchange based on this simple and important principle. EBay brings together buyers and sellers. Match.com brings together people who want companionship. EverQuest.com [an online game with nearly 1 million subscribers paying $15 per month to play] brings together people who like to interact through and explore fantasy worlds.

Third, scaling [growing your business] is a great way to garner more profits per dollar invested; however, scaling only works when a successful process remains a successful

## Smart Tip

Where do eBay and Amazon excel? By enabling customers to develop high degrees of trust in the exchange process, offering great value by making it easier for customers to find a wide variety of items through a one-stop shopping process, keeping promises, and respecting their customers' privacy. Do you do these things? If so, you're on the right track to success.

process in its scaled form. Don't assume that every business process that can be automated and scaled up in some way should be automated and scaled up. For example, using a FAQ section as a means for scaling the availability of customer service may not be enough. Sometimes the customer or the situation requires more assistance than that which is offered by a set of FAQs. Even mighty eBay learned this lesson, as they now offer real-time "live" help through online chat.

> **Smart Tip** *Tip...*
>
> No, you don't have to be on the web, but if you've read this far, odds are high that you either are or you soon will be. But if you still decide not to go online, good luck. You'll need it to compete in an age where consumers routinely look to the net for the shopping information they need.

All this being said, there are situations where scaling online may be extremely effective. For example, consider the case of viral marketing, or getting others to pass along your message or some message that will bring customers to your door. The internet can be extremely effective in this regard. In addition, the web is a great way to scale the number of interactions with a person and the number of people with which you have an interaction— for example, through an electronic newsletter. The master in this domain is Michael Katz of www.BluePenguinDevelopment.com. This can effectively support a permission marketing program.

**McGarvey:** *Why are the B2C [business-to-consumer] e-commerce sites dying?*

**Weinberg:** B2C e-commerce sites are not dying as they were at the end of the dot-com period, circa 2000 to 2001. I am convinced that important B2C services will thrive; B2C is not dead. Many useful and profitable e-commerce sites have emerged or flourished over the past 18 to 24 months. For example, Netflix, which offers DVD rentals via the internet is heading in the direction of profitability; it recently garnered its one-millionth customer, most of whom pay [about] $20 per month. For some firms, e-commerce has invigorated their business. For example, catalog companies such as Lands' End now realize a large percentage of their sales from online orders.

Tried-and-true business principles hold in e-commerce. If your value proposition is weak, then your appeal to customers will likely be weak. In addition, to survive in e-commerce, it is critical to have a clear vision and reasonable plan for success, determination and discipline in execution, and the ability to understand and satisfy consumers. You must not only have a great idea, but also be able to "make it happen." There is a long history of entrepreneurs who developed "greater mousetraps" that did not result in everyone beating a path to their doors.

**McGarvey:** *What niches have yet to be fully attacked by e-tailers?*

**Weinberg:** Over the last two years, I have observed many small businesses filling niches. I still see a lot of opportunity in luxury goods. Some online luxury retailers are beginning to see significant growth. For example, Blue Nile, an online jeweler, grew nearly 50 percent in 2002 and realized its first net profit. Many long-established and premier luxury purveyors such as Gucci, Tiffany, and Rolls-Royce Motor Cars, are online; however, their sites leave much to be desired. I see a great opportunity online for luxury providers who meet the expectations they set for their goods or services.

> **Beware!**
> Never count out brick-and-mortar retailers. Some of them may be dumb, but they aren't dead. And they do have money, domain experience, and deep supplier relationships. When a brick-and-mortar decides to make a move into a space, it can cause real pain to other e-tailers, so always assume that tomorrow you will be competing against them. Know ahead of time how you will prevail!

Another great opportunity for online retailers is in the area of digital downloadable recorded music. The record labels are scrambling to figure out a viable solution to this problem. They underestimated Napster and the wake it created, and they are now behind the eight ball. My bet is on Amazon to bring it all together for the record industry. But I see no reason why a new player could not devise a solution for this great opportunity.

**McGarvey:** *What will the next-generation sites offer that today's sites don't?*

**Weinberg:** Sites in the future will offer increases in speed, fidelity (e.g., the ability to feel items, speech recognition), ease of use, and access for the physically or psychologically challenged.

**McGarvey:** *Why haven't brick-and-mortar retailers "gotten" the web? Will they?*

**Weinberg:** The answer is pretty simple and age-old. They do not get it because they neither use it nor embrace it. I believe that most people realize success because they get immersed in their passions and work their tails off. If brick-and-mortar retailers want to get it, then they need to get everyone in their company online, using the internet and shopping online.

**McGarvey:** *What are two bad e-commerce sites? Why?*

**Weinberg:** Pick any two that make your blood boil or bring out frustration. The most common causes are grounded in content (e.g., limited product information, limited product availability), functionality (e.g., navigation, checkout, customer service), and privacy or security. A site that bothers me is that of Hermès, one of the world's leading luxury good brands. The site provides an irritating shopping experience. Navigation is neither intuitive nor pleasant, and information is minimal. Finding information about the locations of their retail stores—a top-level information item for a retailer—requires a fair amount of detective work. [For curious minds, first click on "customer service," then click on "Returns-Exchanges-Refunds," then click on "To Hermès Boutiques," and finally, click on "Points of Exchange." Hermès should consider adding a link titled "Boutique Locator" to every page on its site.]

**McGarvey:** *Why all the hype over B2B e-commerce sites?*

**Weinberg:** I'm not convinced that there is much hype today, as B2B has been slipping slightly. Nevertheless, relative to B2C, B2B is impressive. In 2001, B2B [e-commerce accounted for] more than 90 percent of all e-commerce, and it [accounted for] more than 15 percent of all B2B commerce [person-to-person selling, trade show selling, catalog sales.]

# Wireless Wonders

In the movie *The Graduate*, the future revolved around plastics, or so the young grad was told. Today, the future definitely revolves around wireless technologies. Find your niche in wireless, and you are on a very fast track to success. "The opportunities today in wireless are much, much bigger than what I saw in the computer business back in 1983," says Phillipe Kahn, CEO of LightSurf, a Santa Cruz, California, company focused on multimedia messaging and mobile content delivery services. "Today's opportunities are tenfold greater."

When Kahn says this, it's a meaningful mouthful. Back in '83, Kahn was a pioneering software developer who created a couple hits—SideKick and Turbo Pascal—for a company he founded called Borland. In 1994, he founded a company called Starfish Software, where he developed a technology called TrueSynch for synching data between devices such as a cell phone and a computer. The possibilities in front of the rugged pioneers who are today defining the wireless information landscape are vastly richer than what he saw in 1983, for one very simple reason: "The numbers were so much smaller back then," says Kahn, who in 1998 sold his TrueSynch technology to cell phone giant Motorola for an undisclosed amount. In the early '80s, PC users were sparse, and that meant the market upside was tiny. But nowadays, explains Kahn, the potential audience for wireless Web products and services is already in the tens of millions of users. "Today's landscape is explosive," he says.

Again, the numbers have it: The wireless Web soon will be in more hands than the conventional Web is. Seem incredible? Shipment of mobile phones has hit a stunning 410 million units, and many of them are Web-ready, contends Datacomm Research, a Chesterfield, Missouri, consulting firm. Factor in access via different kinds of devices—such as wireless computers, PDAs and more—and the number of potential wireless Web users just keeps mushrooming.

You can tap into this. Don't stop thinking until you've found six ways—then get busy implementing the best. Wireless is a wave that hasn't crested yet, but when it does, it will be a monster.

**McGarvey:** *What has fundamentally ailed the prevailing B2C web site business models?*

**Weinberg:** I see many problems. Here are a few:

- Systems should be structured [according to how] consumers think and behave.

- Great ideas are wonderful things. They stimulate other great ideas. A great idea, however, is not enough to build a sustainable enterprise.

- Many firms got hung up on giving product to consumers. Some initial promotions effectively generated awareness and trial. At some point, however, these promotions should have stopped. Aside from credit card fraud, shipping charges are one of the most-mentioned [negatives] for those who have not shopped online (and even for some who have shopped online). Provide free shipping and drop the ridiculous promotions, and I bet sales will do just fine and profits will be much improved.

- Web sites lack personality; they can be sterile. Let's see some faces or caricatures on these sites. Provide cues that bring out human affect—we humans like emotion.

**McGarvey:** *Is Jeff Bezos the smartest e-tailer around? Why or why not?*

**Weinberg:** I believe that he and Meg Whitman [eBay] are the smartest online retailers and marketers who are currently leading internet companies. Meg has a great track record as a marketer and organizational leader. Jeff Bezos has primarily earned his reputation through Amazon. Jeff was an e-commerce groundbreaker, and he has inspired millions to engage the internet as buyers, sellers, surfers, etc. I see great nerve and genius in what he has done and what I foresee Amazon doing in the future.

**McGarvey:** *Is anybody safe from Amazon as Bezos extends his retailing empire into more new categories?*

**Weinberg:** Amazon can flow on and on. I love its model of involving everyone and helping him or her get a piece of the online pie (e.g., zShops, affiliates, even other leading retailers). The internet is partly about creating connections, sharing information, helping people identify their passion, helping people realize their dreams, getting people involved and using their brainpower and voice, and providing access. I believe that Amazon does most of this reasonably well. Ask not what Amazon.com can do for you, but what you can do for Amazon.com.

### Smart Tip

Remember: Amazon offers many ways for you to succeed by helping it get more successful. There are auctions, the low-cost Shops—instant storefronts with fixed pricing—and, of course, the slick Amazon affiliates program. By all means, Jeff Bezos wants to be the top dog on the net, but he is shrewd enough to see that your success can forward his goals. So do as Bruce Weinberg suggests and find ways to help yourself while helping Amazon.

**McGarvey:** *If e-commerce is different in the near future, how will it be? How will it be the same?*

**Weinberg:** Many aspects of e-commerce will be integrated into the ways business gets done and customers are served. It will no longer be perceived as a process that dominates the entire way a firm does business; rather it will be considered an element in an overall business process. The government will play a greater role in regulating e-commerce and will more effectively enforce laws that are violated in an e-commerce context. The issues of privacy and security will remain important. However, a greater proportion of the population will overcome many concerns in these areas and be conducting more of their exchange activities online, such as banking and shopping. This will be facilitated by privacy mandates such as something akin to the "nutritional information" that appears on all food product labels—a succinct and easy-to-understand government mandated "privacy label" will appear on every web site. A variety of devices will begin to get connected to the internet. Think back to the 1967 movie *The Graduate* and say the word "wireless" instead of "plastic."

# Appendix
## e-Business Resources

Here's the blunt truth about e-commerce: Most of what you need to know will not be printed in books or even in magazines and newspapers. One medium that is successfully tracking the rapid developments in e-commerce is the web itself. When you want to know more or need answers to questions, log onto the web and go searching. The information you crave is rarely more than a few mouse clicks away. Here you will find dozens of the sites that deserve tracking.

## Competitive Intelligence

*Fuld & Co.'s Internet Intelligence Index.* Fuld & Co., a research and consulting firm in the field of business and competitive intelligence, has compiled this free index of information from a wide variety of public services. It contains links to more than 600 intelligence-related internet sites, covering everything from macroeconomic data to individual patent and stock quote information, www.fuld.com/Tindex/I3.html.

*Hoover's.* The best content is available for a fee, but there is ample free content for anyone who surfs in. Research competitors, track stock market performance, and keep tabs on IPOs, www.hoovers.com.

*KnowX.* The savvy engine ferrets through public records and reports on bankruptcies, liens, and judgments against individuals and businesses. Costs of reports run from free to $24.95, www.knowx.com.

*Thomas Register.* This is the sourcebook on U.S. and Canadian companies; the book in print or on CD or DVD is free to companies in the United States and Canada, not including shipping and handling charges, and the content on the web is free as well, www.thomasregister.com.

*Yahoo! Finance.* This all-inclusive web site has everything from up-to-the minute market summaries to stock research to financial news—and much of it is free, http://finance.yahoo.com.

# Consumer Web Sites

*BBBOnLine.* The Better Business Bureau's entry into monitoring e-tailers, www.bbb online.org.

*BizRate.* A leader in evaluating e-tailers, www.bizrate.com.

*E-Commerce & the Internet.* Advice from the FTC that pinpoints common frauds, www.ftc.gov/bcp/menuinternet.htm.

*How to Protect Yourself: Shopping on the Internet.* Counsel from Florida's attorney general, http://myfloridalegal.com.

*Internet ScamBusters.* This is a web site and a free electronic newsletter designed to help people protect themselves from internet scams, misinformation and hype; much of the information focuses on internet merchants and consumers, www.scambusters.org.

*SafeShopping.* Created by the American Bar Association, which bills it as "the place to stop before you shop," www.safeshopping.org.

*WebAssured,* Another e-tailer evaluator, www.webassured.com.

# Global Commerce

*Globalization Resource Center.* Compiled by *CIO magazine,* a publication for chief information officers at major corporations, www.cio.com/research/global.

*GlobalEDGE.* Michigan State University's International Business Center's vast library of world trade resources that includes *Country Insights,* an outline of the business climate, political structure, history, and statistical data for more than 190 countries; a directory of international business resources categorized by specific orientation and content; and much more, http://globaledge.msu.edu/ibrd/ibrd.asp.

*Planet Business.* Business resources, arranged by country; a good place to look for foreign contacts, partners and information, www.planetbiz.com.

# Miscellaneous e-Commerce Information

*All Domains.* There's more to web sites than ".net," ".com," and ".gov" domains. Find out about—and buy—international domains here; countries from Afghanistan (af) to Zimbabwe (zw) have domains for sale, www.alldomains.com.

*ClicksLink.* For exploring offbeat affiliate programs—astrology, watch stores, and more, www.clickslink.com.

*Compare Web Hosts.* To help you compare competing hosting services, www.compare webhosts.com.

*Keynote NetMechanic.* For checking your site for bad code and broken links, free of charge, www.netmechanic.com.

*LinkShare.* For signing up for affiliate status with Buy.com, Lands' End, Tupperware, and more name-brand e-tailers, www.linkshare.com.

*Microsoft Central Banner Network.* Formerly known as LinkExchange, and now part of Microsoft's bCentral portal for small business, the Microsoft Central Banner Network remains the web's best banner exchange program, and one of the few still standing, www.bcentral.com.

*Network Solutions.* The primary marketplace for registering U.S. domains, www.network solutions.com.

*TopHosts.* Useful articles and background material to digest before choosing a host, www.tophosts.com.

*Yahoo! Groups.* Still the easiest and best way to set up a free internet mailing list, http://groups.yahoo.com.

# Publications

*Business 2.0.* A monthly look at the forces and players shaping the new economy, www.business2.com.

*Entrepreneur.* Continuing coverage of e-tailing, www.entrepreneur.com.

*The Industry Standard.* The weekly news magazine for the new economy; a must-read, www.thestandard.com.

*Internet Retailer.* News, information and case studies about internet retailing written in an easy-to-read style, www.internetretailer.com.

*Wired.* A cultural magazine that covers e-business, www.wired.com.

# Search Engines

*AltaVista.* A business of Overture Services Inc., AltaVista is a leader in paid inclusion, where, in exchange for a payment, a search engine will guarantee to list pages from a web site, www.altavista.com.

*Dogpile.* A meta search tool that is owned and operated by InfoSpace Inc., Dogpile simultaneously puts your query to more than ten search engines. It's slick, fast, and thorough, www.dogpile.com.

*Google Inc.* One of the best search engines out there, Google's name is funny, but it's a serious hunting tool. Don't miss the "Cache" feature, where Google stores pages on its servers. If a site is down, the page may still be readable at Google, www.google.com.

*Overture Services Inc.* A global leader in commercial search services on the internet. Overture was acquired by Yahoo!, www.overture.com.

*SearchEngineWatch.com.* Useful information about search engines, www.search enginewatch.com.

*Yahoo! Search.* One of the leading search destinations, www.search.yahoo.com.

# Shopping Bots

*BidFind.* Another auction bot, www.vsn.net/af.

*BotSpot.* An ambitious roundup of pretty much all the bots there are, www.botspot.com.

*BottomDollar.com, a Price Grabber site.* An excellent, all-purpose shopping bot, www.bottom dollar.com.

*eSmarts.* Another all-purpose shopping bot, www.esmarts.com.

*mySimon.* A must-see shopping bot, www.mysimon.com.

# Software

*Dreamweaver MX.* The new version of the popular, higher-end web design software, www.macromedia.com/software/dreamweaver.

*FrontPage.* www.microsoft.com/frontpage.

*Interland.* A full suite of tools for building and hosting a complete e-commerce storefront, www.interland.com.

*WebExpress.* This is the David to Microsoft's Goliath. WebExpress is robust, powerful software, and a free trial is available, www.mvd.com/webexpress/index.htm.

*Zy.* Free web-based tools for creating your own site; results can be first-rate, www.zy.com.

## Statistics and More

*E-Commerce Times.* News from the e-tailing front lines, www.ecommercetimes.com.

*eMarketer.* A great news source with an e-commerce focus; lots of stats, www.emarketer.com.

*Nua.* Net-related stats in a readable format, www.nua.com/surveys.

*Shop.org.* An association of online retailers that devotes a section of its web site to the latest industry stats, compiled from more than 200 industry sources, www.shop.org/learn/stats.html.

*Yahoo! Small Business.* A roundup of articles about e-commence and technology targeted to small businesses, http://small business.yahoo.com/resources/articles/technology_and _ecommerce.html.

## Traffic Reports and Ratings

*comScore Media Metrix.* Another take on web site traffic, www.comscore.com.

*Internet Traffic Report.* Measures router volume at various points around the world, www.internettrafficreport.com.

*Nielsen//NetRatings.* Here, web parent companies are ranked by unique audience, among other factors, www.nielsen-netratings.com.

## Venture Capital Firms

*Benchmark.* Said by some to be the top venture capital firm; companies include eBay, eBags. com, Art.com, and 1-800-Flowers.com, www.benchmark.com.

*Kleiner Perkins Caufield & Byers.* The other top VC firm—along with Benchmark— companies include Amazon.com, Drugstore.com, Autotrader.com, iVillage.com, Travelocity.com, and Homestore.com, www.kpcb.com.

*MoneyHunt.* The home page for the TV show that helps entrepreneurs link with VCs and angels, www.moneyhunter.com.

*National Venture Capital Association.* This association's web site contains industry statistics and lists of venture capital organizations and preferred industry service providers, www.nvca.org.

*University of New Hampshire's Center for Venture Research.* The center has created a nation-wide list of venture capital resources to help entrepreneurs find early-stage capital. You can order the list online for $40, www.unh.edu/cvr.

*vFinance.com.* A directory of venture capital resources and related services; a good site for getting info on who's who in the VC world and how deals get cut, www.vfinance.com.

# Web Art

*About.com: Web Clip Art.* Lots of links, http://webclipart.about.com.

*Clip Art Searcher.* Looking for something specific? This meta search tool will scour the web for you, www.webplaces.com/search.

*Free Clip Art.* Free art and links, www.freeclip-art.to.

*Task Force Clip Art.* Some of their images are aimed at businesses, www.nvtech.com/index.html.

# Web Site Building

*Builder.com.* From CNet, Builder.com aims to be a destination for web site creators. Find news, tools and more here, www.builder.com.

*Download.com.* Also from CNet.com, this site allows users to download trial versions and full versions of software, www.download.com.

*Webdeveloper.com.* One-stop shopping for advice and tools for building better web sites, www.webdeveloper.com.

*Webmonkey.* Originally from *Wired* magazine, now a product of Lycos, Webmonkey still does a good job, http://hotwired.lycos.com/webmonkey/e-business.

# Web Site Design No-Nos

*How to Build Lame Web Sites.* Insightful—and sometimes funny—look at bad site design, http://webdevelopersjournal.co.uk/columns/perpend1.html.

*Jakob Nielsen.* The guru of web usability, Nielsen particularly revels in pinpointing the "must nots" of web site architecture. If Nielsen says don't do it, don't, www.useit.com.

# Web Site Tools

*123 Webmaster.* Links to thousands of tools, from CGI scripts to free banner creation, www.123webmaster.com.

*1NetCentral.* This site offers a free, automatic meta tag generator, http://www.1net central.com/meta-tags.html.

*Webmaster Tool Inc.* A directory of tools, many of which are free, www.webmaster tools.com.

*Web Site Resource.* Links to tools, www.wsresource.com.

*Yahoo!'s Credit Card Merchant Services.* Looking for a company to enable you to take credit cards? Here are hundreds. Hint: Just type "credit card merchant services" into Yahoo!'s Directory instead of this long link, http://dir.yahoo.com/Business_and _Economy/Business_to_Business/FinancialServices/Transaction_Clearing/CreditCard _Merchant_Services.

# Wireless Web

*Open Mobile Alliance.* This organization is designed to be the center of mobile service standardization work, helping the creation of interoperable services across countries, operators, and mobile terminals that will meet the needs of the user. To grow the mobile market, the companies supporting the Open Mobile Alliance will work toward stimulating the fast and wide adoption of a variety of new, enhanced mobile information, communication, and entertainment services. The foundation supports WAP, which stands for Wireless Application Protocol. WAP is a secure specification that allows users to access information instantly via handheld wireless devices such as mobile phones, pagers, two-way radios, smartphones, and communicators. WAP also supports most wireless networks. As WAP emerges as a wireless standard, this organization will gain clout, www.openmobilealliance.org.

*TagTag.* Want to make your site wireless web-ready? TagTag is a free tool that will help you do it, http://tagtag.com/site/index.php3.

*Wap Catalog.* A directory of wireless web sites, www.wapcatalog.com.

*The Wireless FAQ.* Previously known as The Independent WAP/WML FAQ, this site covers everything you need to know about WML [wireless markup language], the HTML of the wireless space, and WAP, www.thewirelessfaq.com.

# Glossary

**Angel:** someone who invests his or her money in a start-up.

**Banner:** a graphic image used on a web site as an advertisement; the information superhighway's version of billboards.

**Beta site:** a test site, usually erected in the authoring phase of a web site.

**Bot:** a robot, or program, that automatically does specified tasks.

**Brick-and-mortar (B&M):** a term describing traditional businesses with a physical storefront rather than a cyberbusiness.

**Business to business (B2B):** companies that seek businesses, not consumers, as customers.

**Business to consumer (B2C):** companies that market to consumers.

**Common Gateway Interface (CGI) script:** a simple program that runs on the net; guest books, for instance, often are CGI scripts.

**Clip art:** off-the-shelf images anyone can use; web site authoring programs usually include lots of clip art.

**Cookie:** data created by a web server that's stored on a user's computer to identify that user on return visits to the web site.

▲

**Domain:** the domain name is what comes before the ".com," ".net," or ".edu," all of which are known as top-level domains.

**File transfer protocol (FTP):** the system used to transfer files over the net; you FTP files to your web host.

**First-mover advantage:** the built-in advantage of being the first business in a particular category.

**Host:** a company that provides space for storing (hosting) a web site.

**Hyperlink:** a connection between one object and another; also known as a link.

**Hypertext markup language (HTML):** a code that creates web pages.

**Internet service provider (ISP):** the company that provides a telephone connection that lets a user connect to the net; AOL is the leading ISP.

**Link:** a connection between one object and another; also known as a hyperlink.

**Log:** a record of all visits to a web site; a log usually gives a click-by-click report on a visitor.

**Look-to-buy ratio:** a common measurement used in analyzing the effectiveness of an e-tailer; ideally a 1 to 1 ratio—one looker produces one buyer; look-to-buy ratios of less than 10 to 1 are desirable.

**Meta tag:** an HTML expression that defines a web site's content, to be read by search engines and crawlers.

**Mind share:** consumer awareness and loyalty.

**Newsgroup:** an internet message board or bulletin board.

**Ping (Packet Internet Groper):** a net utility that tests web sites.

**Portal:** a web "supersite" that offers links to substantial amounts of information and often to other sites; Yahoo! is the premiere portal.

**Search engine:** a web site that exists to help users find other web sites; Google (www.google.com) is one of the best search engines.

**Spam:** unwanted, unsolicited commercial e-mail.

**Spider:** spiders (also known as crawlers) search the web for information; search engines use spiders to find web pages.

**Template:** a predesigned document; a web page template, for instance, requires the user to simply fill in some blanks to produce a publishable document.

**Term sheet commitment:** a written offer from a venture capitalist that sets out how much money the firm will invest in a start-up in return for what percentage of ownership.

**URL:** universal resource locator, or, more simply, a web page's address.

**Venture capitalist (VC):** a professional money lender who seeks out high-potential start-ups to fund.

**Webmaster:** a person skilled in creating and maintaining web pages.

**Wireless Application Protocol (WAP):** the standard underlying programs that run on cell phones.

**Wireless Markup Language (WML):** the underlying computer code that produces pages that display on the wireless web.

**Wizard:** a help tool (usually in step-by-step format) that steers the user through to completion of a task.

**WYSIWYG (what you see is what you get):** when the computer screen reflects exactly what the final output will be for a printed page or a web page.

# Index